Ethical Sex

Ethical Sex

Sexual Choices and their Nature and Meaning

Anthony McCarthy

Fidelity Press

South Bend, IN

2016

Published by *Fidelity Press* in South Bend, Indiana
www.culturewars.com

Printed and bound in the United States of America
    by St. Martin de Porres Dominican Community

Cataloguing in Publication Data is on file with the Library of Congress

Anthony McCarthy
    Ethical Sex: Sexual Choices and their Nature and Meaning
        p. cm.
        Includes bibliographical references and index
        ISBN 0-9289891-17-0

Table of Contents

Preface
by Josef Seifert

This splendidly and engagingly written book deserves wide attention and careful reading. It defends in an intelligent way – brilliantly debating views opposite to the author's own – a number of important and, I believe, very true theses about human sexuality and sexual ethics. The author, Anthony McCarthy, shows that the sexual sphere is sharply distinguished from other sources of bodily experience and touches the human person in a different and profound way that cannot be reduced to its procreative aspect, even though it is not to be separated from it.

The book dedicates serious attention to a polemic against the position of philosophers with whom McCarthy has, however, much in common; in particular, Germain Grisez, Joseph Boyle, John Finnis and William May (hereafter GBFM).

Many of the author's objections to the views of GBFM are very well taken, particularly his critique of their counterintuitive claim that among the fundamental human goods of life and health, play, 'religion', knowledge etc. and particular instantiations of these goods there is no hierarchy whatsoever, and that admitting such a hierarchy leads to consequentialist ethics. GBFM thus link their defense of the existence of intrinsically wrong acts to the absence of any hierarchy among the basic human goods and their instantiations. McCarthy argues that this approach is mistaken and that admitting a hierarchy of goods and their instantiations can and should be held in common with a belief in moral absolutes. (One might

1

indeed say that otherwise, absolute moral imperatives towards human persons – such that one ought not lie to them, kill or torture them, despise or hate them – could only exist if one did not recognize God as an infinitely superior being. However, the opposite is the case.)

The author criticizes GBFM – with whom however he basically agrees, including on such delicate issues as the intrinsic wrongness of contraception – on several grounds. He develops fairly broadly the view that some of the GBFM arguments for the wrongness of contraception are ill-conceived, offering a variety of interesting arguments for his position. Probably the most significant basis of his disagreement with GBFM is that these authors do not sufficiently take into account the objectivity and moral (I would say morally relevant) character of human nature, which, McCarthy holds, needs to be understood in order to understand the intrinsic moral rightness or wrongness of human acts (a rightness or wrongness that cannot be simply derived from the consequences of these acts, as consequentialist ethics would claim). Thus he writes: "Many harmful things, after all, are not intended precisely qua harmful, but are intrinsically wrong for all that. And the sexual capacity in particular has a profound relation to reason, or, as Brock neatly puts it, 'it has its own nature and it is part of human nature. It cannot but have a moral meaning'." In particular, McCarthy tries to show that GBFM fail, at any rate in their contralife argument, to elaborate the "inherent goodness of the marital act – an inherent goodness that contraception is said to pervert." Thus he objects: "If we cannot understand the wrongness of contraception without a prior understanding of the value of the marital act, then this suggests that the whole GBFM project has started off on the wrong track (or that the wrongness of contraception and IVF is illusory)."

Moreover, he argues that if the essential moral inseparability of the unitive and procreative aspect of the conjugal act were only due to the contralife element of contraception, one could not oppose the separation in the inverse direction of the unitive and procreative meaning of the conjugal act: The rejection of IVF, which separates the generation of new human life from the conjugal act, cannot be justified on the basis of the contralife argument. In fact, infertile couples use IVF precisely *in order to have children; that is, in favor of human life,* whereas in contrast it would be quite permissible to intervene with the aim of stopping a life being thus conceived.

McCarthy writes:

> "...if I were to see eminent and wealthy fertility expert, Dr W. Inston, at one of London's glamorous IVF clinics, about to inject a single sperm into an ovum in a petri dish, and I grabbed his arm to prevent the procedure, would I be exhibiting a contralife will? I certainly can envisage the IVF (or rather ICSI – introcytoplasmic sperm injection) created baby – I foresee his/her coming to be, and I will against it. More realistically and less dramatically, we can imagine a couple who have agreed to try IVF, but, at the eleventh hour, decide that it is wrong to produce a child in such a way. Do this couple exhibit a contralife will in grabbing the doctor's arm to stop conception going forward?"

I have warned the author and publisher of this book in advance that I have the firm principle of writing prefaces for new books only according to the motto of the International Academy of Philosophy – Instituto de Filosofía Edith Stein:[1] *diligere veritatem omnem et in omnibus, to love all truth and to love it in everything.* Therefore I cannot abstain from some critical remarks on the book for which I have the honor to write this Preface.

While the criticism Anthony McCarthy makes of GBFM's too exclusive emphasis on the anti-life aspect of contraception is quite justified, one might object to McCarthy's own treatment of the contralife argument. First of all, he presents a certain caricature of the anti-life argument against contraception put forward by GBFM, which leads him to reject this argument too readily, instead of recognizing its great value and weight as a partial ground for objecting to contraception. He writes:

"The central claim that GBFM make about the wrongness of contraceptive acts appears to be that a couple that choose such acts can be said to be choosing against the life of a new possible person." And he adds that GBFM (whose work he quotes in the following) claim that "'in and of itself, a contraceptive act is nothing but contralife', that 'insofar as contraception is contralife, it is similar to deliberate homicide', and that insofar as a will is contralife it embodies a 'practical (though not necessarily emotional) hatred of the possible baby they project and reject, just as the will to accept the coming to be of a baby is a practical love of that possible person'."

In his justified critique of an *exclusive basing* of the rejection of contraception on its contralife character (at least in one particular strand of GBFM's thinking) McCarthy not merely argues

---

1   Also of the International Academy of Philosophy in the Principality of Liechtenstein and at the Pontificia Universidad Católica de Chile.

against an *exclusive basing* of the critique of contraceptive acts on their anti-life aspects, but for most of his book seems to reject altogether the anti-life argument present in the old Canon Law of the Catholic Church and in GBFM. Such a wholesale rejection fails to recognize the positive insights that lie in pointing out the contralife aspect of contraception. This aspect can be argued for without claiming that this is the *only valid* ground for objecting to contraception[2] (which McCarthy recognizes that GBFM do not claim). McCarthy, I believe mistakenly, thinks that from the GBFM rejection of contraception in virtue of its anti-life character it would follow that Natural Family Planning (which, as he rightly points out, is not always or essentially morally wrong), would be just as wrong as contraception.

Perhaps an elaboration of his many positive insights, which are less fully developed than his critique, would have shown him that NFP is *not*, while contraception is, essentially contralife. Perhaps it might also be helpful to make less use of unduly formal methods of analytic philosophy in his critique of GBFM and present even richer and deeper analyses than those already contained in this remarkable book. But as McCarthy is an extraordinarily open-minded and

---

2   See for example my "The Problem of the Moral Significance of Human Fertility and Birth Control Methods. Philosophical Arguments against Contraception?" in *Humanae Vitae: 20 Anni Dopo*, Acts of the Second International Congress of Moral Theology, Rome, 1988, pp. 661-672; and " Una reflexion filosófica y una defensa de *Humanae Vitae. El don del amor y de la nueva vida*" in: Benedicto XVI, Karol Wojtyìa, Carlo Cafarra, Antonio Mᵉ Rouco Varela, Angelo Scola, Livio Melina, Alfonso López Trujillo, Fernando Chomali, Josef Seifert, *A cuarenta años de la Encíclica Humanae Vitae, Cuaderno Humanitas* No 19, Pontificia Universidad Católica de Chile, Octubre 2008, pp. 49-59.

deep-searching philosopher, he will no doubt, after the unquestionable success of this first edition, give us a second edition which achieves all of these purposes splendidly.

That McCarthy most seriously aims at a true, rich, and adequate view of "ethical sex" is shown not only by some superb phenomenological passages in his text in which he interprets the philosophy of the body propounded by Karol Wojtyìa and Dietrich von Hildebrand, but also by one paragraph in his book in which he himself withdraws his seemingly total rejection of the contralife argument of GBFM, writing:

"An account of the kinds of acts that constitute chaste acts – acts of full committed union and, perhaps, responsible parenthood – might be the account we are looking for. Such an account need not deny that contraception insufficiently respects the life-giving nature of acts of sexual intercourse (i.e. their teleology and meaning), and is, in this sense, contralife. On the contrary, it may give us a better idea of just *how* such contracepted acts are contralife (i.e. fail to respond appropriately to the value of life/fertility), and in a way free from the difficulties into which the GBFM account falls."

October 30, 2015

Granada, Spain

Josef Seifert

Acknowledgments

During the writing of this book I have incurred many debts which I cannot repay. The greatest academic debt is to my friend and former colleague Helen Watt who always generously gave time to discuss the text with me as well as offering crucial support and inspiration through difficult times in the writing of it. I am also grateful to Geoffrey Hunt of the University of Surrey and St Mary's University for his generous support. I dedicate this book to my late father and to my mother.

The following either made helpful comments on parts of the text or, much more often, provided general and much-needed encouragement: John Atherton, DL d'Avray, Elizabeth Bell, Daniel Blackman, Lynette Burrows, Mark Chabot, Nicholas Denyer, Edward Feser, JLA Garcia, Justin Gudgeon, Colin Harte, Peter Hitchens, Gregor Hoefter, David Jones, Mike Jones, Jacqueline Laing, David McLoughlin, Maria MacKinnon, Johanna McCarthy, Nadia Megnin, Fiorella Nash, David S. Oderberg, Thomas Pink, Alexander Pruss, Piers Paul Read, Fiona Robertson, Roger Scruton, Robert Sungenis, Claire Tapia, Alan Thomas, Anthony Towey, Lucinda Utley, Tim Wilkinson, Huda Yusuf and my brother William McCarthy. Special thanks are due to my employer the Society for the Protection of Unborn Children (SPUC) and especially to John Smeaton, who always showed faith in me, Linda Davidson who gave me my title, and Robert McKenzie for IT help. Without SPUC's generous support this book would never have been completed. All errors in the text are, of course, my own; a good share of any merit is down to those who engaged with me and gave of themselves, even as they disagreed with me.

Most importantly of all, I should mention my immediate family – Dorota and Michal, two extraordinary people in their very different ways, who have had to endure a great deal that they shouldn't during the book's completion, as indeed have I. I only hope that the book gives some indication of how much its author values the deep bonds he has tried to defend here, even if others do not.

Note to the reader

This book is essentially a work of philosophy and some content is of a fairly technical nature. Readers who would prefer to avoid such content can skip chapters 1 and 4, without serious loss to their understanding of the overall argument.

Introduction

The degree and kind of a man's sexuality reaches up into the top-most summit of his spirit.

Friedrich Nietzsche, Beyond Good and Evil

Don't you know that your bodies are members of Christ? Should I remove the members of Christ and make them members of a prostitute? May it never be! Or don't you know that the one who is joined to a prostitute is one body with her? 'For the two' he says, 'will become one flesh'. But the one who joins himself to the Lord is one spirit with him. Run from fornication! Every sin a man may do is outside the body, but he who commits fornication sins against his own body. Or don't you know that your body is a temple of the Holy Spirit who is in you, which you have from God, and that you are not your own."

St. Paul, First Letter to the Corinthians

Th' expense of spirit in a waste of shame
Is lust in action; and, till action, lust
Is perjured, murderous, bloody, full of blame,
Savage, extreme, rude, cruel, not to trust,
Enjoyed no sooner but despisèd straight,
Past reason hunted, and no sooner had
Past reason hated as a swallowed bait
On purpose laid to make the taker mad.
Mad in pursuit, and in possession so;
Had, having, and in quest to have, extreme;

Introduction

A bliss in proof, and proved, a very woe,
Before a joy proposed; behind, a dream.
All this the world well knows, yet none knows well
To shun the heaven that leads men to this hell.

William Shakespeare, Sonnet 129

Enjoy your own sex life (so long as it damages nobody else) and
leave others to enjoy theirs in private whatever their inclinations,
which are none of your business.

Richard Dawkins, The God Delusion

virtue alas is no more like the thing that's called so, than 'tis like
vice itself. Virtue consists of goodness, honour, gratitude, sincerity,
and pity; and not in peevish, snarling, straight-laced chastity.

John Vanbrugh, The Provok'd Wife

More souls go to Hell because of sins of the flesh than for any
other reason.

Claimed to have been said by Our Lady of Fatima to seer
Jacinta

In virtue of its profound centrality and intimacy, as also of its mys-
tery, sex is capable of a particular relationship with love, the most
spiritual and the deepest of all experiences.

Dietrich von Hildebrand, In Defence of Purity

In semine hominis esse quiddam divinium.

Aristotle

any great improvement in human life is not to be looked for so long as the animal instinct of sex occupies the absurdly disproportionate place it does therein.

John Stuart Mill

the vices opposed to prudence arise chiefly from lust, which is the principal species of intemperance.

St. Thomas Aquinas

Thick or Thin?

Ought sexual activities, desires, pleasures to be assessed only according to general moral principles which apply to other areas of our lives? For example, is consent enough to justify our sexual choices? And if so, does that make sexual ethics different from other areas of ethics–or alternatively, does it make it the same as other areas, if we are inclined to think the rest of ethics is as 'thin' as that?

Bernard Williams famously talked of people and societies which conceptualized their moral experience using 'thick' ethical concepts such as cowardice, brutality, chastity, fidelity, and perversity. He says of these concepts,

> They are characteristically related to reasons for action.
> If a concept of this kind applies, this often provides
> someone with a reason for action, though that reason
> need not be a decisive one... We may say, summarily,
> that such concepts are "action-guiding." At the same
> time, their application is guided by the world. A concept
> of this sort may be rightly or wrongly applied, and peo-

> ple who have acquired it can agree that it applies or fails
> to apply to some new situation....Some disagreement at
> the margin may be irresoluble, but this does not mean
> that the use of the concept is not controlled by the facts
> or by the users' perception of the world.[1]

By contrast, a 'thin' concept is a more general prescriptive concept such as rightness, goodness, and obligatoriness which is minimally 'world-guided'. Williams imagines a hypertraditional society where the members lack thin ethical concepts and use only thick concepts. However, for Williams it seems that, "if the hypertraditionalists reflected on what they did, this would destabilize their practice and they would lose their knowledge." As Alan Thomas points out though, "the hypertraditionalists lost not their truths, but their concepts. They were unable to endorse the concepts they originally used without irony. They could not form the perspectival judgements, using perspectival concepts, which articulated the truths that had been available to them." In such a situation "someone who rejects the concept of chastity as a means of conceptualizing sexual behaviour may refuse to judge a sentence deploying the concept as either true or false as a means of registering the rejection of the concept."[2]

Whatever we may think of Williams' reflections on what is ultimately a phenomenological distinction, few of us can doubt that for many the 'thick' concept of chastity does not feature in their ethical thinking, as opposed to other concepts which occupy prominent places. Even those who take very seriously the role of virtue concepts in our ethical thinking tend to disregard chastity as a useful concept. *A fortiori*, a consequentialist such as Peter Singer can famously observe, ethics is not a set of prohibitions particularly concerned with sex...sex raises no unique moral issues at all. Decisions about sex may involve considerations of honesty, concern for others, prudence, and so on, but there is nothing special about sex in this respect, for the same could be said of decisions about driving a car. (In fact, the moral issues raised by driving a car, both from an environmental and from a safety point of view, are much more serious than those raised by sex.)[3]

Specialness of Sex

In the history of civilisation such views about sex and sexual values are rare across cultures and arguably non-existent when implicit assumptions are examined and revealed. Singer's oft-cited view is now fairly standard among sexual ethicists and moral and political philosophers in the Western World, many of whom in no way share Singer's radical consequentialism. Indeed, one will find neo-Aristotelians, virtue ethicists, neo-Kantians and devotees of any other philosophical school one cares to think of espousing Singer's bluntly put view that at most any moral rules that apply solely to sex do so merely externally and contingently.

So, for example, it is worth quoting at length Mortimer J. Adler, a philosopher of Aristotelian, even Thomist, sympathies,

> no sexual acts which yield mutual pleasure to consenting individuals can be condemned as perverse or unnatural. But this must not be interpreted to mean sexual behaviour is subject to no moral restrictions whatsoever. On the contrary, it is subject to the same kind of moral restrictions that are applicable to other forms of playful activity, indulged in for the sake of the pleasure that at-

tends them. The intemperance that manifests itself in the disposition to prefer the pleasures of the moment to a good life as a whole, or that consists in habitual overindulgence of sensual pleasures, can defeat an individual's pursuit of happiness...The vicious character of the libertine operates against success in the pursuit of happiness to the same extent and in the same way that the vicious character of the drug addict does, or the alcoholic, the glutton, the money-grubber, or anyone else who has the *bad habit* of seeking a real good to a degree or in a manner that is not good for him...To the question, Is this act of fornication good or bad?, there is...no general answer. Rules cannot be formulated to govern such matters. But good habits do govern them.[4]

The further you abstract from different moral phenomena the easier it is to assert their identity. Indeed, some traditional ethicists defending Thomist conclusions about sexual morality have shown a tendency to treat sexual ethics as essentially having to do with 'moderation' or 'self-control' or 'temperance', thus assimilating the virtue of chastity under another and more general heading. Of course it does not follow that those who do not treat sex as morally unique or special thereby necessarily hold that it is morally lacking in importance, or indeed that those who treat it as special necessarily hold that it is morally important.[5]

Someone might hold, for example, like the sexual revolutionary Wilhelm Reich, that sex has become, due to inhibiting 'morality' and 'supernatural religious experience', extraordinarily important and yet hold that the Singerite position is basically right in claiming that that there is nothing special per se about the norms which govern sexual ethics. For Reich, it is just that sexual 'repression' is enormously damaging to character and civilisation (a view held in stark contrast to the view of Freud and that of his slightly more orthodox disciple Herbert Marcuse, who assents to Freud's view of the necessity of sexual repression in the foundation and history of civilisation–while, however, holding that at this stage of history there need be no real tension between a civilised social order and libidinal gratification).[6]

Alternately, one could easily imagine a hippy commune which thought permissive sexual behaviour required similar moral principles to be applied to it as another very special activity such as the communal taking of psychedelic drugs (principles for 'sacred' activity say). Perhaps they believe that both practices enable people to get in touch with the sacred life-force of the universe such that violating principles enjoining such practices would be especially wrong. Here the 'specialness' of sex would not be unique even if rules applied to it differed from general moral rules. This would contrast with an imagined heretical Christian sect which *did* recognise the uniqueness as well as the specialness of sex in claiming that the Gospel injunction to love meant that there was always a strong obligation to 'love' (sexually) all those with whom one came into contact. Such a sect could not be faulted for not treating sex as unique.[7]

Alternately, forms of temple prostitution in the ancient world, so claimed Herodotus, had special rules attached to them because sex took on a unique and religious significance. The rules attached to sex here need not have been seen as of merely local application, and would have been in place because religious people viewed sex as special and unique. Such a belief would be very different from the Singer position, while this view of 'sacred sex' would be of precisely the kind furiously denounced by the prophets of the Old

Testament.[8] Indeed, that denunciation itself might well be taken as a sign of recognition of the extraordinary nature of sex and what the Hebrew prophets saw as something uniquely dangerous. That such practices might be associated with apostasy and 'whoring after strange gods' only adds to the idea that for the Hebrews sex appears to have taken on a special and perhaps unique significance.

Jonathan Webber, on the other hand, holds that sex is not morally special ("how could a phenomenal quality make any moral difference?") and that there is no specifically sexual morality. Webber concludes his paper 'Sex' by stating,

> For universal participant consent to be sufficient for
> moral acceptability in the sexual domain...it must be suf-
> ficient for moral acceptability in our lives generally. This
> is not to say that it must be sufficient for moral accept-
> ability in every area of our lives. Some areas might be
> morally special in ways that mean the general rule does
> not apply there. But the sufficiency of consent must nev-
> ertheless be the general rule if it is to be the sexual rule.[9]

Webber is unsure whether there is any such general rule and throws up examples which suggest that universal participant consent is not generally morally sufficient.[10] One reason Webber offers for his rejection of traditional notions of sexual morality (those that might make sexual ethics 'special') is that,

> Understanding paedophilia, bestiality, sadomasochism,
> or homosexuality as perverse...does involve seeing it as
> a redirection of sexuality away from its natural path of
> adult intra-species heterosexual intercourse. Analysing
> the concept of perversion as a means to understanding
> sex, therefore, puts the cart before the horse: that concept

is parasitic on the view that sex has a natural teleology,
a view that has been very influential in the history of our
society. One might as well argue that our concept of fornication shows sex to be paradigmatically marital. Without support from the analysis of perversion, moreover,
there seems no justification for privileging any kind of
sex–procreative, communicative, or any other–as paradigmatic.[11]

In Chapter 2 we will examine arguments concerning natural
teleology and in the following chapters we will consider the role
of social functions as they relate to an account of paradigmatically good sex. Webber seems to be wrong, though, to talk in this
context of the cart before the horse. Surely when examining sexual
perversion and paradigmatically good sex the cart is examined
alongside the horse just as in examining the concept of injustice
we are necessarily examining at the same time the concept of justice and in examining the concept of theft we are necessarily examining at the same time property rights. Each can illuminate the
other even if one or another concept can sometimes be considered
alone. A similar point might be made in response to philosopher
Graham Priest who believes that "sexual perversion is ...another
notion that needs to be assigned to the scrap-heap" on the grounds
that, as far as he is concerned, "sex has no particular aim or goal...
that automatically grounds a moral evaluation."[12] Yet the recognition of something as perverse, rather like our experiences of disgust or shame, might not rely on any well-worked-out theory as
to what is being deviated from while still being an experience of
a real disvalue (someone regarding coprophilia as perverse may
find the concept of perversity useful in trying to move towards the
thought that maybe sex has a purpose which, whatever it is, is not
being fulfilled in such a case). Our experience of disgust, while

often less moralised than our experience of perversity, nevertheless can come to us before we have a worked out theory as to why certain things disgust us and how many things which elicit disgust might represent that which is disturbing to our nature and in need of investigation. In some cases, investigation might include moral investigation, and even if such investigation is inconclusive, that does not make valueless the concept and experience of disgust or, arguably, perversity.[13]

Rape

However, even those who both believe in the unique and special nature of sexual phenomena and who believe that there is a specific sexual ethic and/or virtue which governs sexual willing and activity might take a minimalist view of that specialness. Such a position is still distinct from the outright denial of specialness most vividly set forth by Alan Goldman, who takes a Singerite view on the lack of 'specialness' of sex.[14] For Goldman,

> ...rape is always a sexual act and it is always immoral. A rule against rape can therefore be considered an obvious part of sexual morality which has no bearing on non-sexual conduct. But the immorality of rape derives from its being an extreme violation of a person's body, of the right not to be humiliated, and of the general moral prohibition against using other persons against their wills, not from the fact that it is a sexual act.[15]

Not unrelatedly, Goldman defines 'sex' and 'sexual desire' as follows: "sexual desire is desire for contact with another person's body and the pleasure which such contact produces; sexual activity is activity which tends to fulfil such desire of the agent."[16] Such an obviously absurd description will, of course, empty sex of any meaning (partly by seeming to include an enormous number of things in the category of sex, e.g. giving my son a hug). And this would seem to be an example of someone so concerned not to treat sex as morally (and perhaps non-morally) 'special' in any way that he must trivialise the very concept along with that of sexual violation. However, a virtue ethicist such as Raja Halwani will accept, minimally, that rape is a *sexual* violation[17] while, according to his virtue theory, as opposed to a standard liberal theory, promiscuity, open marriages, prostitution and homosexual activity can all be manifestations of sexually virtuous behaviour. In taking this position he has not had to operate with a description of sex as extraordinary as Goldman's, and he does, according to his virtue theory, preserve a certain specialness for sex, even if that 'specialness' allows for a level of permissiveness that suggests that sex is not *very* 'special'–i.e. it is not generally governed by rules so very different from general moral rules or by a virtue which is specific in the sense of being restrictive in any very focused way. So, while a virtue ethicist like Halwani is not governed by mere 'consent' constraints he can nevertheless in practice assimilate much of sexual morality to something which looks rather like a standard liberal position.

It is interesting to note, though, that the concept of rape seems to be one which even the most hard-headed 'Singerite' has difficulty in dismissing as something that is not importantly a *sexual* violation–i.e. a violation of a distinctive kind. It is difficult to account on such a view for the extraordinary role that rape has played throughout history as a paradigm example of one of the basest possible offences.[18] Indeed, it is worth examining in some detail a classical story of rape–the story of Lucretia–not least to emphasise the historical role of rape and ask why it seems to occupy a position in various societies so much more significant than that of assaults of other kinds.

20

The Rape of Lucretia

As far as we know across all cultures historically and up to the present day, shame is especially associated with sexual matters. Bernard Williams alerts us to the fact that,

> The basic experience connected with shame is that of
> being seen, inappropriately, by the wrong people, in the
> wrong condition. It is straightforwardly connected with
> nakedness, particularly in sexual connections. The word
> *aidoia*, a derivative of *aidos*, "shame," is a standard
> Greek word for the genitals, and similar terms are found
> in other languages.[19]

The story of *The Rape of Lucretia* has come down to us in various forms. English readers may have first come across the story in Shakespeare's moving retelling or by viewing Titian's painting *Tarquinius and Lucretia*. In many of the standard accounts, the virtuous and noble Lucretia had proven herself to be a model wife as compared to the wives of the principal men of the army. One of these men, Sextus Tarquinius, in Livy's account "inflamed by the beauty and exemplary purity of Lucretia, formed the vile project of effecting her dishonour" (Chapter 57-58). Humiliated by the fact that his own wife lacked the virtue of Collatinus's wife Lucretia, Sextus goes to and is received into Lucretia's house. While she sleeps he approaches and threatens to kill her with his sword while also entreating her to submit to his sexual passions. Livy writes,

> When he saw that she was inflexible and not even moved
> by fear of death, he threatened to disgrace her, declar-
> ing that he would lay the naked corpse of the slave by
> her dead body, so that it might be said that she had been
> slain in foul adultery. By this awful threat, his lust tri-

umphed over her inflexible chastity, and Tarquin went off exulting in having successfully attacked her honour.

When Lucretia finally sees her husband and his companions she cries,

> ...what can be well with a woman when her honour is lost? The marks of a stranger, Collatinus, are in your bed. But it is only the body that has been violated: the soul is pure; death shall bear witness to that. But pledge me your solemn word that the adulterer shall not go unpunished.

The men pledge their word to punish Sextus Tarquinius, urging,

> that it is the mind that sins not the body, and where there has been no consent there is no guilt. 'It is for you', she said, 'to see that he gets his deserts: although I acquit myself of the sin, I do not free myself from the penalty; no unchaste woman shall henceforth live and plead Lucretia's example'. She had a knife concealed in her dress which she plunged into her heart, and fell dying on the floor. Her father and husband raised the death-cry.

Nicholas Denyer, in a fascinating paper called "Why Did Lucretia Kill Herself?" notes that the excellence which Lucretia is more possessed of than the other wives is *castitas*–a word which, while lying at the root of our word 'chastity', covers more than this word. Denyer tells us,

> Lucretia's superiority in *castitas* was initially demonstrated, not by anything obviously and immediately sexual, but by the fact that she was found, like any good

Roman lady, working late into the night at her wool,
while the other wives were found at a luxurious banquet.
The virtue so proven (*spectata castitas*) provokes the humiliated Sextus Tarquinius to attempt to destroy it. But
while *castitas* may not be confined to the sexual, it certainly includes a sexual element. Lucretia's faithfulness
to her husband in matters of sexuality is of a piece with
her working at her wool while other wives are party-
ing...The Latin word for what Sextus Tarquinius does to
Lucretia is *stuprum*, 'dishonour' or 'disgrace'. The word
is not confined to sexual disgrace...in being termed a *stuprum*, the rape of Lucretia was classified, not primarily
as a sort of bodily harm, like a bruising or a stabbing or
the breaking of a bone, but an injury to her reputation. It
was thought to harm her chiefly by lowering the esteem
in which she could be held. And the rape was thought to
injure her reputation, however reluctant she had been,
however involuntary her part in it.[20]

In many accounts of the rape of Lucretia the rape is understood as carried out by brute force. Livy's account suggests an act
coerced through a threat to honour (that is through the fear of being thought to have committed adultery). In order to successfully
coerce Lucretia the threat of death would not work, but a threat to
honour succeeds, specifically honour as it relates not only to sexual
behaviour but also to sexual violation. Either way, a strong notion
of shame attaches to Lucretia, either due to a forcible violation
where questions of consent are utterly irrelevant, or due to coerced
consent through a despicable and compelling threat.[21]

It appears to be held by the men in Livy's story that there is
no guilt accruing to Lucretia (though in the case of coerced sex

at least, Lucretia may be latently ambivalent about her role). But there is certainly, in her mind, something like shame even if she has done no wrong 'in the mind.'[22] And that shame 'of the body' seems to be particularly acute in sexual matters–so acute that Lucretia appears to commit suicide as a form of pedagogy (or possibly as a form of self-punishment or bid to prove her honour: in the Livy account she makes a paradoxical and ambivalent claim of innocence).

For St. Augustine, Lucretia is quite wrong to commit suicide (indeed, if she is innocent of sexual wrongdoing she has merely murdered an innocent–herself). Augustine contrasts the Christian view with that of Roman pagans who held Lucretia to be superior in virtue to Christian women who had been raped.

> We maintain that when a woman is violated while her soul admits no consent to the iniquity, but remains inviolably chaste, the sin is not hers, but his who violates her...What shall we call her [Lucretia]? An adulteress or chaste...If she was adulterous, why praise her? If chaste why slay her?...since she killed herself for being subjected to an outrage in which she has no guilty part, it is obvious that this act of hers was prompted not by the love of purity, but the overwhelming burden of her shame...and this matron, with the Roman love of glory in her veins, was seized with a proud dread that, if she continued to live, it would be supposed she willingly did not resent the wrong that had been done her...Not such was the decision of the Christian women who suffered as she did, and yet survive...Within their own souls, in the witness of their own conscience, they enjoy the glory of chastity. In the sight of God, too, they are esteemed pure,

and this contents them...they decline to evade the distress
of human suspicion...[23]

Augustine talks only of Christian ladies, but the story of Susannah, immortalised in Gentileschi's painting and recounted in Chapter 13 of the Book of Daniel provides an eloquent pre-Christian example of a woman with a similar attitude to the Christian women praised by St. Augustine–in her case exemplifying a reversal of Lucretia's order of concerns.

The accounts give powerful testimony to the idea that shame can be associated with something done to one which is not something chosen but rather inflicted. Whichever account of the Lucretia story we take, it becomes clear that an act of violation (though in one version involving coercion rather than physical force) is enough to bring about shame to such a degree that someone might feel impelled to kill herself. And that act is one of *sexual* violation. St. Augustine accuses Lucretia of pride, the greatest sin for Christians, and contrasts this with the attitude of violated Christian ladies who do not assign this kind of prime importance to unwilled sexual violation or external factors such as the opinions of others.

Rape, Shame and Guilt

Shame differs from guilt in important ways, according to a convincing and influential account of Bernard Williams. For Williams, "If we come to understand our shame, we may also better understand our guilt."[24] Contrasting shame with guilt Williams observes,

> What arouses shame, on the other hand, is something
> that typically elicits from others contempt or derision or
> avoidance. This may equally be an act or omission, but
> it need not be: it may be some failing or defect. It will

lower the agent's self-respect and diminish him in his
own eyes. His reaction...is a wish to disappear, and this
is one thing that links shame as, minimally, embarrassment with shame as a social or personal reduction.[25]

Shame, then, might be seen as something bound up with the
experience of impotence and, unlike the case of guilt, there is no
necessity for an 'internal witness.' Guilt typically involves an internal judgement of one's choices, including deliberate thoughts,
which informs one that a set of standards one identifies with has
been violated. If sex is special and has an especial link with shame
then in some sense it should come as no surprise that feelings of
guilt may be especially prevalent in this highly sensitive area–an
area where even before we get to voluntary acts we are dealing
with self-perceptions of 'personal reduction.'

If shame is something acutely felt by rape victims, even those
who do not feel their chastity even ambiguously compromised,
then we need to understand why rape is so often taken to be such a
serious matter.

Rape has been classified as a crime against humanity in international law,[26] the wrongness of which does not depend on physical damage to the victim, or even psychological damage.[27] A victim
of such an assault could be unconscious and never aware of what
had happened. Nevertheless, he/she would have been seriously
wronged and the law would take far more seriously what had been
done than it would any non-sexual physical assault which inflicted
comparable physical damage.

The sexual assault of rape is ordinarily defined in terms of lack
of consent and that is how I will use the term.[28] Rape here refers to
an act of specific sexual assault whereby one person, without the

consent of another person, intentionally applies force of some kind directly or indirectly to that other person, in order to engage in sexual intercourse with him or her. The term also applies to acts of sex performed on those unable to consent.

In defining rape in terms of lack of consent we need to be clear that it is still something very different from other breaches of consent. It is fairly uncontroversial that when it comes to property there are acceptable non-consensual expropriations that are not theft (e.g. state penalties or taxation).[29] Similarly, there are non-consensual 'breaches' of confidences in certain circumstances which are justifiable and even required. While lack of consent is what defines the above examples, rape, also defined by lack of consent, isn't like this. Coercive sex as punishment, for example, is always rape and is nowhere regarded as acceptable in the way fines and the revealing of confidences can be. And while a rape victim's subjective attitude plays a role in determining whether a rape has occurred, it is not the victim's *desires* that determine this, but wholly and simply the absence of consent.

At this point it might be worth raising the issue of whether rape is taken so seriously not just because it is an expression of contempt or some other negative mental stance - lots of things are - but more fundamentally because it parodies the expression of something important and hence is an offence not just against the person raped but against society, which has an interest in maintaining the meaning of sexual intercourse. It is one of the purposes of this book to give an account of sex that is rationally sustainable and that might make sense of our intuitions in this area.

In order to arrive at such a general account, however, we need to be clear on the relationship between the alleged significance of sex and consensual and non-consensual forms of it. David Archard, in a valuable exploration of the issue building on the work of Susan Brison, writes:

> Non-consensual sex is of an entirely different order
> from consensual sex. What is wrongful is sex-without-
> consent. The wrong is not measured as sex from which
> consent has been subtracted; the wrong of rape is the
> indivisible wrong of non-consensual sex. Susan Brison
> points out (pp. 6-7) that thinking of other offences as
> action-types without consent exposes the oddity of doing
> so in the case of rape. Try, she suggests, thinking of theft
> as 'coerced gift-giving' or murder as 'assisted suicide
> minus consent'. She adds that 'In the cases of both theft
> and murder, the notion of violation seems built into our
> conceptions of the physical act constituting the crime,
> so it is inconceivable that one could consent to the act
> in question'. It is easier to think of rape as a violation if
> one does not simply think of it as sex–and the very same
> kind of sex as we have as consenting parties–but with
> the consent subtracted.[30]

In other words, sex should not be seen as a simple and invariant factor in both rape and consensual sexual intercourse. Following on from my earlier point about the unconscious victim being seriously harmed, I would agree with Archard when he rejects the view that those who care little for the meaning of sex are somehow less fundamentally harmed by rape. As Archard says,

> the inference is solely warranted by the disputed as-
> sumption that the harmfulness of non-consensual sex is a
> function of the value of consensual sex.[31]

The wrong in raping someone in a 'persistent vegetative state' is, of course, different in some important ways from that of raping someone conscious and aware that they are being violated. But what the cases have in common is the fact that a fundamental immoral violation has taken place, irrespective of how active the mental capacities of the victim are at a given time. If we replace 'rape' with 'murder' in these examples, it should be clear that the wrongness of the act is not dependent on the exercisable mental capacities of the victim, but rather on the fatal violation of a core good of that victim, namely his life. Such thoughts lead us to the idea that our various radical capacities (even if unactuated, as in the case of someone in PVS) have the value that they do because they are the radical capacities bound up with being a human being - a being described by Aristotle as a 'rational animal'. A being with radical capacities has interests which he need not know he has but which can nevertheless be violated (a baby being killed, a senile man being humiliated, etc.). The value of an actuated capacity is not something that can be understood separately from the value of the whole organism which is defined by a set of radical capacities or overall orientation (we will look at this further in Chapter 2).

If this view of human persons is correct, then we are in a better position to make sense of why rape appears to be such a serious crime, the seriousness of which is difficult to account for on views which make 'harms felt' or 'victim's views of the importance of sex in human life' the decisive criteria for judging the harm of rape. Archard proposes that sex is one of those basic interests that is particularly important because it is close to

> the centre or core of the space that, metaphorically, defines the self. If our sexuality is an interest which defines who and what each of us is, then it is at the very heart of our self-identity. In consequence, rape attacks and damages something crucial to our being and personhood...

> On the spatial model, our interests in our sexual bodily
> integrity and in our sexual self-determination are at the
> heart of our being. Sex and sexuality are central to who
> we are...To put things all too bluntly and simply, on the
> spatial model, rape is very wrong for violating what we
> are.[32]

Liberal thinkers like Archard will often talk of sex as being "at the heart of our being" and "central to who we are" but do not make clear why this is so or whether this is true of all people or only people who choose to see it thus, or what aspects of the whole range of phenomena called sexual are part of that 'heart'.

Throughout this book we will be exploring from different angles the question of the relevance of sex and its ethical foundations. What we note here, however, is that such a view about the centrality of sex appears to have a great deal of philosophical but also phenomenological and literary and cultural support - not to mention near-universal historical and contemporary support amongst people from extremely diverse backgrounds.

While in recent times it has become common for academics and books and newspapers and hugely popular TV action series to portray various forms of brutal torture as morally unobjectionable, rape is not portrayed in anything like this way. Rape is not even discussed in such terms, whereas torture is, apparently, a subject that *can* be so discussed. Heroes can, apparently, torture people (see, for example, the highly-regarded show '24') but never rape them. Some will say that you can torture a suspect in a 'ticking time' bomb situation, but is anyone saying one can rape such a person? Moreover, it is generally accepted that one can crack someone over the head, cut off a limb, inject poison into them, in order to save their life from illness–but does anyone argue, if such a thing can be imagined, that one can rape an ill person to save their life?

Our attitudes to rape may well suggest that sex is 'central' and if shame is the kind of phenomenon suggested above it might be thought that shame has something to tell us about the nature of the human person. For Karol Wojtyla (later Pope John Paul II),

> Only the person can feel shame, because only it of its
> very nature cannot be an object of use (in either mean-
> ing of the verb to use). Sexual shame is to some extent a
> revelation of the supra-utilitarian character of the person,
> whether the person is ashamed of the sexual values con-
> nected with its own body or of its attitude to such values
> as persons of the other sex, its fixation on them as mere
> objects of enjoyment.[33]

These kinds of consideration, while they might fit well with our intuitions in this area, must be seen in light of certain metaphysical foundations and the following chapters of this book will aim to explore these as far as is possible. It is worth noting here that, almost uniquely, attempts to discuss metaphysics in relation to sex are very often met with negative responses (including, it must be said, from those who seem to think rational discussion of sex should be substituted by immediate psychological assessments of the characters of those they disagree with!).

Sex and Phenomenology

In closing, I think it is worth thinking carefully and deeply about the 'specialness' of sex. Aurel Kolnai and Dietrich von Hildebrand make use of phenomenology to try and carve out a special place for sexual ethics. Kolnai even goes so far as to say,

> It is because we experience *sinful sexual experience*
> *itself* in sexual sin, and not primarily the logical web of
> relations and their oppositions, that there is inherent in
> this attitude of moral disapprobation an importance and
> absoluteness which has no parallel.[34]

For Kolnai, as apparently for St. Paul (see opening quotes),
sexual sin involves par excellence some kind of 'dirt' within oneself - sexual ethical responses presuppose a reference to *'sexuality
as dirt.'*[35] And phenomenologist Dietrich von Hildebrand always
insists on the essentially 'deep' nature of sexual sin, which quite
unlike other kinds of sins, is something which "goes to the root
of bodily existence."[36] In our own time, Roger Scruton has also
stressed such phenomenological points, writing that,

> It is because a woman is damaged in her sense of self
> that the experience of 'date rape' is so traumatic. The
> victim will often feel shamed, humiliated, her sexual-
> ity sullied and spoiled. Something has been stolen from
> her, and this thing is not her body, but herself. All those
> commonplace descriptions...demand a metaphysical
> exegesis, and the place to begin this exegesis is by
> examining the state of mind of the seducer. For the
> violated woman frequently describes her experience as
> an encounter with evil...The work of negation has been
> wrought...on her *embodiment*–on her sense of her body
> as the physical outreach of the self. At a certain mo-
> ment the seducer appears in his true light. He is not, his
> victim realizes, taking pleasure with me, but on me and
> against me. His pleasure appears bestial and the victim
> too is transfigured in her own eyes into something bes-
> tial.[37]

All of the above suggests that sex 'matters'. Aristotle himself tells us '*In semine hominis esse quiddam divinium*'. And if sex really does matter, we had better get our thinking on it right. If sexual ethics cannot be simply assimilated to other areas of morality - or is perhaps even paradigmatic of morality (though not in such a way as to be merely assimilated to that of which it is a paradigm!) then sex cannot be trivialised or ignored.

Chapter 1
Contraception as Contralife

"If anyone for the sake of fulfilling sexual desire or with premeditated hatred does something to a man or to a woman, or gives something to drink, so that he cannot generate, or she cannot conceive, or offspring be born, let it be held as homicide."

Pope Gregory IX[1]

In their paper "'Every Marital Act Ought to Be Open to New Life': Toward a Clearer Understanding,"[2] the influential Catholic philosophers Germain Grisez, Joseph Boyle, John Finnis, and William May (hereafter GBFM) propose an argument that they believe will (i) explain what constitutes a contraceptive act and (ii) explain why such acts are always morally impermissible. Their argument attempts to explain the wrongness both of contraceptive acts within marriage, and of contraceptive acts outside of marriage, by reference to the 'contralife' character of such acts in the context of what is known as the New Natural Law Theory.[3]

It may come as a surprise to readers that this opening chapter is concerned with somewhat more abstract matters concerning the general approach to moral reasoning proposed by these authors. However, the experiences people may have with sexual value/disvalue and the importance such values may occupy in human life are not to be understood in a vacuum, but need to be somehow situated in a general theory of ethics. Beginning with the GBFM argument is useful in opening the discussion, even if some aspects of GBFM's overall theory and its application to sexual ethics may fail to convince on closer examination.

The framework for GBFM's argument involves a method of evaluating individual human acts (which, for these writers, necessarily involve some kind of choice) in terms of certain aspects of human fulfilment or 'basic human goods'.[4] What makes the GBFM paper distinctive is GBFM's separation for purposes of moral evaluation of contraceptive acts from acts of sexual intercourse, and their refusal to analyse these two acts as one and the same human act–i.e. an act of contraceptive sex.

Another distinctive feature of GBFM's argument that contraception is necessarily contralife is that it does not rely on any prior theory of what constitutes specifically *marital* goods in the light of which contraception must be assessed.[5]

Basic Goods

To see the GBFM paper in its proper context it is necessary to outline briefly the authors'[6] more general theory of the basic goods–sometimes referred to as the 'New Natural Law Theory' or theory of the Grisez-Finnis school. Adopting as a starting point and directive for action Thomas Aquinas's[7] formulation of the self-evident first principle of practical reasoning that "the good is to be pursued; the bad is to be avoided" (a principle which plays a role analogous to that played by the principle of non-contradiction for theoretical reasoning) the theory proposes that careful reflection on what motivates human agents, regardless of location or time, reveals a limited variety of real basic intelligible human goods (values) which are realisable for human beings. The list of these basic goods is made up of the most general and distinguishable features of human activities that constitute human flourishing. These 'basic goods' are, in the words of Germain Grisez, "aspects of persons, not realities apart from persons…the basic goods by which they [persons] enjoy self-fulfilment must be aspects of persons, not merely things they have."[8] The practical intellect (as opposed to the speculative intellect) is said to grasp these basic human goods directly in non-inferential acts of understanding. These basic human goods correspond to the "inherent complexities of human nature."[9]

The basic goods are, as one commentator surmises, "kinds of goods that we can intelligibly conceive any or every human agent as acting *towards* or *for the sake of,* in and of themselves, and with no further objective beyond those goods in mind."[10] They are, in other words, non-instrumental goods (although they may also be used instrumentally). John Finnis categorises these basic forms of human goods as Life, Knowledge, Play, Aesthetic Experience, Sociability (friendship), Practical Reasonableness, and 'Religion.'[11] As the basic goods provide ultimate reasons for acting they are, according to the Grisez-Finnis school, incommensurable. In other words, instantiations of differing basic goods present in options for choice cannot be weighed up against one another; for each can be a distinct and ultimate reason for acting. There is no more fundamental good by which we compare the relative values of the basic goods.

Practical Reasonableness is one of these basic goods, and from its requirement (namely the 'self-evident' principle that good be done and pursued and evil be avoided) the Grisez-Finnis school derives a series of practically applicable moral principles which Finnis terms the Basic Requirements of Practical Reasonableness.[12]

Practical Reasonableness, in the words of Finnis, "...both is a basic aspect of human well-being and concerns one's participation in all the (other) basic aspects of human well-being."[13]

Given that the purpose of practical reasonableness is to advance human flourishing, to act directly against (i.e. to destroy, damage or impede) any aspect of human flourishing is of itself practically irrational. The Grisez-Finnis school therefore holds, as *one* of the basic requirements of Practical Reasonableness, that one can never be morally right in choosing directly against a basic human good. One may pursue a basic human good in action, or one may at least respect it (i.e. not damage it), but may *never* choose to damage such a good. As Finnis observes in *Natural Law and Natural Rights*:

> Reason requires that every basic value be at least respected in each and every action. If one could ever rightly choose a single act which *itself* damages and *itself* does not promote some basic good, then one could rightly choose whole programmes and institutions and enterprises that themselves damage and do not promote basic aspects of well-being, for the sake of their 'net beneficial consequences'.[14]

GBFM take it that to aim for 'net beneficial consequences' is to adopt an incoherent general objective for action, because the incommensurability of the basic goods means that consequences of actions cannot be commensurably evaluated.

Much more can be said about this approach to ethics, but a number of points should here be noted. The approach, though attractive in its focus on human flourishing, invites searching questions as to how we are to understand concepts of 'damaging, destroying, or impeding' a basic human good, especially, for our purposes in this chapter, that of life.

We need to ask which acts count as 'direct' attacks and whether all such acts are truly immoral. For example, in the case of capital punishment actions that do seem to be 'direct' attacks on the good of life have been and are approved in certain circumstances by many, including the religious tradition out of which the Grisez-Finnis theory arises (even if that Church has increasingly frowned on the use of capital punishment in practice).[15] Yet on the Grisez-Finnis account it is difficult to see how such actions could ever be morally justified. Similar problems crop up with regard to what are usually taken to be morally licit actions of armed police or soldiers in just wars: even where such people are not intending to kill aggressors, they are at least intending to do serious bodily harm.

Furthermore, how is one supposed to characterise actions that 'impede,' for example, the basic good of play, and why need such actions always be necessarily wrong?

Incommensurability

As well as providing answers to such questions, the theory needs to give a clear account of the practical implications of the 'incommensurability' of the basic goods. With regard to the contraception case, GBFM posit that, as there are no goods commensurable with the basic good of human life, one can never make a rational choice against life. It would only be rational to choose against the basic good of life for the sake of a greater good, but given the incommensurability of any other good with this (or any other) basic good, such a choice could never be indicated.

GBFM apply their theory of basic goods to contraceptive acts, to which they object on the ground that they are identifiable as necessarily contralife choices–i.e. choices made directly against the basic good of life. As contraception is, according to GBFM, a contralife choice, it is, necessarily, irrational.

The fact that couples do try to calculate whether to bring about a child at some given time, and appear to compare that to the option of *not* bringing about a child at that time does not, according to GBFM, mean that their calculations are in fact rational. In comparing two possible futures, one in which a baby comes to be and one in which he/she does not, the couple appear to be calculating on the basis that they "*know* that the future without the baby will be rationally better,"[16]–and, say GBFM, this they cannot know.

However, this approach seems fraught with difficulties. Such high standards for knowledge claims threaten to call into question any knowledge claims based on future probabilities for medium-term decisions.[17] All of us make, all the time, exactly these kinds of decisions, based on reasonable projections of future probabilities.

Consider also a couple that decide not to conceive a child in January but to conceive one in March instead. They do this for reasons of the mother's health. Cannot the mother claim that, in choosing to have the baby later in the year, she is comparing one life against one life–and, all other things being equal, doing so for reasons of health? In which case, cannot she be said to be choosing the same amount of life (beginning two months later) plus the good of health? Given this, it certainly appears that the choice to try and conceive in March overrides the rational appeal of conceiving a child in January.

If GBFM refuse to concede the above, then it follows that the sorts of commensurating decisions that GBFM *do* allow as rational are not possible either. Why is it rational (*ceteris paribus* and with no better options) to crash your aircraft into a field that is less densely populated than a neighbouring field? Such a decision is rational according to GBFM because the pilot's "comparison of possible futures established the rational preferability, in terms of saving human lives, of steering towards the less densely populated area."[18] However, it is unclear how the loss of V's unique and irreplaceable life in field 1 is being compared to the instantiations of X, Y, and Z's lives in field 2. The value of X, Y and Z's lives in field 2 may *exceed* but does not *include* the value of V's life.[19] Put another way, proposal (a) "to crash into field 2" does not have all the beneficial features of proposal (b) "to crash into field 1" *and some more*. Moreover, how is one supposed to identify the 'future benefits' of the pilot's decision, following GBFM's approach? Yet GBFM in this case wish to characterise the pilot's decision as rational. If that decision over apparently 'incommensurable' futures can be rational, then why cannot other such decisions?

In light of these examples we can ask regarding incommensurability: if a chooser is to be a virtuous chooser, i.e. one who aims to make those choices most fulfilling of human nature, then he must be choosing with an eye to greater or lesser value (which is not to say that value can be identified independently of what it is virtuous to prefer). And the virtuous chooser is precisely a chooser who is good at identifying just how valuable certain choices are. The same applies to GBFM's point about side-effects and the Golden Rule.[20] Here the morally praiseworthy application of the Golden Rule to situations requiring a calculation of the possible benefits/burdens of side-effects requires an agent to be virtuous–and a virtuous agent is precisely the agent who can identify correctly which instantiations of goods are most important.

An example might be the following: While playing dominoes I notice that a person in the same room is drowning in the bath. It appears that I have a duty to save this person, and in so doing stop playing dominoes. I have this duty, according to the Grisez-Finnis school, not because life is a greater good than play (or because this instantiation of life is a greater good than this instantiation of play), but because, following the Golden Rule, I should do unto others as I would have them do unto me (on this see also George (1999)). However, the proper application of this rule assumes that I am not a domino-playing fanatic, who thinks that playing dominoes is so important a good that even if I were dying, I would urge others to carry on playing dominoes rather than save me. In order for the rule to be properly applied we implicitly assume a *virtuous* agent of the kind I have described. This is not to deny that the virtuous agent is bound by certain non-negotiable demands concerning particular virtues and their related goods. It is merely to note that the GBFM view of incommensurability seems far too strong to account for some actions that seem morally required.

The Contraceptive Act

Having briefly considered incommensurability and the theory of basic goods it is important now to be clear how GBFM define a contraceptive act. The authors state that:

> ...to contracept one must think that (1) some behaviour in which someone could engage is likely to cause a new life to begin, and (2) the bringing about of the beginning of new life might be impeded by some other behaviour one could perform. One's choice is to perform that other behaviour; one's relevant immediate intention (which may be sought for some further purpose) is that the prospective new life not begin.[21]

This definition shows that GBFM see contraception as only loosely related to intercourse: a sexual act and a contraceptive act are, in their view, two separate acts. The definition contrasts with a definition which takes intentional contraceptive acts of sexual intercourse as the basis for a definition of contraception.[22]

One of the reasons for setting up the debate this way is that, by focusing upon the intention of those who contracept, their chosen human act can be properly analysed in terms of intentionality. GBFM appear to define contraceptive acts in a way that captures what Pope Paul VI in *Humanae Vitae* #14 condemns, namely any act, "which either before, at the moment of, or after sexual intercourse, is specifically intended to prevent procreation – whether as an end or as a means."

In order to stress what their definition of contraceptive acts includes, GBFM state that contraception is not defined by a pattern of outward behaviour. An example they give is of a population-controlling dictator who for his own purposes 'contracepts' by adding a fertility-reducing chemical to the public water supply. The dictator's behaviour is, on GBFM's account, contraceptive; that is, he makes a choice the moral object[23] of which is to impede the beginning of the life of possible persons. The moral object of the choice is what renders his behaviour contraceptive. Such behaviour, on this account, necessarily exhibits a contralife will. Couples who drink the water and subsequently have intercourse, insofar as they did not drink the water for contraceptive reasons, would not be contracepting, although their intercourse would be infertile.

Whether the dictator's own actions should be brought under the term contraceptive is an interesting question. It does seem confusing to say, with Janet Smith,[24] that the dictator has turned the marital acts of the water-drinking victim couples into contracepted acts (albeit non-culpably contracepted acts)–unless contracepted acts merely means acts physically incapable of procreation (in which case it might be better simply to speak of physically sterile acts). What the dictator cannot do is turn anyone else into a contraceptor by such means, for it is not in his gift to impinge upon the moral objects of the chosen behaviour of others by means of acts of which they are unaware. All he may do is render sexual acts physically infertile. However it seems that we *can* usefully say of the dictator example that not only parents but society needs to welcome (a) fertility and (b) new lives. On the assumption that contraceptive and other sterilizing acts are in some sense immoral, the dictator might *corrupt* married couples and destroy their marital acts at the subjective level (promoting contraception and not just secretly changing the water) *or* he might fail to respect the goods that couples' own actions *do* respect (i.e. a) and b)).

There appears to be a moral difference between a couple choosing to perform an act of contraceptive sex, and the dictator choosing to pollute the water hoping to sterilise others. A common argument against contraception, based on characterising contraception in terms of contraceptive sex acts, will say that the couple are intentionally doing something to their marital act which renders it non-marital and that this rendering differs radically from what the dictator is doing, as he is simply incapable of rendering anything non-marital without engaging the couple's own intentions.[25]

An example to elucidate this seeming difference might be the following. Imagine a dictator who, in introducing his fertility-reducing drug into the water, somehow ensures that it will only affect the fertility of non-married couples. He does this because he thinks it is unjust for people to have children out of wedlock. He also believes it to be immoral for any couple to contracept their own acts of intercourse, because, according to him, in so doing the couple, married or not, render their acts opposed to the good of marriage.

Now imagine a non-married couple contracepting their sexual act with a similar motive to the dictator sterilising the water i.e. to avoid a child being born out of wedlock. The couple have turned one type of act (their act of merely non-marital intercourse) into another type of act entirely (a *contracepted* act of non-marital intercourse). The couple have not, of course, turned an otherwise marital into a non-marital act, but rather, have further distanced their non-marital act from a marital act as GBFM and the Catholic Church to which they belong would understand that act.[26] In so doing the couple have affected their characters differently from the way in which the dictator has affected his.

A common approach to the question of contraception would see the couple's act but not the dictator's as coming under the heading of specifically sexual immorality. Is the dictator being sexually immoral in some way? We might imagine a case where the dictator does not even know what marital meanings the sexual act is meant to express–he may merely have some hazy idea that normal sexual intercourse is loosely connected with the possibility of conception.

But if this is the case, is the dictator's wrongdoing to be characterised as merely a case of illicit use of power, such as illicitly sedating a couple would be? Is it only the illicit use of power over the couple that would characterise the wrongdoing of the dictator in a case where the dictator, with perhaps a relatively benign *further* intention, sought to prevent the couple's sexual act from being fertile? Or is his wrongdoing to be characterised more specifically as a species of sexual wrongdoing? It might be argued that the dictator does not relate properly to certain couples' reproductive well-being and in this sense behaves somewhat analogously to a couple who contracept their sexual act. However, there are very real differences too.

On the GBFM account, what makes both the couple and the dictator contraceptors is their possession of a contralife will. Any further difference in the moral nature of their acts is, for GBFM, extraneous to the question of whether they are engaging in the type of wrongdoing known as contracepting.

Such an account of contraception cannot properly exclude the following type of case. Imagine an aunt expressing to her niece disapproval of her niece's intention to have a child. The aunt foresees that some behaviour of her niece is likely to result in a new birth, and believes rightly or wrongly that her verbal expression of disapproval will make this eventuality less likely. Is she, on the GBFM definition, a contraceptor? If she is a contraceptor she is surely a worse one than the dictator, for she is directly attempting to influence the intentions of her niece and not merely whether or not she has a child.

Would it matter if her advice to her niece not to have a child were grounded in a recognition that the niece, for very good reasons, had a *duty* not to have a child? GBFM might try and argue that their use of the word "impede" in relation to new life rules out cases such as this, but they provide no definition of the word "impede" or any independent reason for thinking that such cases should be ruled out by their definition.[27] Lawrence Masek imagines a case where a father, fearing his daughter and son-in-law may not chart their fertility correctly (they have a serious reason to avoid pregnancy), adds an anovulant drug to his daughter's drink. The couple do chart correctly and the father's intervention is superfluous. For Masek, the father "does not commit an injustice by frustrating someone's desire to become pregnant. In this case defenders of *Humanae vitae* cannot circumvent the contralife will argument by appealing to the injustice of using contraception on others. (To emphasize that the woman and her husband are not victims of an injustice, one could add that they would welcome her father's intervention if they knew about it)."[28] This argument, however, misses the point that an assault is still an assault even if the victim or victims would not object to it if they knew. And a virtue ethicist might say that such an assault is precisely against the virtue of justice. And surely something qualifies as an assault that involves a non-consensual thwarting of - or attempt to thwart - a function: in this case the non-trivial matter of a woman's fertility.

If it can be shown that GBFM's definition of contraception is in important ways inadequate in drawing a distinction between contraceptive acts and the practice of 'Natural Family Planning' (NFP), which GBFM follow the Catholic Church in seeing as licit in principle, there will be no reason to include the above cases under the term of contraception. For, if contraception has such a wide meaning, inclusive of many activities GBFM and the Catholic Church regard as licit, then clearly GBFM will no longer be merely defending the teaching of *Humanae Vitae*, but actually rejecting it as too lax.

One reason given by GBFM for treating contraceptive acts independently from sexual acts is that by doing so, "one cannot argue that since marital intercourse is good, contraception involved in it can be acceptable. If the contraceptive act and the marital act were one and the same human act, that argument might succeed, since that one act could be analysed with two effects."[29] This, GBFM believe, would make this approach open to the objection that the 'principle of double-effect' might justify such an act.

However, many of those who object to contraceptive sexual acts will deny that such acts are marital in nature, precisely because they have been deliberately rendered contraceptive.[30] Such an account, which I have called the contraceptive sex act account, allows that 'taking a pill' is an act of contraceptive intent (assuming that is why the pill is taken) and that 'having sexual intercourse' after taking the pill is acting with an intention that may well confirm the original intention (i.e. the intention to render infertile any possibly fertile sexual act). So, while there are two acts–the taking of the pill and the sexual act–the contraceptive sexual act is one that confirms the prior intention embodied in the pill-taking act.[31]

Necessarily Contralife

Given their wide definition of contraceptive acts, GBFM proceed to argue that "every contraceptive act is necessarily contralife." A couple, according to them, "in choosing contraception as a means to [a] further good... necessarily reject a new life. They imagine that a new person will come to be if that is not prevented, they want that possible person not to be, and they effectively will that he or she never be. That will is a contralife will. Therefore, each and every contraceptive act is necessarily contralife."[32] As GBFM put it elsewhere, "the contraceptive acts seeks to impede *the beginning of the life of a possible person*."[33]

Obviously an account of the wrongness of contraception in line with Catholic teaching will need to exclude the actions/omissions of couples who licitly practice NFP, but we will come to that later. The central claim that GBFM make about the wrongness of contraceptive acts appears to be that a couple that choose such acts can be said to be choosing against the life of a new possible person. GBFM further state that "...in and of itself, a contraceptive act is nothing but contralife,"[34] that "insofar as contraception is contralife, it is similar to deliberate homicide,"[35] and that insofar as a will is contralife it embodies a "practical (though not necessarily emotional) hatred of the possible baby they project and reject, just as the will to accept the coming to be of a baby is a practical love of that possible person."[36]

Possession of a contralife will presumably means at very least something formal, such as 'having an attitude that does not appropriately value the good of life,' or 'having an attitude that relates to the good of life inappropriately.' However, GBFM imply that a contralife will is something more than this. They state that, "an essential condition of the immorality of deliberate homicide is that it involves a contralife will,"[37] and further that, "contraception is similar to deliberate homicide, despite their important differences, precisely inasmuch as both involve a contralife *will*...the contralife will that contraception involves also is morally evil, although we do not claim that it is usually as evil as the homicidal will."[38]

However, a homicidal will is a will that aims at depriving an identifiable individual or individuals of the good of life, thereby harming him/her/them.[39] For GBFM the contralife will involved in contraception is a refusal to help to bestow the benefit of existence on a *possible* person, but I take it that this does not involve a 'harm' to any such person who will not in fact exist: there is a major difference between an action that harms by depriving a real future person, and an action that fails to benefit a possible person.[40] True, a choice of failing to benefit can be a wrongful harm in some circumstances where there will be a real future victim (and even where there will not be there may be a failure in generosity involved). However, what the distinction shows is that the term contralife operates in far too wide and formal a way to capture what is an "essential"[41] condition of a homicidal will.

Indeed, there is a question as to whether it is correct to characterise the contralife will as an "essential" condition of a homicidal will if by that we mean a non-trivial condition. We might say that a homicidal will is a will directed to the end that a particular person or actual future person or persons be (effectively) harmed by depriving them of life. But, if I will to kill X I am willing against X's life (even if I may not be willing to 'harm' X as such–I may not believe death will be harmful). There is no reason to suppose that there need be a separable 'contralife' component of the homicidal will which acts as a 'condition' for the homicidal will, except in the trivial sense that life is inappropriately related-to (at least if the killing is unjust). Similarly a theist might argue that an essential condition of any sin is that it involves a will opposed to God's law, such that insofar as one type of sin involves such a will, it has that in common with any other sin. Here what is constitutionally a sin need not be something *intended* to violate God's law as such, even if it is known that it will do so (the relationship between one's intentions and awareness of this kind is discussed further in the Appendix).

Admittedly GBFM's understanding of 'contralife' will is narrower than our imagined 'contra God's law' will; nevertheless, there are multifarious ways in which one might have what GBFM term a contralife will. The aunt in our earlier example may have a contralife will insofar as she takes verbal steps to discourage her niece from conceiving: if there is no moral reason why her niece should not conceive, then the aunt relates inappropriately to the good of potential new life. However, what of a couple who *do* have a duty not to have a child, but nonetheless will to conceive one? Surely their will must also be, in some sense, contralife, in that they relate inappropriately to the good of life by their very pursuit of that good (we might say, they value life but fail to respect it).

A couple, on the GBFM account, have a contralife will if they intend their extra-marital sex not to result in conception. According to GBFM, a couple who practise NFP with the intention that no child come to be, and choose the not-coming-to-be of a child as a means to achieving their further goal of avoiding baby-related burdens, have a contralife will. A couple who refuse to bestow the good of life on a possible person, if such a formulation makes sense, and use contraceptive means to achieve this goal also have a contralife will.

These examples make it clear that there are many different ways of possessing a contralife will. They should also make clear that the attempt to draw a close analogy between a homicidal will and a merely contralife will is misconceived.

Possible Persons

A number of further objections can be made to the GBFM account. Firstly, the idea that a couple necessarily 'imagine' a possible person whom they make sure, by their actions, will not come to exist, does not seem to be justified. There is no reason to think that 'contracepting' couples necessarily have such thoughts.[42] What are the identity conditions for such a possible person? Just how specific does the imagining of the possible person have to be, and does the specificity of the couples' visualisation of the possible person they are choosing against affect the level of moral wrongness of the contralife choice made against that possible person?[43] As concerns the possible baby that results from contracepted sexual intercourse being unwanted/hated, GBFM would need to establish that this practical hatred is a necessary motivation for the couple to undertake a contraceptive act, not just that it is a likely later reaction to any actual baby that does in fact come to be.

In translating precise definitions into predicate logic we need a criterion of identity. As Frege argued, if we are to use the symbol *a* to signify an object, we must have a criterion for deciding in all cases whether *b* is the same as *a*, even if it is not always in our power to apply the criterion.[44] Not only can we have no object without an identity; we can have no *naming* of an object without a *criterion* of identity. No such criterion for the 'imagined' or 'foreseen' possible person is provided by GBFM. This is an important point, for the wrongness of contraception on the GBFM model runs along the lines that it is illicit to will against the good of life of so-and-so. However, the most one might will against in fact would be a range of possible persons one of whom will, in coming to exist, fall under the described range.

Can we make intelligible the notion of practical hatred for a person who does not yet exist? Imagine two families, the Pascals and the Molinas, who are involved in a long-running blood-feud. One day a member of the Pascal family, Rufus, poisons the well of the Molina family with the intention of killing the future yet-to-be-conceived grandchild of the Molina's. Cannot Rufus be said to have, at least, a malicious intention towards the future Molina grandchild? In a sense this seems a reasonable assumption, but needs to be qualified. Surely the most Rufus can be said to have is a conditional general attitude to any possible future Molina grandchild. As a general intention this is condemnable but even here, Rufus cannot be said to have a practical hatred for a person who may never come into existence. Rufus' intention cannot be characterised as "there exists x–I intend to make sure that x doesn't exist," precisely because x does *not* yet exist. Moreover, Rufus can only will against a range of possible persons. One may always ask the question, of someone who refers to "the future Molina grandchild," "why do you suppose that there is only one (non-existent) future Molina grandchild?"[45] So the most that Rufus may have is a negative general propositional attitude towards a range of possible persons.

The analogy with contraception breaks down, however, when we remember that the contracepting couple is acting precisely to ensure that the possible person is not actualised, whereas Rufus is doing nothing to prevent the coming-to-be of the future grandchild, and may even welcome his/her coming to be so that his evil plan can be realised. Whereas Rufus wills harm to one of a range of possible persons he anticipates will be actualised, the contracepting couple wills against a range of possible persons who they will never to be actualised. Rufus' will can here be called homicidal in a way in which the contracepting couple's can't be.

Admittedly, Grisez and Boyle[46] do not now use the word 'imagine', and talk of the couple necessarily 'foreseeing' a baby coming to be. This seems more hopeful insofar as it jettisons the idea of active imagination of a specific possible person and is more suggestive of the idea of a range. The theory, however, runs into its biggest difficulties with the NFP/contraception distinction.

GBFM appear to be making the counterfactual claim that if sperm X were to enter ovum Y at such-and-such a point, and at such-and-such a time, and at such-and-such a temperature etc., we would have a specifiable possible person. Given this, GBFM then seem to be saying that a contracepting couple must be necessarily foreseeing such a specifiable possible person, and acting so as to prevent his/her coming into being. Of the status of such a being GBFM say: "the possible person whose life is presented is no mere abstraction but an absolutely unique and unrepeatable individual who would exist if he or she were welcomed rather than prevented."[47] According to GBFM, such an intention to prevent is always wrong because it entails a contralife will. It entails a contralife will because a couple, in choosing to contracept, is doing no more and no less than impeding the beginning of the life of that specifiable possible person (or, at least, a narrowly specifiable range of possible persons).

However, we need to ask here how the intentional relation to the specific possible person or persons involved in the case of the contracepting couple can differ from that involved with an NFP couple. The overarching choice in both these cases is "not to cause [or "not to help to cause"] the initiation of new life" as the result of a chosen sexual act. GBFM appear, in characterising contraceptive acts in terms of an intentional relation to the bringing into being of a possible person, to cast their net too widely. The argument is that both a contracepting couple and an NFP couple can have good reason not to cause the initiation of new life, due (for example) to the burdens that a baby's coming-to-be would bring about. To contracept in order to achieve this goal is, for GBFM, never morally licit because contraception necessarily involves intentionally impeding the beginning of a possible person's life. NFP, however, on the GBFM account, need not be contralife, although it *can* be chosen with "contraceptive intent."[48]

The distinction of importance for GBFM is the following. To contracept is to choose to prevent the beginning of the life of a possible person–it is "a choice *to do something*, with the intent that the baby not be, as a means to a further end." However, the noncontraceptive choice of NFP[49] differs because "It is a choice *not to do something*–namely, not to engage in possibly fertile sexual intercourse–with the intent that the bad consequences of the baby's coming to be will be avoided, and with the *acceptance as side effects* of both the baby's not-coming-to-be and the bad consequences of his or her not-coming-to-be. In this choice and in the acceptance of its side-effects, there need be no contralife will. The baby who might come into being need not be projected and rejected."[50] The authors further add: "[T]rue, not choosing to realise that good– and, indeed, choosing to avoid the burdens one anticipates if one were to realise it–means *not willing* that the good be realised, but it does not mean *willing* that the good *not be realised*."[51] The claim is that the NFP couple can be, "choosing not to realise something they have good reason to choose to realise [a baby], but whose realisation would conflict with avoiding something else they have good reason to avoid [the burdensome side-effects of that baby's coming-to-be]."[52]

Against this, it can be objected that the contracepting couple and the NFP couple stand in the same intentional relation to the beginning of new life, at least in the sense that both couples intend that life not be conceived. The contracepting couple, like the NFP couple, may well characterise their decision to contracept as a decision to choose against the burdens that the coming-to-be of a new baby will bring about. GBFM say that this necessarily involves for the contracepting couple a contralife will because it necessarily involves the intention to impede the coming-to-be of a new child. The NFP couple are said to be willing only against the bad side-effects that the coming-to-be of a new baby will bring about. But how is one to make sense of the idea that one can try to avoid the effects of having a baby without trying to avoid having a baby? According to the NFP couple's plan, their *means* of avoiding the effects of having a child is *that they not have a child*. One of the propositions a couple must go through en route to reaching the intended outcome of their plan (not having those burdensome baby side-effects linked with the baby's coming-to-be[53]) is the proposal: *not having a baby*.[54] The deliberate removal of the necessary causal precondition of avoiding the baby side-effects cannot be characterised as a mere side-effect of the couple's plan.[55]

Masek's Defence

Lawrence Masek, in an ingenious defence of the GBFM thesis argues that a couple using NFP and desiring that human life not begin do not have to be intending the non-existence of human life either as an end or as a means. He proposes three examples to defend this claim:

> *Case 1:* A baby has an illness that causes both earache and constipation. A pediatrician informs the baby's parents that the two symptoms cannot be treated simultaneously. The parents need to choose which symptom to treat first, but the pediatrician says that each symptom causes an equal level of discomfort and that there is no medical basis for choosing one over the other. The parents toss a coin to determine which symptom to treat first.

> *Case 2:* The baby's situation in case 2 is the same as the baby's situation in case 1. The parents are about to toss a coin to determine which symptom to treat first. They then consider that they have a long car trip planned and that treating the earache first would make the car trip easier, since it would reduce the hassle of changing dirty diapers on the trip. The parents therefore choose to treat the earache first.

> *Case 3:* Parents of a healthy baby are planning a car trip. They add a chemical to their baby's food in order to impede the baby's digestion, in order to

cause constipation, in order to reduce the hassle of changing dirty diapers on the trip.

Masek tell us, "I see no reason that the parents act wrongly in case 1. If they may toss a coin in case 1, I see no reason that they may not consider the effects of each option in case 2. In case 3, however, the parents do act immorally since they intentionally impede their baby's health as a means to having fewer hassles on their trip."

We can cautiously agree with Masek that these judgements "seem intuitively plausible."[56]

One does not need to reject the idea (strongly argued for by Frances Kamm[57]) that an effect can motivate an action without being intended, in order to reject Masek's arguments with regard to contraception and NFP. What we need is to examine the examples Masek gives, and others, in the light of questions about contraception.

It would seem that the difference between Case 2 and Case 3 is like the difference between (3) contraception ('deliberate constipation'[58]) and delaying sexual activity along NFP lines (2).

For Masek it is unreasonable to say that the couples in cases 1 and 2 'intend' the baby to be constipated. For when you choose when a particular bad side effect happens (constipation), you need not be intending it.

However, this becomes more difficult to argue the more useful to you is the aspect that guides your choice (as opposed to e.g. situations where that useful aspect is a mere 'defeater of a defeater', as Kamm would call it). Let us imagine two cases involving fertility-affecting treatment, which is more directly related to contraception than Masek's cases:

> *Case A:* A woman needs treatment that will
> make her temporarily infertile (a bad side-effect
> of some morally good medical treatment). The in-
> fertility is unwelcome (or at least, not particularly
> focused-on): it is simply a bad side-effect. She
> will choose when to have the treatment and so will
> choose the time when she has that bad side-effect.

> *Case B:* A woman doesn't want a baby and
> chooses the same treatment that the woman in
> Case A receives, but regards the 'side effect' as the
> doctors see it as a bonus. She generally objects to
> contraception (i.e. rendering otherwise fertile acts
> infertile), but wants infertile sex with her husband
> when he comes back from his lengthy naval post-
> ing. In this case she is *intending* to make herself
> infertile. This is not a mere side-effect. Her actions
> differ from those of the NFP couple who use infer-
> tile or fertile times for intercourse, because here the
> woman is *choosing to make a fertile time infertile.*

In light of these relevant examples what might be said about Masek's points? Certainly it can't be the case that you intend side-effects which are still altogether unwelcome but which you shift to a less bad time, e.g. I will shift agonising pain to Thursday rather than Wednesday. Surely it is ludicrous to say I am intending ago-nising pain as an effect of my operation!

However, when the 'side-effect' is welcomed and seen as conferring a benefit overall, it is a different story, e.g. when the secondary effect of infertility is brought about so as to 'benefit' the woman at a time of her choosing. If you time the 'side-effect' to get the perceived benefit (as opposed to minimising perceived harm) then how can we say this effect is not intended?

In an NFP case similarly, there is certainly an intention that children not come to be. To claim that the NFP couple are merely not choosing to do anything to achieve something is to mischaracterize what they are doing. NFP can be adopted by a couple precisely because they intend that a new child not come to be on the grounds that the burdens this would bring about are serious enough for them to avoid having a child at that time. By deliberately refraining from intercourse when the woman is thought to be fertile, the couple intend precisely not to bring about a new child.[59] While the use of contraception actively prevents (or lessens) the possibility of a new child coming to be, the NFP couple in contrast are said to act licitly in avoiding by omission a new child coming to be. However, the NFP couple, insofar as they are pursuing that strategy, are not just omitting to actively bring about the coming-to-be of a new child, they are *intending by omission* that a new child not come to be.[60] This is precisely the rationale behind the adoption of NFP.[61]

The distinction, for GBFM, between the NFP couple and the contracepting couple in their intentional relation to the existence of new life is difficult to see. Certainly the authors when writing about euthanasia[62] see as morally equivalent deliberate active euthanasia and euthanasia by deliberate omission (as opposed to 'letting die' without intending death). Is the idea then that the NFP couple must somehow try to intend only to avoid the burdens of the possible baby's coming-to-be, without intending that baby's not-coming-to-be? But as we have seen, the avoidance of the coming-to-be of the baby is integral to the plan of refraining from intercourse. If we do accept the GBFM position here, then cannot the couple using a condom who also will to avoid the bad side-effects of pregnancy be said to be not necessarily willing against conception itself? If that is the case, then GBFM must characterise such couples as non-contraceptors, which is highly counterintuitive.[63]

The only way to distinguish NFP and contraception, on the GBFM account, appears to be that with contraception the couple seem to be foreseeing and directly choosing against a relatively specific possible person. So, with a barrier contraceptive, the couple (assuming full knowledge of sexual reproduction) are said to be willing against any possible person that would result from any of the sperm that would have otherwise penetrated the woman's ovum. But even here there are, on average, over 40 million sperm per ejaculate that might fertilise the women's ovum at any of the many possible times: as with the NFP couple, it may be claimed, their refraining from intercourse during a certain period cannot be said to be a direct willing against a clearly specifiable possible person, given that there is *no* clearly specifiable possible person.

However, if we accept this distinction, then surely we must accept that the couple using an ovulation-impeding contraceptive (e.g. the Pill) are also not directly willing against a clearly specifiable possible person (leaving aside abortifacient effects they may realise are possible and positively intend should there be 'breakthrough' ovulation). In point of fact, the couple who have sex after taking the pill are even more distanced from a specific possible person than the NFP couple. For the NFP couple are deliberately refraining from sexual activity due to the fact that they believe a particular ovum at a particular time will be present, whereas the pill-taking couple are having sex when they believe no ovum will be present at the time of sexual activity. So, the pill-taking couple, insofar as they relate to possible persons, are further distanced from a specifiable possible person than the NFP couple–who stand in closer relation to the possible persons that would result from ovum x being fertilised, at time y, by one of over 40 million sperm. Again, the NFP couple are omitting to act at time y, but it is an intentional omission adopted on the grounds that they intend that none of a range of possible persons come to be. GBFM might have other grounds for rejecting pill-usage (such as that it temporarily suppresses healthy functioning), but that position would be independent of their contraception/contralife argument.

Moreover, the NFP couple, in refraining from intercourse at a certain time, with the intention that a new baby not come to be, could be said to be choosing that a specifiable possible person (i.e. the person that would have resulted if they had chosen to have sexual intercourse instead of refraining) not-come-to-be. The NFP couple intentionally omit to have intercourse because they seek to avoid any such intercourse causing the beginning of a new person's life.

If the claim were that the difference between the NFP couple and the contracepting couple is that these couples have a different intentional relation to the sexual activity and its being a possible cause of new life (the NFP couple has an intentional relation to *abstain* from sexual activity–something GBFM themselves note), then we have a rather different argument from the one proposed by GBFM which is concerned too broadly with the intentional relation to the "beginning of new life."[64]

Rape Case

On the GBFM account, then, there appear to be no cogent grounds for excluding the licit practice of NFP from the category of contraception. On top of this GBFM also have difficulties with the case of pregnancy prevention after rape. The latter is generally accepted by Catholic commentators on these issues, and various Bishops' Conferences or their Committees have said that a woman who has recently been raped is quite within her rights to seek to evacuate the rapist's sperm from her body.[65] GBFM have this to say on such an action: "…the measures that are taken in this case are a defence of the woman's ovum (insofar as it is a part of her person), against the rapist's sperm (insofar as they are parts of his person)."[66] The question here is whether a woman in this situation is, according to GBFM, morally permitted to prevent the conception of a specific possible person.

Imagine a woman who either knows or does not know that she is fertile. She is much more likely to try and rid herself of the rapist's sperm if she believes that by not doing so she risks the conception of a possible person. But if that is the case, then she very definitely is willing against a possible person. She foresees the possible person coming-to-be (sperm X, Y, Z etc. entering her ovum), and she acts in such a way that that possible person does not come to be. Such action, on GBFM's account, exhibits a contralife will. Likewise, if I were to see eminent and wealthy fertility expert, Dr W. Inston, at one of London's glamorous IVF clinics, about to inject a single sperm into an ovum in a petri dish, and I grabbed his arm to prevent the procedure, would I be exhibiting a contralife will? I certainly can envisage the IVF (or rather ICSI – introcytoplasmic sperm injection) created baby – I foresee his/her coming to be, and I will against it. More realistically and less dramatically, we can imagine a couple who have agreed to try IVF, but, at the eleventh hour, decide that it is wrong to produce a child in such a way. Do this couple exhibit a contralife will in grabbing the doctor's arm to stop conception going forward?

One of the authors of the paper, Germain Grisez, has written further on this subject and suggested that conception should be understood as the completion or continuation of sexual union, and that the victim of the rape is justified in resisting the continuation of that union.[67] Such a position implies, however, that a rape victim who does *not* attempt to have the rapist's sperm removed from her may be consenting to (or at least not resisting) the completion of that sexual union even though she is now in a safe environment. So the rape victim is not only justified in having the sperm removed, but would appear on this view to have a *duty* to have it removed (insofar as this is practicable).[68] However, Grisez does not state this implication, making only the weaker claim that a woman in this situation can be justified in having the sperm removed.

It is difficult to make sense of Grisez's attempted solution to the problem of rape victims and contraception. He makes the claim that "…women who are victims (or potential victims) of rape and those trying to help them are morally justified in trying to prevent conception *insofar* as it is the fullness of sexual union" (emphasis added).[69] If conception simply *means* the completion of sexual union then we appear to have a simple identity statement, such that, insofar as a couple knows that conception is the fullness of sexual union, in willing against the fullness of sexual union they are necessarily willing against conception (i.e. the coming to be of a new human being). If the fertilisation process includes conception we also appear to have a problem of symmetry. For, if a woman may licitly will against the fertilisation process *qua* the end of the process (conception), then cannot a contracepting couple will against conception *qua* the beginning of a (gestational) process and as a means to their end of avoiding pregnancy burdens?

However, what Grisez *can* say is that there are two separable events here–1) the fertilisation process, and 2) the moment of conception; and that the second event is related to the first as an effect is related to a cause. Up to the moment of conception then, we have a part of the man (sperm) engaged in the fertilisation process. The fullness of sexual union is therefore achieved just prior to conception, and conception is an effect of that union. At the moment of conception, the part of the man (sperm) breaks up and the sexual union ceases. On Grisez's account, the rape victim can licitly will against the completion of sexual union *qua* sexual union, and not at the same time necessarily be willing against conception.[70]

Whether this is psychologically plausible (assuming accurate knowledge on the part of the woman as to what constitutes fertilisation and conception) is extremely doubtful. Nevertheless, even if we were to accept this account, there are further problems. Imagine a couple who plan to have sexual intercourse and then stop midway so that they do not begin a fertilisation process. On this account, the couple might be able to say that they had no intention against conception (they might even welcome conception), but that, for whatever reason, they were willing against the fertilisation process only. Perhaps such a couple could be criticised by Grisez for intending incomplete sexual acts–but this would be to criticise them on grounds other than that they are contraceptors. If one were to say that this example is hugely psychologically implausible, then one undermines the plausibility of the rape victim case also.

Conclusion

Given the inadequacies of the GBFM thesis in accounting for the distinction between contraception and NFP, and the permissibility of pregnancy prevention in cases of rape, it would appear that a different approach is needed in defining, and putting a case against, contraception. By attempting to provide an account of contraception that is not reliant on a prior theory of marital goods, or presuppositions about the inherent values and meaning of the sexual act, GBFM have to adopt an externalist account as to the wrongness of separating the unitive and procreative meanings of the sexual act.[71] They do account for the 'inseparability thesis', but only by pointing to what they take to be the wrongness of on the one hand, contraception, and on the other, IVF/AIH (artificial insemination by husband). Contraception, they claim, is always wrong, and for the reasons their paper has summarised. But, as I contend, their account is inadequate as it stands. Moreover, what the failure of GBFM's account suggests is that it is difficult to give an account of the wrongness of contraception that is entirely separable from an account of the inherent goodness of the marital act– an inherent goodness that contraception is said to pervert. If we cannot understand the wrongness of contraception without a prior understanding of the value of the marital act, then this suggests that the whole GBFM project has started off on the wrong track (or that the wrongness of contraception and IVF is illusory). With IVF also, is it so evident that we can understand the alleged wrongness of IVF without also having some notion of how children should in fact be conceived–i.e. by a marital act? While it is *prima facie* wrong to make a human being a product of technological manufacture, it might be difficult to account for the repugnance felt toward this procedure without some prior understanding of how children ought to be brought about–i.e. by marital union.

The GBFM account attempts to explain what they see as the wrongness of contraception as applied to both marital and non-marital acts. However, it may be possible to account for this perceived wrongness by giving a *prior* account of how marital acts instantiate marital goods, and by demonstrating that sexual acts outside marriage which are contracepted are somehow further distanced from marital goods than non-contracepted sexual acts outside of marriage.

An account of the kinds of acts that constitute chaste acts – acts of full committed union and, perhaps, responsible parenthood – might be the account we are looking for. Such an account need not deny that contraception insufficiently respects the life-giving nature of acts of sexual intercourse (i.e. their teleology and meaning), and is, in this sense, contralife. On the contrary, it may give us a better idea of just *how* such contracepted acts are contralife (i.e. fail to respond appropriately to the value of life/fertility), and in a way free from the difficulties into which the GBFM account falls.

Chapter 2
Natural Law, Functions, Teleology

As every instrument and every bodily member subserves some partial end, that is to say, some special action, so the whole body must be destined to minister to some plenary sphere of action. Thus the saw is made for sawing, for sawing is a function, and not sawing for the saw. Similarly, the body too must somehow or other be made for the soul, and each part of it for some subordinate function, to which it is adapted.

Aristotle, On the Parts of Animals

This chapter aims to give an account of sex which takes biology and the human body seriously as a basis from which to address questions in sexual ethics. In exploring the biological function of sex, it lays the foundation for the concept of the *social* function of sex and the institutions related to sexual activity discussed in later chapters. Some readers may, however, prefer to skip this chapter, and go directly to Chapter 3 with its expanded focus on more social questions.

In exploring, in the last chapter, GBFM's argument concerning contraception, it should have been clear that all four authors reject what is called "ethical naturalism." By ethical naturalism I mean the theory that moral truths are in some sense primarily derivable from 'theoretical' truths concerning natural properties[1] (of which more below). GBFM's 'anti-naturalist' approach to natural law, basic goods and practical reason will have various consequences for questions in sexual ethics, beginning with contraception.

The description of a contraceptive act that GBFM put forward, as we have seen, accounts for its wrongness in terms of the contralife will which, they claim, any contraceptive choice necessarily involves. For GBFM the object of any given act is what the agent chooses specifically to bring about.[2] In rejecting naturalism GBFM appear to have little time (references to 'impeding' notwithstanding) for arguments that take seriously moral reasons relating to the misuse of 'natural functions' as a basis for seeing certain sexual acts as morally problematic.

In this chapter, I lay out a natural law framework taking account of these different approaches to naturalism, and examine the role of teleology, functioning and flourishing in giving an account of the good. Having done this, I focus attention on the 'function' of reproductive organs and activity and investigate *prima facie* reasons against thwarting normal performance of functions, especially human bodily functions and especially human sexual functions. Positing that how people relate to their fertility is of special moral importance, I examine the place that considerations of 'function thwarting'[3] should have in our thinking about sexual ethics.

Natural Law and Practical Rationality

Natural law theory, as traditionally understood, is more than just a theory of practical rationality[4] even if that is our primary concern here. By a theory of practical rationality I mean a theory which firstly, gives an account of how to identify reasons for action and secondly, gives an account of how choices between possible actions are governed by rational standards. A natural law theory of practical rationality seeks to explain how the fundamental reasons for action (i.e. certain goods) are connected in some way in the nature of human beings. In conjunction with this, "a natural law theory asserts that the requirements of practical reasonableness, those standards the following of which makes action fully rational, are justified by reference to features of the goods that are the fundamental reasons for action."[5]

There is, however, dispute concerning the goods that constitute fundamental reasons for action. The dispute generally concerns i) how the goods are supposed to be grounded in human nature and ii) how the goods are known.

Naturalists[6]

I will now examine two schools of 'natural law' theory.

'Naturalists' hold that, following the self-evident first principle of practical reason that good is to be done and pursued and evil avoided, we derive the first principles of natural law, which specify the basic goods or forms of human flourishing which are to be pursued. The naturalist claims that such a derivation is made via a theoretical reflection on nature, specifically human nature. These first principles, though derived from theoretical premises, are primary in the practical order.

Such a position rests on a denial of the principle, popular in English-language philosophy, that one cannot logically derive an 'ought' from an 'is', or, put another way, that one cannot derive a practical judgement from a non-practical judgement.[7]

Various arguments are made against this principle. Some assume that a fact/value distinction lies behind the 'is/ought' distinction and go on to claim that "normativity [is] built into the very fabric of reality in the first place" and that there is no such thing as a "'value-free' catalogue of the facts on which the system of morality rests."[8]

One way of explaining away the 'fact/value' distinction is to see values as facts (or vice versa). By taking seriously Aristotelian ideas of essence, natural kind (substantial form),[9] dispositional property,[10] and final cause[11] it can be argued that values are merely the "ends of a natural process."[12] In other words, some argue that the good is the end to be attained, which is the development of an essential dispositional property. More simply, 'goodness' refers to the natural property 'being a development of things' natures'. In Lisska's words, "a value is the further development of a dispositional fact. Disposition and end are in the same category of natural properties, the former the formal cause, the latter the final cause."[13]

Human nature (and indeed all entities defined by their natures) can be characterised in terms of essential properties, some of which are dispositional. These dispositional properties tend towards specific ends. Human flourishing is, on this view, determined by the harmonious completion of those dispositional properties determinative of human nature. The 'end' – human flourishing – is, by definition, 'good'. Such an approach presupposes that moral norms are founded upon a human anthropology, which takes into account a particular biology.[14]

What counts as a human good will depend on how human nature is structured. Theoretical reflection on this structure and its tendencies will, on this account, give us a conception of the human good which can then be employed by practical reason (seen as purely deliberative of means) in order to determine how an agent ought to act.

Fundamental differences in the structure of human nature would have meant that human goods in their current form would not have existed. For the naturalist, the strong grounding in human nature of the basic human goods provides grounding for practical deliberation. As human nature is seen as made up of dispositional properties, those dispositional properties will play a central role in determining the goods. As dispositional they are understood in terms of their tending towards certain ends. So on the naturalist view teleology is centrally important for our understanding of the ethical.

An objection to this approach (aside from worries over is/ought type problems) is that it is unclear how the specific 'dispositional properties', realisation of which contributes to 'flourishing', are picked out. It is unclear, for example, how we understand which dispositional properties contribute to human flourishing without first grasping what goods/ends those properties tend towards. If the end of a dispositional property is first defined in terms of a 'good,' the problem appears soluble, but how we come to knowledge of the good remains to be explained (e.g. is the truth grasped by theoretical or practical reason?).[15] Moreover, we still need to distinguish tendencies from, say, liabilities to decay, and how can we do that except by first identifying good activities tending towards genuine benefits? If prior evaluative criteria are used to pick out those dispositional properties that are, in themselves, worth developing, then the question arises as to what role is played in the theory by already-identified human nature and constituent nontrivial dispositional properties. The choice to adopt a particular definition of human nature will have been guided by a prior belief that x is a good worth pursuing, and not by any entailment from a previously identified dispositional property of human nature.

An essential dispositional property is understood as something that a being has in virtue of the kind of being it is. Such properties are not just any dispositions (accidental to the 'natural kind') but rather are those properties which flow from the very essence of the being in question. We are able to gain knowledge of the essence of a thing through those properties.

Anti-Naturalists

But, it might be asked, how do we come to the knowledge that certain realised dispositions fulfil an essence and that these constitute goods? Anti-Naturalists of the Grisez-Finnis school answer that question by claiming that fundamental practical truths are underived. The first principles of natural law are self-evident and are grasped through practical reason.[16] By practical reason is meant something more than mere deliberation of means chosen by an actor toward certain theoretically discovered ends. For, as Grisez says, "primary principles of practical reason cannot be derived from antecedent knowledge."[17] Our knowledge of the human goods is grasped through practical reason in the following manner: "… the way everyone comes to know them: by insights that grasp the self-evident truth of the practical principles."[18]

This approach certainly appears to solve the problem of how to pick out the relevant dispositional properties. Practical claims are not derived from (supposedly) theoretical premises about capacities/tendencies/inclinations, although these are conditions that allow for practical reason to grasp a basic good.

The claim of 'anti-naturalists' seems to be that in order to appreciate what is 'good' an agent must have experienced an activity that is beneficial to him: without this practical experience/input, he cannot derive what he 'ought' to do from certain (purportedly) theoretical facts about human nature. Even if 'facts' about human nature are regarded as descriptive of 'dispositional properties', it is argued that the 'final ends' which pick out those essential dispositional properties are grasped by a prior experience of 'benefit'.

Practical experience of benefit and practical perception of things as to-be-desired,[19] on this picture, is a form of practical knowledge that cannot be derived from purely theoretical premises.[20] And yet, while it may be true that practical experience of benefit may be grasped in a very general way in relation to one good, it is surely possible, once a person has had such a practical experience of benefit, for him/her to come to understand theoretically that other activities can be beneficial. A suggestion might be put to someone who has experienced benefit practically that activity X is, like already-experienced activity Y, beneficial. It is not as though each 'basic good' can be discovered only practically. The anti-naturalist need only be committed to the idea that there is some moral knowledge that cannot be fully accounted for by theoretical knowledge. And this seems plausible insofar as it is difficult to see how we are to understand 'benefit' without this practically experienced input.[21]

One of the problems with the Anti-Naturalist (AN) account is that it is unclear what exactly the connection is between a basic good and a state of complete human flourishing. For the Naturalist the state of human flourishing is, as we have seen, the final cause "based on the structure of the formal cause."[22] The connection is unclear on the AN account. To argue that the grasping of a basic good is a matter of epistemology, from which one can work back to an ontological account of capacities of human nature is to make a move that requires explanation, especially given that one has identified as 'self-evident', and therefore underivable, certain practical principles.[23] As Mark Murphy puts it: "If the only relevant notions of 'explanation' depend on derivability, it follows that one cannot justifiably assert that natural law is strongly grounded in human nature if the principles of natural law are in no sense derivable from human nature."[24]

One way of accounting for the connection between the class of judgements about human nature and the principles of natural law is to view the connection not as one of entailment, but rather as a relation where one set of propositions is partially constitutive of the other set. On this picture, popular in philosophy of mind, we might say that being happy 'naturally expresses itself' in a smile. As John Haldane points out, such statements are not inductive. Rather, he suggests, certain natural facts about human beings are partly definitive of psychological notions.[25] If this is correct, by analogy we might account for the connection between facts about human nature and the principles of natural law by saying that ethical claims make essential reference to facts about human nature. This may be a way in which we can save rational derivation without at the same time asserting relations of strict logical entailment. What are said to be conceptual differences between the types of judgements may, if we accept the difference, rule out deduction from one set to another set, but rational derivation (understood in terms of essential reference) can still account for a very tight connection between the judgements.[26]

Teleology

In describing the Naturalist account of goods, we referred to natural kinds and dispositional properties in the context of flourishing. This metaphysical underpinning of the Naturalist account of Natural Law[27] assumes that anything that is in any way an agent acts for an end. As Aquinas has it:

> ...an agent does not move except out of intention for
> an end. For if the agent were not determinate to some
> particular effect, it would not do one thing rather than
> another: consequently in order that it produce a determi-
> nate effect, it must, of necessity, be determined to some

certain one, which has the nature of an end. And just
as this determination is effected, in the rational nature,
by the "rational appetite," which is called the will; so,
in other things, it is caused by their natural inclination,
which is called the "natural appetite." (*Summa Theologica* I-II, q.1 a.2).

The principle enunciated here is intrinsic to understanding what
it means for something to *act*. If an agent is to act at all (whether
that agent is rational or non-rational) it must be aimed at something. Insofar as an act is definite its aim must also be definite.
Every act is itself in some way an end. However, as Stephen Brock
has pointed out: "If something is subject to an activity, not out of
any inclination, but out of sheer compulsion, or merely at random,
then it will not have made any contribution to it. Hence it will not
be an agent of it."[28] So the principle helps us to decide what is and
is not to be counted as an agent. And being an act's agent means
"being its source, that from which the act takes its start."[29]

While many may be disinclined to accept this account for inanimate agency, when we talk of *biological* entities such an account
is certainly at least plausible. When describing biological organisms we need to remember that efficacy cannot be divorced from
finality. In other words, teleological explanation of the action of biological organisms cannot be simply reduced to purely mechanistic explanation.[30] In attempting to explain the order present in the
behaviour of an animate being we need to explain how this order
comes about. Reference to final causes lends itself to explanations
of how something acts 'for the sake of' the order which is brought
about. The laws through which we explain the behaviour of particular organisms are teleological in form even if often no explanation
of this teleology is offered by those who recognise these laws. The

very recognition of (naturally) necessary and sufficient conditions for acts presupposes teleology.[31] The observation that there are certain conditions under which elements of a process normally appear, and that there are characteristics of a subject that correspond to its capacity for undergoing the process under such conditions leads us to note the characteristic of a tendency.

Hume's account of causality[32] which seeks to explain the concept of causation as a result of experiences of repeated observation of successive events giving rise to the mind expecting one event when perceiving another, does not satisfactorily account for the need, in order to explain motion, for essentially and irreducibly composite entities.[33] Moreover, teleological accounts of causality offer explanations for the distinctions between direct and indirect agency and can give us an account of notions such as interference and prevention, which Hume's approach seems unable to provide. By talking of direct agency we spare ourselves the necessity of requiring a general rule stating a connection of instances, a rule which, of itself, cannot explain the existence of a given effect. Focus on direct agency offers an immediate explanation (e.g. of something becoming hot by the presence of something already hot)[34] without need of a general rule stating a connection between the instances in question. This is especially important for, as Brock puts it: "there may be no such rule, or it may suffer a host of exceptions."[35]

If we accept the soundness of the idea that entities in nature have tendencies or natural ends in the sense that they can be said to have intentionality (directedness), then we can talk sensibly of an organism having a function. By attributing (sub) functions to certain features of organisms the 'organisation of an organism' can be described.

Those who are uneasy in talking about the function or functions of a *human being as such* will often accept as uncontroversial the claim that human or animal organs exhibit functions, insofar as clear sense attaches to the idea that they are 'for' something and that, consequently, they are not 'for' other things. Such organs are, in usual circumstances, parts of an organism. Furthermore, they are parts of an organism insofar as they exhibit (or tend to) functional activity. As Murphy puts it: "…some feature of the part's activity, that activity which constitutes its functioning…makes it part of the human."[36] This seems eminently plausible. A dry-gangrenous finger, for example, neither contributes to the organism nor is contributed to by the organism. It therefore no longer constitutes a part in so far as it has completely ceased to function. A tumour neither contributes to the functioning of an organism nor is it contributed to, in any teleological way, by the organism as an individual organism. Our understanding of what it is for something to be part of an organism is that it contributes to the organism and/or is contributed to by the organism. Similarly, and perhaps even more clearly, we understand the parts of artefacts in terms of their functionality and their contribution to the overall function of the artefact (a bicycle, for example).

Functions are understood as goal-directed and are understood through their contribution to certain goals through particular causal pathways. Aristotle famously wants to say of an organism, to the features of which various (sub) functions are attributed, that it must itself have an overall function.[37] The thought appears to be that in order to explain or make intelligible the goal-directedness of the various sub-functions, it must be intelligible to say that the organism as a whole has a function.[38] If the organism as a whole has no function how can we explain a) that there is an organism present at all (as opposed to a group of objects spatially close but not united) and b) that the various sub-functions are parts of the organism on account of how they serve the functioning of that organism.

If we accept the above then it follows that the organism itself must have a function. A sub-group of functioning parts is part of a whole in virtue of the functions involved, and everything that is a part of the whole on account of its function contributes to some function of the whole. Clearly this does not mean that that there is one simple function of the organism to which all the sub-functions contribute. Rather, it is only because of their being parts of the organism on account of what they do that each of them serves at least one of the functions of that organism. It is the organism that unifies the diverse functions, even if the function that makes of that organism a unity is merely an inclusive function unifying the diverse functions. So the organism has a single (if compound) unifying function.

Functions, Flourishing and the Good

Functioning might be analysed in the following way: A Bs in order to C. Given a teleological understanding, the above claim should include a notion of 'goal-productivity' (i.e. A's B-ing tends to promote the obtaining of C) and the aetiological condition that A B's because A's B-ing promotes the obtaining of C.[39] Such conditions placed on 'in order to' statements help us to capture what we mean when describing teleology in nature, at least at the organic level. Further, a necessary condition for the truth of 'in-order-to' statements is an appeal to 'goodness' – for such statements are correct only within a value-centred system. So the obtaining of C for any given function is *pro tanto* good for the organism.

The first condition is not sufficient for functioning to be present. Michael Levin[40] imagines an accidentally incurred heart lesion which might be necessary for the heart's pumping blood if it is otherwise diseased; but the lesion is not there 'in order to' pump blood. So we need to say something more in order to capture what it is about a function which distinguishes it from simple efficient causes – even those which have good results. A function of a human heart is to pump blood if and only if there is a state of affairs (the blood's circulating) such that the heart pumps in order that this state of affairs may obtain.[41]

Of course a human heart may fail to do this, just as a lesion is not the 'kind of thing' that is ordered to pumping blood. So we want to say something like, a human heart is the *kind of thing* that B's in order that C may obtain. This takes care of a malfunctioning heart which, although it may not successfully ensure that C obtains, remains the 'kind of thing' that does this. And there need be no problem in defining a natural kind in functional terms. This seems an example of what Aristotle calls commensurate universal definition[42] (e.g. the terms whole and part define each other, as do the terms necessity and contingency).

What, then, might be the connection between functioning and flourishing? Flourishing is clearly a value notion. Flourishing is good in some way. And the goodness of flourishing cannot be purely instrumental – flourishing is valuable (or at least has some of its value) 'in itself'.

The overall human function fulfils these criteria. The human being functions 'in order to' achieve C. But there is nothing in the theory that precludes C from being identical to 'human functioning'. And if C is a 'good state of affairs' then human functioning is simply a good state of affairs.

Human functioning is good, and not merely instrumentally. Human functioning does not seem to be the kind of thing that requires there to be a *further* state of affairs that qualifies it as good. The unified functioning of a human is good in itself, apart from any instrumental value. The functioning of a human constitutes his or her flourishing, just as the functioning of a non-human animal constitutes that animal's flourishing.

The Good

It might be countered here that there is no clear sense in which we can talk about an 'objectively good state of affairs.' What might such a phrase mean? Insofar as good is an evaluative term is it not also a subject-relative term? And if a term is subject-relative in what sense is it objective? Such a question needs to be asked in the context of function statements which implicitly refer to 'flourishing,' seen as an objectively good state of the human (or non-human) organism.

Some have suggested that to say of a state of affairs that it is good (or bad) means that it 'ought (or ought not) to exist'. However, as JLA Garcia points out "While it is hard to see what sense to give to the thesis that a state of affairs ought not to exist…there is no serious problem in understanding the claim that something ought or not to be desired."[43] If something ought to be desired, it ought to be desired by someone. Garcia, as we will see later in this book, holds that for a desire to be morally good is for it to be related to a virtue – and virtues in turn are best seen as related to roles.[44]

On this account, moral good and evil are in a sense prior to the desirability and undesirability of states of affairs since the latter are understood in relation to the former. The obvious objection that might be made to such a view is that surely it is the 'value' of the state of affairs that determines the moral value of the desire for it. However, while it might be said that state of affairs x is bad or at least such as to make it morally bad to desire, it does not follow that the immorality of the desire is somehow dependent on some prior badness of the state of affairs. Perhaps it is just the fact that the state of affairs is bad to desire for a particular person (or even in the abstract for any person) that makes it bad.

Desiring such a state of affairs for a particular person is what would be a sign of being a bad friend, family member, fellow human, etc. Such an approach has clear advantages in terms of intelligibility over theories which merely assert the existence of basic intrinsic value.[45]

In judging the objective value of states of affairs we are, on this account, saying that what the virtuous person would prefer is what constitutes the value.[46] And to desire a bad state of affairs means to have a morally bad desire contrary to a virtue or virtues. This form of evaluator relativity can take account of both the subjective-relative nature of values and their objective status.

Such an approach to 'the good' allows us to say that the flourishing of an organism is *pro tanto* 'virtuous to desire'. So we come to knowledge of flourishing via, in the first instance, the practical input of 'experienced benefit.' Flourishing is good, and by good we mean that which is virtuous to desire (desirable – i.e. good – is defined in relation to a rational perceiver).

All things being equal it is virtuous to desire the flourishing of any organism, human or otherwise. That said, while it is virtuous to desire the flourishing of a rat *pro tanto*, there will often enough be overriding considerations (i.e. the flourishing of other creatures, not least ourselves!) which mean that we ought to desire other states of affairs than rat flourishing *simpliciter*.[47]

Applications

If we are justified in seeing the term function as an irreducibly evaluative term,[48] and are further justified in seeing a human being (or any organism) as necessarily having a unitary-complex function, and in identifying successful functioning qua organism with flourishing, then it follows, as a conceptual truth, that it can't be good *pro tanto* to directly or in effect thwart that function.[49] And it can't be good *pro tanto* to directly or in effect thwart a sub-function that is necessarily part of the unitary-complex function of the human being. By thwart I mean, use in a manner contrary[50] to its purpose (and not merely use for something other than its purpose/ purposes).[51] And what holds for human functions also holds for the functions a non-human animal possesses. Everything else being equal, we should not desire that an animal not flourish.

Aristotelians can and do hold that the overall plausibility of this view is an *a priori* plausibility. In other words, its force derives from its following from certain general theses (as outlined concerning realism about substantial forms, teleology, functions, flourishing). If the theory is correct then if in a certain case it seems intuitively implausible to say that directly thwarting a natural function is in some way in need of moral justification, the problem may lie with our intuitions, not with the theory.

And in fact the theory does not appear to entail such counter-intuitive conclusions, at least for the most part. In most cases the theory does in fact fit our intuitions and any historian could tell us that people generally have always been able to make some sense of the idea of a 'natural' or 'unnatural' preference, aim, action and so on.

In considering more problematic cases, we need to assimilate them to the clearer ones, rather than assimilate the clear cases to the allegedly problematic ones. A clear example of simple function thwarting is given by Michael Levin.[52] He suggests that pulling out all of your teeth in order to make a necklace would be an act obviously contrary to the function of teeth and, *pro tanto*, not good (on my account not virtuous to desire i.e. harmful to flourishing of the organism).

If it is bad *pro tanto* to thwart/disable a function permanently it is also bad *pro tanto* (though necessarily less bad *ceteris paribus*) to thwart that same function temporarily. The teeth extraction case is a clear case of permanent thwarting and perhaps seems particularly shocking because of the various social meanings we associate with eating. A case where thwarting a function seems even more radically problematic is interfering with brain function. Of course a brain has a whole series of functions. But to do something to a brain so that, for example, the human whose brain it is comes to hold a series of false beliefs about important issues (let's say, the existence of God, or his own existence)[53] would seem to be a paradigmatic case of function thwarting that is morally problematic. We might even say that such function thwarting could never be justified, at least if the effect was permanent.

Similarly many people will find it intuitively plausible to say that permanently blinding oneself is not morally licit, unless the overall health of the organism demands it (i.e. the overall physiological flourishing of the organism justifies the thwarting of that particular function). And even here, not everyone will accept that deliberately and permanently blinding oneself is acceptable if the threat comes from another human being who viciously demands this, rather than relating to natural processes that cause or will in the future cause disease. If we admit that there needs to be a serious overriding reason in cases like these to justify such drastic action this suggests that function thwarting or permanent disabling is *prima facie* morally problematic.

It is important to remember that there is nothing about the theory that entails that every thwarting of a natural function is equally serious. We are rational and social animals, and the 'rational' and 'social' parts of our nature are 'higher' and more important than the generic 'animal' parts: more obviously bound up with our flourishing qua humans and more relevant to those aspects of the good for us that we typically see as morally significant. The above examples seem to bear this out intuitively. So thwarting those functions that have more of a rational and social aspect to them is more contrary to the good for us than thwarting some generic 'animal' function.[54]

An example of a 'lower' or animal function might be earwax.[55] Earwax functions to keep the ear canal clean and moist. People sometimes like regularly to clean the wax out of their ears, and it turns out that this can cause the tissues inside the ears to become irritated and in some cases even infected. This is a good example of something that is both clearly contrary to the good for us in one sense – it tends to keep a bodily organ from functioning as it should – but which is so minor a part of our 'animal' nature and so distanced from our rational and social natures that thwarting this particular function is something that might be fairly easily justified. By contrast, the brain case imagined involves the person using an organ that is inherently rationally oriented in a way contrary to goods that have a serious moral importance (closely bound up with our core, defining dispositional properties as rational beings), rather than just generic animal importance.

Unity, Goods and Enjoyment

I have assumed throughout this discussion that the human person simply *is* the living human organism, at any stage of life. This position has clear advantages, though I will not focus on these here. For example, many have pointed out that such a position, in the words of Helen Watt, "avoids the peculiar dilemma of finding ourselves with two candidates for personhood occupying the same space: the organism which seems to acquire the supposed person-making feature, and the entity supposedly 'created' by that feature's acquisition." Watt further points out that the position "also avoids the unease we feel in saying that one and the same entity fluctuates in its moral status depending on whether a particular function has already been acquired and/or is currently possessed. It allows us to accept the common-sense view that immature humans have objective interests, and rights that those interests not be unjustly thwarted."[56]

Given this conception and what we have said with regard to the connection between functions and flourishing, we can agree with David Braine that "the proper subject of human morals is the human being, not just the "rational being as such" or "person"…"

On such a picture it should not be surprising to find that what Braine calls the "shape of human morals" will be affected not only by the fact that human beings are creatures of a rational type, but also by what arises "from patterns which belong to his specific form of animal life."[57]

Building on a holistic conception of man and what we have said about 'basic goods' being constituents of flourishing (good functioning), and the fact that such goods are, in Oderberg's useful phrase, "terminal points of teleological explanation," it should be clear that these goods are not only non-instrumental; they are also goods which are naturally appreciated by the subject of them. The appreciation or enjoyment of these goods has an (objective) physical aspect. And it is precisely this aspect that conditions, in an important way, what counts as an appropriate appreciation of such goods. This is so because, as Braine has argued, insofar as human flourishing consists of the appropriate appreciation/enjoyment of certain goods, physically conditioned, it is a structured integrated whole.[58]

So, the particular structure of human nature determines what are or are not goods for that nature. These goods are primarily constituted by what it is virtuous to prefer (i.e. they are goods relative to a rational perceiver). Given this, our appropriate enjoyment of certain goods, as embodied beings, is what the virtuous person would desire.[59] For the goods enjoyed by the person are structurally related to the kind of being he or she is. And these non-instrumentally enjoyed goods are primary in deciding what it is good to want or desire.

Given what we have said about the nature of human beings as substantial forms,[60] and how goods are related to this nature, it is important to recognise that there is a value in the human organism itself, irrespective of active mental attributes. To kill another human organism (i.e. end the life of a being with the human form of animality) is to directly attack a non-instrumental good: it is to do something wrong or at least seriously harmful and thwarting of good – even if that human person or at least some part of that person perdures (as many religious people believe). This point bears out the general truth regarding basic goods – namely that they must be individually respected.[61]

But the value the organism possesses in itself means that activities of the organism have value, at least insofar as they serve the flourishing of the organism.[62] And this applies to 'automatic' subfunctions of the organism as well as rationally chosen activities. If we accept that there are intrinsically good types of chosen activity such as eating, thinking, speaking, hearing, engaging in sexual intercourse – i.e. actions which successfully exercise functions and can *pro tanto* serve overall flourishing – then we need to examine intuitions about whether there are appropriate ways of achieving the ends of functions which respect the 'animality' of human nature i.e. the nature that is intrinsically valuable.

Just as our objective best interests are determined by our nature as the kind of rational beings we are, so our objective best interests are also partly determined by this 'animal-side' of that nature.[63] As rational animals there is an appropriate way in which knowledge can be gained. While 'infused' knowledge is good qua end achieved, the good appropriate *means* to the end of knowledge-gaining, given the kind of beings we are, is knowledge we discover in a *human* way through mental activity, reasoning, induction, deduction – i.e. active use of the mind. Such a good is realised by us in terms of who we are, and there is value in the fact that the knowledge has been discovered by us through active use of our human rational apparatus.[64]

Similarly, there are good kinds of activity the ends of which are appropriately achieved in ways which respect the animal side of our being. Eating using jaws, teeth, tongue; speaking using lips, mouth, tongue; reproducing through use of reproductive organs – all of these things involve goods realised in an appropriate way determined by our animal nature.

Activities which deviate from the norms bound up with (though not directly derived from) our animal nature may show disrespect for that nature. Acts which structurally bypass a function that is part of our animal nature, when aiming to achieve the end of that particular function are *prima facie* morally problematic, and their problematic character will vary according to the importance of the function's role in overall human flourishing. While they need not be 'function-thwarting' in the sense of deliberately *frustrating* a function or acting contrary to an end of a function while using some related capacity, they are means to a good which fail to some extent to recognise the animal-side of our nature or, to put it another way, our special human form of animality.

An analogy which makes the general point with regard to the adoption of appropriate means for certain ends might be the following. In order for the end of justice to be served, criminals ought to be punished by the state for their crimes. Imagine a state faced with this duty pondering how to achieve this end. Imagine further that the state has two options open to it. Both options will achieve the right end (an appropriate sentence for someone found guilty of a crime). One option involves having a court system with evidence gathered and presented openly, with advocates for and against the defendant, witnesses called and questioned. In short this option involves making use of a sophisticated form of procedural justice in order to reliably achieve the end of a just result. The other option is to consult a particular person who has strong intuitions which are then used to determine the guilt or innocence of the accused, and any sentence that might be deemed necessary in the case of guilt. Let us imagine that the latter option produces exactly the same acquittals, convictions, and sentences as the former. Even so, it seems that the latter approach has not served justice in the way that the former has. In the former case the end is achieved through means appropriately and importantly tied to the end to be achieved. In the latter case the end is seemingly detached from the means, which are not appropriately geared to the end. In some ways, even the end reached will differ due to the different means adopted.

An example closer to our concerns with bodily functioning would be the relation between sexual intercourse and conception.

A married couple aiming for the end of a child through the use of IVF can achieve that end, as can a married couple who conceive sexually. But the IVF couple cannot achieve the end as an outcome and symbol of bodily unity – as something expressive of a body-unifying marital act. So the end – in this a case a new human person – in some sense differs because of the means, at least in the sense that the child cannot express via its origin a particular, marital significance.

So, if a particular structure of human animality not only dictates an end that is good for the human animal, but also connects that end to certain appropriate means that respect (do not structurally bypass) the very human animality which conditions the end, then we can see that, at least *prima facie*, those means ought to be chosen. Moreover, the more important is the end in terms of human flourishing, the more important it is that the appropriate means are employed, lest they distort the appropriate realisation and appreciation of the end.

Reproductive Organs

The physical differences between the sexes reveal, from a natural viewpoint, the complementarity of the sexes and the way in which human sexuality is ordered toward physical union. Sexual desire would not exist without this end, and the sexual organs cannot be adequately defined except by reference to their reproductive (and reproductively unifying) function.

This reproductive function means that, put bluntly, a man's penis is for sexual intercourse with a woman in such a way that she receives semen in her vagina.[65] That is what it is for in the first instance – though as we shall see, there is a whole world of spousal and parental meaning which accompanies this act.[66] To deliberately thwart this function – that is, to use the penis in a way contrary to this end – would be *pro tanto* bad, contrary to flourishing. Thwarting the function would be using it in such a way that semen was deliberately released outside such a context. This would be a use "contrary to the end"[67] of the organ in a way in which simply not using the penis in a way intended to lead to ejaculation would not be.

The functioning of our reproductive organs is clearly related to that aspect of the good of health that is fertility. To deliberately and directly thwart our fertility is, at the very least, to attack[68] an aspect of our health, or at least its successful exercise, which makes up part of our flourishing.

However, it might be argued that, as in the case of earwax, we can fairly easily justify thwarting (at least non-permanently) a particular function insofar as it is part of our generic animal nature. The question I wish to raise is – where should we locate the use of reproductive organs on the scale of 'generic animal organs' as opposed to organs aimed at higher functions?

A man or woman who deliberately sterilises him or herself permanently is clearly acting *pro tanto* against human flourishing. If reproductive functions are seen as like any other function, however, such a procedure might be justified in order to save the person from death or other grave harm.[69] The overall flourishing of the human being would justify such a procedure according to the principle of totality: the intervention may be an attack on a healthy organ but is made in accordance with the overall good of health – the same basic good. Certainly, almost everyone would agree this is permissible outside the context of chosen sexual acts i.e. where the person is incapable of consent in the case of severe mental disability (discussed below). But outside of an extreme threat of death or grave harm it seems intuitively plausible to say that permanently disabling this particular function is particularly morally serious. If the reproductive function were seen to be more a 'generic animal function' it would be difficult to account for this intuition. If it is seen as merely a matter of health then it hard to see why there should be a distinction made between sexual organs and other 'animal' organs.

We might test various intuitions with regard to sterilisation. A monk or nun vowed to celibacy would still have his or her flourishing damaged or diminished in being sterilised. In the same way an infertile monk or nun is less healthy than a fertile monk or nun even if he or she may never actually use his/her reproductive capacity.[70] Certainly deliberate sterilization (say, as part of a medical experiment) would seem to be wrong.

Yet there seems to be more to the thwarting of reproductive functions than health considerations. Even if we are not referring to reproductive-type acts there seem to be other considerations to take into account with the thwarting/disabling of reproductive organs.

When talking about the reproductive function of reproductive organs we are talking about functions that in many cases are rarely if ever exercised in comparison to many other functions (for example, hearing). Yet a man who has been castrated, even if he never had any intention of engaging in reproductive type activity, is commonly seen, across many varied cultures, as in many ways more damaged than a man who has lost a kidney, say – and not just in terms of generic health. Which sex we are seems ultimately determined by an 'animal' feature of ourselves and it seems that this is not something we can freely change. As David Braine puts it, "it is not proper to regard the body as an object in regard to which we are master, freely to determine of which sex it shall be."[71] This doesn't even go far enough – for not only is it not 'proper' in a normative sense, it seems that it is simply not possible. And a sex-change operation (actually a mutilation and not an actual 'change' of sex) is something very different from operations involving other organs, such as a heart operation, for example. The difference might be accounted for in terms of a theory of inherent meanings (or, if we prefer, social functions or social teleology) associated with certain natural functions and the place those functions have in our rational choices in relation to our overall flourishing.

While a reproductive organ has a 'pre-rational' inclination toward its proper object (its function), when we are interested in the proper use of faculties we have to take into account human rational desires that follow on from apprehension of an object as good – for, as Aquinas says, something is desired, not because it suits the act of this or that faculty, but because it suits the whole animal (*Summa Theologica* I, q.80. a.1). The pre-rational functions of reproductive/sexual organs need, ultimately, to be understood, as we saw earlier, in terms of the unitary-complex function of the human being. This does not mean that the faculties themselves do not have a specific and valuable *telos*. It does mean that these specific functions, as we have seen, help to make up the overall function of the organism (something we shall look at further in the following chapter on meanings).

The relation of the body to sexual desire and the specifically reproductive organs might shed light on why such organs possess a special significance in terms of the overall function of the organism. As David S. Crawford has pointed out, "sexual acts in fact rely on the sexualised body for their very possibility. But the body is only sexual insofar as it is a male body or a female body."[72] Following this it is undeniable that "…we experience desire generally, and sexual desire in particular, as arising from our most intimate personal life. *I desire*, not a sub-personal or purely material part of me. But sexual desire clearly is rooted in and lived out in the sexualised body, which, as we have just seen, depends on the correspondence of masculinity and femininity." If sexual desire is merely some ungrounded and free-floating 'spiritual' reality is hard to see how it can be 'sexual' desire.

As rational creatures and sexual creatures, human beings have desires bound up with their rationality. As the human body is sexualised, the human person is a sexual person – even if through some medical condition he or she may have problems connected with the specifically sexual organs. The sexualised body which grounds sexual desire also determines the goods for the organism – goods bound up with that organism's various functions.

The desires that we associate with the person in regard to his or her sexual organs share much in common with other, not explicitly sexual desires – e.g. the desire for union, in some form, with another. Whereas the reproductive function necessarily involves co-operation with another in order to be activated, so too do other desires for union (for example, in non-marital friendship). Kevin Flannery makes the useful point that "sex (the manifestation of particular desire) is not physical exercise, the lack of which impedes general human flourishing. Human sexuality, which is qualitatively different from the sexuality of mere animals, is much more like (although not identical to) a particular calling or talent… What matters is not the satisfaction of various isolated propensities of the psyche but that, whatever a person does, it fit into a rational scheme."[73] These observations suggest that the active perversion of sexual faculties may carry a much stronger *prima facie* objection than the perversion of certain other faculties, as the use of these faculties is much more obviously bound up with the rational goods of the human person.

Clarifying Perverse Use of Faculties

Alexander Pruss has attempted to formulate a definition of perverse activity in general relating to natural faculties or functions:

> It is perverse to act with and through one's faculty F at t in a way that per se makes F be such that none of F's natural functions can be exercised at t.[74]

Notice that this formulation focuses on acting "with and through" a particular faculty and so is not concerned with defining as perverse[75] actions which thwart a faculty or function externally (for example, using a deodorant is not necessarily perverse on this model).[76] So while it is perverse (and wrong *pro tanto*) to use a faculty contrary to its purposes, it is not necessarily wrong to disable a faculty *simpliciter*. But it seems plausible to say that it is perverse in some way to disable a faculty in using that faculty, and it is plausible, given our relationship to our bodies and their role in determining what is good for us, to say that to perversely use our bodies may be at least morally questionable, as suggested above.

This is interesting because it is suggestive of an idea that certain actions *through* a faculty have inherent meanings (and in a more obvious way than actions *on* a function). In the next chapter we will examine the question of inherent meanings in the context of what counts as good and rational sexual activity – that set of activities which is the particular concern of this book. Nevertheless, even without examining in depth the inherent meanings of certain kinds of activities, we can make sense of claims about the purposes of faculties: such faculties/purposes are in some sense bound up with human flourishing. They are so bound up with it that their misuse is rightly called perverse and is, *pro tanto*, bad – not virtuous to desire.

Now if the above formulation successfully captures our intuitions about some paradigmatically perverse activity, and if there are reasons concerned with human good and good functioning on the Thomist model outlined, and if the more important the capacity the stronger the reason to object to perverse activity, it seems that we have a basis for rejecting some such activities, at least *prima facie*. Why sexual activity may be importantly different from other bodily functioning is a question calling for a richer account of the social function of sexual activity – and I take it that talk of inherent meaning is talk of social functions (as opposed to mere descriptions of biomechanical function).

Sterilisation

In the light of the above, it would seem, intuitively, extremely perverse to deliberately sterilise oneself or another permanently, at least for reasons unconnected with overall healthy functioning.[77] Insofar as sexual activity is rational activity incorporated into a life aimed at overall flourishing, the deliberate permanent disabling of a very important function for a reason unconnected with the overall health of the organism seems, *prima facie*, hard to justify. Sterilisation certainly appears to be perverse activity even if done 'externally' by others in ways that do not coopt sexual functions (Pruss's formulation stipulates sufficient but not necessary conditions for perverse activity).

In the next chapter, I will examine the case of sterilisation in the light of a theory about the inherent meanings of chosen sexual activity. What I would like to consider now is the question of sterilisation in relation to a seriously intellectually disabled adult. Here, sexual activity is taking place, on the woman's part, at the sub-rational level: she is not 'acting' voluntarily and we cannot talk of freely chosen sexual acts to be adjudged by the norms of rationality. Principles for what it is reasonable to do in prospect of, during or after freely chosen sexual activity cannot simply be transferred to the very different situation of a sexual attack.

In Chapter 1, while examining rape, I briefly discussed questions relating to a rape victim defending herself from an attacker by 'contracepting' the act – i.e. taking a pill to prevent the rapist's sperm causing conception. In the case of a disabled mature woman with a mental age of 5 there is no chosen sexual activity on her part as she is mentally incapable of choosing an act under that description – i.e. she is incapable of choosing sexual activity as a good/rational type of activity in general (what this means will be explored further in this book).

The man choosing to have sex with the woman is raping her in the sense that she is incapable of giving true informed consent. A result of the sexual activity may well be that she is impregnated. This impregnation will cause her psychological and other harms as well as being socially undesirable. In that case, so the argument goes, might it not be appropriate to sterilise the woman in order to preserve her from otherwise unavoidable and foreseeable harms?

The good being appealed to for the woman is a social good and the idea is that this social good trumps her health good thereby justifying a mutilation of the woman (i.e. a tubal ligation). There is nothing wrong with the woman's tubes (they maintain their inherent *telos* – i.e. are healthy not dysfunctional) and the woman will be no less healthy in being impregnated. Any distress caused by the impregnation will be due to incomprehension or misperception of successful teleological functioning: it is not equivalent to distress caused by a genuine pathology, and is more equivalent to the distress felt by a transsexual at his/her body, seen as being of the 'wrong' sex. It is understandable and in a sense appropriate that the woman is distressed – but her distress is not a distress appropriately related to the harm done (qua uninvited pregnancy) insofar as she does not understand what it is to be a mother or how the situation lacks an appropriate context. The kind of mental distress caused to the woman is a part of her mental disability – even though she may partly realise the very real harm done to her.

The woman's brain is impaired whether or not she is pregnant – her distress is not over some additional health problem. Mental disability by definition increases the tendency to certain harms (which would include the harm of misperceiving pregnancy). But the actual suffering of those harms does not make the sufferer more or less healthy per se.

The proposal is to attack the woman's health through a permanently mutilating operation as a means to achieving a social good. This is different from a case where, say, the woman has a reproductive system that is pathological insofar as if she became pregnant she would die or be seriously injured. In such a case it seems permanent sterilisation might be permissible as a last resort, for it is done to serve her overall health interests – and it is done on an already malfunctioning system. It cannot be said that the girl's *health* has been attacked, when the ligation is performed precisely in order to preserve her health from an existing threat.[78]

But it seems also that sterilisation would be justifiable in principle if the reproductive system was healthy but the heart was malfunctioning such that any pregnancy might result in death. For here, although the area being 'attacked' is healthy in itself, it is being 'attacked' in order to protect another part, or rather the human being as a whole, from fatal consequences. Just as surgeons in removing a cancer will also intentionally remove healthy surrounding tissue as a means to their end of a successful operation and containment of the pathology, so here they operate on healthy functions for the overall good of the organism where there is a pathology elsewhere (similarly one could remove healthy eyes if perception would for some reason result in death).

What does not seem justifiable, at least in the case of an innocent human being, is to attack health instrumentally for a good not relating to health. One does not have to agree with the Grisez-Finnis school on the complete incommensurability of the basic goods to agree on that.[79] If we agree that of their nature, individual virtues (relating to differing goods) make non-negotiable demands, and further agree that there is, in some sense, a unity of the virtues such that no practice of any virtue can be strictly incompatible with a practice of another, then we can see that there will be actions relating to particular virtues that are always ruled out. It is virtuous to desire health. I can never subjugate or instrumentalise entirely that particular virtue to another virtue. Different virtues make different demands on us – but must always be compatible. And it cannot be virtuous to desire a direct attack on a particular good – at least of a permanent and disabling kind, and at least in the case of an innocent person – even in order to advance a separate good of that person.

This is not to deny that social harm is a genuine harm. It clearly is. But a direct attack on health of this sort is always incompatible with a particular virtue, where it is not an intervention aimed at *preserving* healthy functioning. Another way of saying the same thing is that the teleology of any particular good must be respected to some minimal level and not sacrificed for the sake of another good. When I refer to attack[80] I do so in the context of a permanent sterilising act – it is much less clear that temporary suppressions are ruled out (it seems that I can blind myself for one hour as part of a socially useful experiment but that I am not permitted to permanently mutilate myself by having my eyes removed for the same experiment).

These examples show that, when it comes to permanent sterilisation, there are strong reasons to regard it as a direct attack on the good of health, regardless of what we might also say about the operation in the context of meaningfully chosen sexual acts. That it is an attack on that aspect of the good of health that is oriented to the co-operative bringing about of new life means that it is an attack that is particularly serious in terms of human flourishing.

Such an attack must be differentiated from the mere suppression of a faculty, not least because it is possible to suppress the functioning of a faculty in order to preserve overall healthy functioning of an organism. If temporary suppression of a faculty is wrong in such a case, it is wrong for reasons other than as an attack on health.

A woman who is about to be raped might licitly take a pill (leaving aside complications such as the risk of an abortifacient effect) in order to suppress her fertility so that a new life will not be conceived through such an assault. She suppresses her healthy fertile functioning in order to prevent a social harm. But she has merely suppressed her fertility in this case. The suppression here is not connected to safeguarding her overall health, but done in order to prevent a social harm (conception from rape). So, it might be argued, in suppressing her fertility she is attacking her reproductive health for non-health-related reasons.

But temporary suppression need not be characterised as an 'attack' on the good of health that is always and everywhere wrong. If it is not an 'attack' and can be done for a significantly serious reason, since it does not constitute a deliberate serious injury, that reason does not have to relate to overall health. Where there might be a problem with temporary suppression will be where such suppressions radically alter the inherent meanings of *freely chosen sexual acts*, thereby changing their moral character.

Intended direct temporary suppressions will not always be wrong, but when they *are* wrong it will of course be for other reasons than permanent damage to health. The suppressions need to be understood in light of their effect on the meanings of particular acts – meanings understood in a richer way than mere health or bodily functionality. And it is possible, as will be argued, that some suppressions, when they are chosen in relation to certain kinds of intended acts (when someone contracepts their own sex act) will also violate a specific virtue related to a specific basic good – the good of marriage. But being raped is not 'acting' and taking the pill is a temporary suppression of healthy functioning outside the context of a freely chosen sexual act. Any permanent attack could only ever be justified in terms of a health good, and never (qua permanent disabling) for the sake of another basic good.[81]

Conclusion

In this chapter I have tried to lay out a basic approach to moral theory building on the comments made in Chapter 1 on the GBFM model. By drawing out the importance for our moral thinking of notions of functions and flourishing, and how the concept of the good must be understood in terms of virtuous desirability, I have aimed to give a minimal account of the values at stake which relate to our bodily functioning at a pre-rational level – its relation to overall human flourishing – and also at the level of rational use of the faculties involved.

In offering this account, I have focused mainly on successful biological functioning and have not focused so much on the vital social meanings connected with reproductive functions in particular. It is to these social meanings that we will now turn.

Chapter 3
Marriage and Meaning

Even concubinage has been corrupted: - by marriage.

Friedrich Nietzsche, Beyond Good and Evil

The anthropologist Mary Douglas, in her book *Natural Symbols*, boldly states:

> The social body constrains the way the physical body is
> perceived. The physical experience of the body, always
> modified by the social categories through which it is
> known, sustains a particular view of society. There is a
> continual exchange of meanings between the two kinds
> of bodily experience so that each reinforces the catego-
> ries of the other. As a result of this interaction the body
> itself is a highly restricted medium of expression. The
> forms it adopts in movement and repose express social
> pressures in manifold ways. The care that is given to
> it, in grooming, feeding and therapy, the theories about
> what it needs in the way of sleep and exercise, about
> the stages it should go through, the pains it can stand,
> its span of life, all the cultural categories in which it is
> perceived, must correlate closely with the categories in
> which society is seen in so far as these also draw upon
> the same culturally processed idea of the body.[1]

I quote this at length because it is illuminative in its suggestion
of the importance of social institutions in constraining or encourag-

ing bodily expression and how the body and the functions of the body are viewed. For Douglas is interested in the feedback loop between social structures and beliefs about bodies and their functions/meanings.

Douglas goes on approvingly to summarise Marcel Mauss, stating that, "Every kind of action carries the imprint of learning, from feeding to washing, from repose to movement and *above all* sex. Nothing is more essentially transmitted by a social process of learning than sexual behaviour and this, of course, is closely related to morality" (my emphasis).[2]

What Mauss importantly doesn't say here is that some social norms with regard to the body are bad for people's health, or their flourishing in general, while others are good. Social input to bodily behaviour can promote or combat flourishing outside as well as inside the sexual ambit – a point I will return to later. Suffice it to say that we learn to speak via society, but both the good of society and the good of our health dictate what are better and worse ways of using our voice-box, the proper use of which is about more than instinct. Thus we learn how to perform bodily actions, but hopefully we learn how to perform them right.

Mauss is generally taken by Douglas as saying that there is no 'natural' behaviour, for all actions carry the imprint of some sort of learning (note that by 'natural' here is meant not what relates immediately to 'natural law' and human flourishing but something more akin to 'instinctive,' in some very basic sense).[3]

Roger Scruton in discussing *homo faber* notes, apparently in accordance with what Douglas and Mauss suppose regarding 'nature,' that

Sexual desire is a social artefact. Like language and like morality, it is born from social relations between human beings, and adds to those relations a structure and firmness of its own. It does not follow from this, however, that sexual desire is 'merely conventional,' or not a part of human 'nature.' For some artefacts are natural to human beings: in particular, all those which stem directly from social existence and which form the basis for the construction of personality. We could indeed imagine a human being 'outside society', but this *homo faber* would be, not a natural phenomenon, but a freak – a creature in whom the normal human potential had been frozen or destroyed…Sexual desire is as natural an artefact as the human person. There could, perhaps, be human beings without this response. But the collective endeavour which paints our face on the blank of nature also generates desire, as one of the fundamental links between embodied persons…There is no normal human sexual development which avoids the predicament of desire, and no normal development of a person which avoids the acquisition of 'gender'. Persons are essentially desirous, and desire essentially personal.[4]

In referring to how some artefacts are 'natural' to human beings what Scruton says here could be compatible with the view that the body itself bears signs from the beginning of the 'natural' functions and flourishing which will involve learning and social interaction for their fruition. Moreover, social functions which truly 'embody' human flourishing are 'natural' in a way that goes beyond mere social convention, though not, of course, in a way that denies the importance of such conventions – any more than the idea of essence does.

Meaning as Social Construct

Gareth Moore, in making use of Douglas and Mauss, takes what they say about social structures to argue for a much more radical position. He writes initially:

> Sexual nature is a social and cultural matter, not merely biological; we can expect it to have all the variety we find in social matters.[5]

Later he extends the thought, claiming that:

> Sexual acts are indeed capable of bearing meaning. But meaning is a human affair, a result of human social structures and of human conventions. To try to ground the meaning of sexual activity in the creative activity of God is to make a fundamental mistake.[6]

This *a priori* denial of natural meaning, for that is what it is, comes at a very high price. If human social structures and conventions are not in any way bound by 'natural meanings' (or the "creative activity of God") and are more like words (a comparison Moore makes[7]) then it is difficult to see why Moore appears to take it as a given that sex has a biological meaning at all, even if not 'merely' so. Why assume that a particular society with particular social structures and human conventions could not dislodge this 'imposed meaning,' so that bodily 'functioning' was seen as inapplicable to 'sex' in this new sense?

If Moore were correct he would need to explain why he (presumably) takes it as a given that human organisms themselves with their overall function of coordinated life are not merely socially constructed, though any sub-functions or functioning(s) of the organism simply *must* be socially constructed.[8] He would also need to show that there is no such thing as 'fitness' such that, for example, a social convention that women breast-feed their babies as an expression of maternal care and bonding was no more or less 'fitted' to the activity than a social convention that women breast-feed their babies as a completely alienating activity expressive of hatred toward the baby. For Douglas, the body and the social body interact, and while she stresses the social body's 'imprint' of learning, she is not thereby denying the essentially symbiotic relationship. Indeed she says, "The physical body can have a universal meaning only as a system which responds to the social system, expressing it as a system...The two bodies are the self and society: sometimes they are so near as to be almost merged; sometimes they are far apart."[9] For Moore it appears that the latter is entirely determinative of the 'nature' of the former. So he can say, with regard to the significance of sex, "Just as the meanings of words change over time in the same society, as people come to use words in changing ways, so the meanings of human acts can change with changing institutions and habits...Sometimes people who find certain words and symbols emblematic of a community they find oppressive or benighted deliberately set out to change the way they are used, or urge that they be abandoned altogether. Sex is no exception to this common phenomenon."[10]

On this account, the physical structure of a sexual act is irrelevant in helping to determine its goodness, at least insofar as goodness is bound up with what is 'natural' in some sense for human beings. The most Moore might say is that sex is 'natural' only insofar as it recognises certain social conventions, such that the word 'natural' is no longer connected to any fixed idea of human nature or essence.[11]

Alexander Pruss has pointed out that the view that there are no inherent meanings to sexual activity is more common than the view that physical objects are mere social constructs. The latter view is rare because it seems obvious that the physical provides our paradigm of objectivity.[12] In fact, the analogy put forward is not as close as it might be, as what needs to be compared is the social construction of the *meaning* of sexual activity with the social construction of the meaning of physical objects, for example, a human body that is 'healthy' or 'ill.' Whatever one might say about this, when it comes to sex it is undeniable that it is, fundamentally, *about* the physical/bodily, the biological and teleological/functional, which is the basis for its real, objective importance. It is no accident that handshakes cannot function as sex and we cannot just decide to make them do so.[13]

Species of Act

Perhaps one attraction of a more restricted version of Moore's view (other than, for sexual revolutionaries, its utility in undermining traditional sexual morality[14]) is that certain chosen physical actions (e.g. picking up a daisy) are morally indifferent *as such*. There is nothing about the physical structure here that helps us to judge whether the act of picking the daisy is morally good or bad.[15] That judgement will depend upon much wider consideration of situations, of the actor's further intentions, role in society and so on. Moore might simply extend this to sexual acts and say that these acts in themselves have no 'meaning' and therefore the intrinsic physical structure of any particular sexual act[16] is irrelevant, or at least indeterminative, in judging whether it is morally choiceworthy.

In examining Aquinas's discussions of sexual ethics and the moral objects of acts Stephen L. Brock makes the following point about the role of (chosen) physical structures in moral evaluation:

[I]n some cases the condition of the object that constitutes an act's natural or physical kind constitutes a
determinate moral kind as well. Sometimes it is indeed
sufficient to know that someone performed a certain kind
of physical act voluntarily, in order to ascribe to him an
action of a definite moral quality. A clear example, in
Thomas, is that of sexual acts other than heterosexual
copulation, the acts "contra naturam." The relation of
such acts to the sexual power differs from that of heterosexual copulation. They differ in physical kind. What
gives them this difference also gives them a different
relation to reason. According to reason, the good kind of
sexual act is the marital act. There are also bad kinds of
heterosexual copulation – for instance simple fornication
– which is bad just because the object is not the agent's
spouse. This of course is not a physical condition.[17]

Marriage as Standard

For Aquinas, it is marriage which is that standard with respect
to which sexual activity is judged to be good or not, a standard
that applies to all human beings by virtue of their rational nature.[18]
Marriage is a social institution, and it is this institution which
makes sexual activity reasonable activity. While we can talk of a
function at a physical level (the penis is 'for' [or partly for] ejaculating semen; the voice box is 'for' emitting sound) we can also
talk of the social functions these serve in the context of human
flourishing at both the personal and the societal (common good)
level, in order for them to be successfully used (e.g. the penis is
'for' ejaculating semen in the context of a sexual act celebrating
the institution that is marriage for the good of the couple and offspring; the voice box is 'for' [in certain contexts] emitting sound

in order that a person may communicate e.g. by making true statements about the world etc.). In other words, there is a chain or hierarchy of purposes, and the activity will tend to be unreasonable unless in ascending the hierarchy you reach the right kind of purpose to justify that kind of action.

What is the institution of natural marriage and why is such an institution required by the common good? What is the relationship between the marital act and the institution of marriage? How can some (sexual) acts be said to 'damage' the institution of marriage? In exploring these questions, I hope to show why the achievement of certain goods depends upon a) restricting certain acts uniquely capable of realising those goods to the institution of natural marriage and b) recognising that marital acts occupy a privileged place within marriage.

Sacramental Marriage

In order to go some way to achieving these goals, it is appropriate to reflect on a theologically-grounded view of marriage – though one which nonetheless makes room for a view about the natural goodness of marriage. The Catholic Church holds that marriage, as an arrangement of nature, is of Divine origin. According to the Council of Trent, Christ brought marriage, ordained and blessed by God, to the original ideal of indissoluble monogamous marriage (Matthew 19:3-11) and elevated it to the dignity of a sacrament. The essential properties of a sacramental marriage i.e. a marriage between two baptised persons are unity, monogamy, and indissolubility.[19] Such properties serve the purpose of marriage, the generation and rearing of offspring, and the mutual love and unity of the spouses (I will have more to say on marital love later in the book). On this understanding, the rightness of monogamy is established as it and it alone guarantees the fulfilling of the purposes of marriage and is a faithful image of Christ's everlasting union with His Church. Aquinas, supporting this understanding, adumbrates the requirements and goods of sacramental marriage. "Now the figure must correspond to the reality which it signifies. But the union of Christ with His Church is one of one bridegroom with one bride to be kept forever. For, of the Church it is said, One is my beloved, my perfect one. Nor ever shall Christ be parted from His Church for so He says Himself, 'Lo, I am with you, even unto the end of the world.' And so the Apostle, 'We shall be forever with the Lord.'"

Matrimony therefore, as a sacrament of the Church, must be of one husband with one wife to continue without separation. This is what Aquinas means by the faith whereby husband and wife are bound to one another. The Church holds that there are three goods of sacramental marriage: offspring (proles), to be reared and educated to the worship of God, faith (fides) whereby one husband is tied to one wife, and sacramental signification by the indivisible union of the matrimonial connection, making it a sacred sign of the union of Christ with His Church.

Natural Marriage

While these reflections apply to Christian marriage, it is also true that the Church has pronounced that natural marriage; that is, marriage between the baptised and unbaptised, or between two unbaptised persons, is presumptively intrinsically indissoluble due to God's ordinance made at the institution of marriage. So even though natural marriage allows for extraordinary exceptions to indissolubility, it is not said to be dissoluble through civil law. On this understanding, the institution of marriage is seen qua institution as a direct creation of God and therefore as having a special moral status.

The Church's understanding of so-called natural marriage and the proposition that the institution is of directly Divine origin plays a definite role in normative reasoning about sexual ethics and marriage. Someone holding to the Divine Origin (DO) account is bound to hold that it cannot be right to alter fundamentally by mere human fiat an institution so founded. However, while the DO of the institution might only be known through Revelation perceived with the eyes of faith, it does not follow that the obligations flowing from marriage are obligations purely religious. As Joseph Boyle, to whom this analysis owes much, has pointed out, "The obligations of marriage are moral obligations, even if MICG [what I am calling DO, Boyle terms 'Marriage is an Institution Created by God'] can only be known by religious belief. For institutions generally create obligations, and they do so not primarily in virtue of their origins but in virtue of their function in social life. When institutions are morally legitimate, that is, compatible with relevant moral norms, the obligations they create are genuine moral obligations."[20]

On Boyle's understanding, insofar as the institution has a morally legitimate role in society it can create moral obligations regardless of belief in the DO model. Those who do not accept the DO account will not see themselves as bound by additional religious obligations not to tamper with the institution but would still be bound from tampering with the institution by other moral norms governing marital relations and procreation.[21]

Clearly, in the world in which we live, arrangements called marital are many and varied and, as a descriptive matter, it looks as though marriage is not *an* institution, but rather is a set of similar institutions which have Wittgenstein-style family resemblances to one another. As a descriptive matter it also seems that the institution, like other institutions, can be redefined, altered, and tampered with.

However, with the DO picture it seems we *are* talking about an institution different from other institutions, and indeed, other quasi-marital institutions. The Catholic Church holds that marriage is a natural institution,[22] and insofar as it is a matter of morality, a matter of natural law as well as participation in Divine law. Boyle draws an analogy by citing the Ten Commandments, including those not related to marriage, which are naturally known as well as (in the view of believers) divinely handed down. Thus the DO interpretation of marriage appears to include a moral and not only religious prohibition of tampering with the form of marriage, such that the form cannot be tampered with without violating moral norms applicable to anyone.

If marriage is seen primarily as a matter of natural law, we need to identify the basis for criticising those forms of marriage which violate the set of moral norms which provide for a fixed form of marriage. On this view, theology is not most basic in understanding the foundational moral justification of natural marriage. Rather, there must be something about the very character of natural marriage which generates moral obligations which are themselves morally necessary.

Role of Marriage

What might be the philosophical justification for a moral prohibition on tampering with a particular form of marriage? Many will simply deny that marriage is an institution in any sense radically different from other human institutions – bearing in mind that institutions regardless of their origin can in certain circumstances impose moral obligations.[23]

William Godwin, in his *Enquiry Concerning Political Justice*, wrote,

> The institution of marriage is a system of fraud…marriage is an affair of property, and the worst of all properties. So long as two human beings are forbidden by positive institutions to follow the dictates of their own mind, prejudice is alive and vigorous. So long as I seek to engross one woman to myself, and to prohibit my neighbour from proving his superior desert and reaping the fruits of it, I am guilty of the most odious of monopolies.[24]

Godwin supplies a whole battery of reasons as to why marriage fosters cowardice and unhappiness. But a central concern of his, and of others who take a less dim view of marriage, is the question why, if marriage is *simply* dealing with sexual activity among people, it requires any socially prominent institution at all?

One obvious answer is that sexual intercourse of a generative kind can cause, or help to cause, babies and, as Boyle points out, there are compelling moral arguments for establishing socially regulated institutions for the procreation and raising of children. It is this connection to having children which requires that there be such marital institutions. Furthermore, procreation and the raising of children are not a purely private concern of parents but part of the common good of society. Another way of putting it would be specific human goods which can only be secured through (or in) certain institutions, and requirements of practical reasonableness that only those institutions can satisfy.

So the claim of what might be called the 'traditional moralist' is that the institution of natural marriage is necessary in order to honour a natural moral precept. The Kantian philosopher Alan Donagan suggests the following general moral consideration; namely that "Those who voluntarily enter into sexual relations from which a child is born are reasonably held to fail to respect the child as a rational creature if they refuse to provide for its upbringing." From this kind of consideration he tells us that the fundamental (Kantian) principle of morality yields a precept of responsibility: "It is impermissible for human beings to voluntarily become parents of a child and yet refuse to rear it to a stage of development at which it can independently take part in social life." This precept presupposes that it is "impermissible for human beings voluntarily to become parents of a child they cannot rear."[25]

The rationale behind the precept is simply that in order for a child to lead a life befitting his or her dignity he or she will need protection, care, nourishment, and education. On the traditional view, the form of marriage that is morally acceptable is one derived from a precept of parental responsibility or true parental love by way of the specificatory premises about what is necessary for the rearing of a child until it can take part independently in social life. One of these premises is that a child's upbringing and sense of security and identity is impaired unless the ultimate authorities in charge of him or her are the natural parents joined in a stable marital union. Certainly, where natural parents cannot assume this natural authority alternative arrangements, such as adoption, have to be made. But these are generally assumed to be unfortunate necessities, intrinsically inferior in some ways to a traditional family structure even where they are otherwise successful. They are also regarded this way by many adopted people themselves.

Quasi-Marital Arrangements

On this basis some argue that there are institutional arrangements other than natural monogamous marriage which can fulfil the precept and not violate any moral norms. Both forms of polygamy – polygyny and polyandry – might be suggested as alternative morally acceptable forms fulfilling the precept. However, when we reflect on our premises concerning what is necessary to raise a child well it appears that the upbringing of children will generally be impaired unless their parents, joined in stable marriage, are the ultimate authorities in charge of them. While two child-rearers are a 'team', three (or more) is an intrinsically unstable number, as there is always the likelihood that two will form a 'team' against the third. Moreover, the value of having important relationships that are fundamentally 'given' (i.e. not chosen at the relevant level) carries with it a social message about obligations to particular persons that do not rest entirely on our choice of those persons as they do in the often lesser obligations one might owe to 'chosen' friends and others. It is good for people to have the security of 'givenness': to begin this way is good for children and prepares them for later chosen relationships that may nonetheless be non-negotiable after they have been formed. Even marriage is a 'given' once chosen, if it is seen as indissoluble.

Polyandry, by confusing the determination of paternity or making it difficult militates against the father carrying out a parental role and creates identity problems for the child. Polygyny, historically a much more common arrangement, as Aquinas suggests, reduces the position of wives to that of servants and more generally is incompatible with the basic moral equality of husbands and wives. Kant stresses this point when he writes, "the relation of the partners in a marriage is a relation of *equality* of possession, equality both in their possession of each other as persons (hence only in *monogamy*, since in polygamy the person who surrenders herself gains only a part of the man who gets her completely, and therefore makes herself into a mere thing), and also equality in their possession of material goods. As for these, the partners are still authorized to forgo the use of a part, though only by a separate contract."[26]

Finally, 'wife-swapping' is likely to undermine confidence in parentage, as it is more realistic to place a taboo on all non-monogamous activity than to confine such activity to specific periods in an attempt to make paternity clear. The benefits for the child, in terms of security and identity, of knowing who the parents are and that they have particular responsibility for him or her should not be underestimated. We can see this from the reports of many who have grown up without these benefits.[27]

Designing Marriage

The moral requirements for bringing new life into being clearly play a crucial role in determining what is or is not a desirable and morally good sexual arrangement. I want to suggest a thought-experiment at this stage. Imagine trying to design an institution that would best protect the interests of children to be brought into the world. First, by making the conjugal/sexual/procreative act a necessary condition for a 'complete' marriage, a consummated marriage, one would tie the natural and appropriate act for generating children to the appropriate institution for the upbringing of children. Secondly, by restricting that act to the institution one would protect children against the possibility of their coming to be outside of the appropriate institution for their upbringing. Such an institution would be justified on account of its relation to children in general, even if, by a natural accident, no children were ever born from a given marriage.

The question for a critic of this 'designed' institution would be, what is it that necessitates lifelong monogamy in marriage? Without the potential relationship to children it is difficult to see 1) why the arrangement should be life-long and 2) why the relationship should be restricted to two people. By privileging what I call the marital act within the institution, such that the very definition of and entry to the institution depends upon the marital act and vice-versa, one protects the rationale for the institution.

Substitutionary Sex

In the light of this understanding of the institution, what should we say of a couple who choose to engage in what are (at some level) experientially similar sexual experiences (e.g. oral sex, mutual masturbation, contracepted sex)? Here, the special connection between the conjugal act (if seen as a sexual act not relevantly morally dissimilar from other consensual sex acts) and the institution of marriage becomes difficult to sustain. Why, for example, ought a couple who choose these relevantly similar forms of sex get married?

We might formulate the thought in the following way:

You ought to marry and/or favor the marriages of others because, among other things, you want, or should want, yourselves and/or others to engage in, to coin two terms for this purpose, PS (consensual and intentional sex of a procreative and socially significant and valuable kind). Insofar as you engage in SS (substitutionary consensual sexual activity) you reduce the rationale for getting married in your own minds and in the minds of others.[28]

So if a couple are intending to gain sexual experiences through a substitutionary[29] form of sex they dilute or endanger their ability to appreciate the relevance of normal sexual intercourse (PS) to the institution of marriage. If the couple view their activity SS in a non-substitutionary way, i.e. as not relevantly similar to PS,[30] it becomes difficult to see why it should be restricted to the institution of marriage, any more than having a meal with someone not one's spouse. But of course sexual pleasure is one of the things (along with structural features) that links SS to PS: it is not realistic to suppose that couples will treat SS as a *completely* different kind of activity. Moreover, a question arises as to whether there is some very important human/physiological good which this kind of pleasure exists to serve and encourage.[31]

It does not appear to be a matter of mere cultural conditioning that for one or other spouse to engage in SS with a third party is something deeply problematic for anyone committed to the institution of marriage. This, plausibly, is because such behaviour involves sexual activity of a type relevantly similar to PS, even if not intended as such. And this point in turn may suggest a built-in significance to sexual activity in general. For it would appear that the motives of people engaging in such activity, while morally relevant, are not conclusive in identifying the damaging nature of such activity in relation to the institution of marriage.

The critic, at this stage, may simply agree and say that the couple who have a tendency to prefer SS to PS, insofar as they do, weaken, in their eyes, the rationale for marriage. And they might be quite happy to accept this eventuality, as many do. They might even follow Igor Primoratz[32] and argue that the structure of the kind of argument I am proposing amounts to, "A is much better than B. Therefore, B is no good at all."[33] Primoratz goes on to say, in his own example where A is "loving sex" and B is "loveless sex," "In addition to being logically flawed, this line of reasoning, if it were applied in areas other than sex, would prove quite difficult to follow...Of course, B can be good, even if it is much less good than A. Loveless sex is a case in point...To be sure, when adherents of the sex with love view reject casual sex, they also claim that other things are not equal: that a person who indulges in loveless sex thereby somehow damages, and ultimately destroys, his or her capacity for experiencing sex as an integral part of a loving relationship…to the best of my knowledge [this] is merely a popular piece of armchair psychology, rather than a claim established by research."[34]

Primoratz is talking about loving and loveless sex in this instance, but his point can just as easily be applied to what I am saying about SS and PS. A couple might argue that PS might be 'better' in some wide sense, and 'better' within marriage, but that they are quite happy with SS and see no strong reason to get married as they are more interested in SS than in PS.

Privileged Acts

It could also be objected that certain *non*-sexual behaviours might also be seen as restricted to, or at least to have some relation to, marriage. Might not such activities outside marriage also be condemned as 'diluting' the rationale of marriage? The significance of holding hands might be one example. However this point seems to rest on certain variable cultural conditions in ways in which activities of type SS do not. There are no societies in which handholding is seen as equivalent to sex: this is surely because of its lack of similarity both experientially and in terms of function.[35] How about presumptive disclosure? Given their particular role, a spouse has a presumptive right to know certain things about the other partner that no-one else does. That is something we would often make sense of within a marriage, but the question is why are we treating it differently from SS or PS?

Well, the presumptive right to know derives from a spouse's role within marriage and the importance of a special form of friendship being maintained. And this in turn is required ultimately because of the possibility of children coming from at least some such relationships, requiring in its turn a lifelong commitment – and that requires parents to have a special openness to one another in the interests of the child and in the couple's own interest.[36] Having said that, the exclusivity here may not be workable if interpreted too strictly, as others outside the marriage may also need certain private information. But it is interesting that even in cases where in practice we all agree we are talking about a mere presumptive right which can be overridden, those cases testify to the institution of which sexual exclusivity is a more workable and systematic witness – and one more closely related to the possibility of a child coming from at least some such relationships. We should bear in mind that the possibility of conception outside marriage, and therefore of the child being deprived of what he/she needs for a stable sense of identity, means that the taboo is particularly useful: a single violation could well have lifelong consequences (unlike many cases of non-disclosure).

Counterarguments

Critics of the traditional position have generally attempted to argue in one or other of the following ways. Some have taken the line that the marital act is not an essential mark of marriage insofar as just about everybody has recognised the validity of naturally sterile marriages. A sterile marriage validly entered into cannot lead to the natural procreation of children, and therefore the natural procreation of children cannot be an essential mark of marriage.

Others, such as Gareth Moore, have sought to locate the significance of the marital act within the institution of marriage. For Moore, it is the institution of marriage that invests meaning in the marital act. Moore goes so far as to say, in his late work, that strictly it makes no sense to talk of the 'natural meaning' or built-in significance of any type of activity. The meaning of any kind of activity is for him entirely context-dependent. Of arguments relying on the idea of built-in significance Moore says, as we saw earlier, "that there are inherent meanings in human sexuality is no justification at all. Sexual acts are indeed capable of bearing meaning, but meaning is a human affair, the result of human social structures and human conventions."[37] Similarly, writers like Michel Foucault see institutions in general, including marriage, as products of prevailing configurations which promote a particular social goal: they are part of a series of contingent social practices and, for Foucault, yet another mask worn by power (power being a crucial concept Foucault unfortunately never seems to have adequately analysed).[38] There is no 'nature' of sexuality, merely a struggle between different social forces aiming to impose meanings upon e.g. sex or language. There is no 'normal', and the widely held idea that heterosexuality is 'normal' is a fiction. Categories such as heterosexuality (and with it institutions like marriage) and homosexuality are socially controlling constructions which should be 'unmasked'.

In answer to Moore's criticism, it needs to be pointed out that, as the previous chapter argued, the 'final cause' or foundational natural purpose of sex is procreation, just as the natural purpose of eating is nutrition. And procreation is inherently heterosexual. We are talking here of 'nature's purposes' (for theists, ultimately, God's purposes), not what a couple may happen to have as their purpose in engaging in sex. Whether something is a procreative type of act is, at least in one basic respect, independent of an agent's intention, for the significance of what he or she does in choosing to engage in intercourse of a procreative or even a non-procreative kind is determined by the central role that procreative activity plays in human life. And certain facts about human biology determine what that central role is (hence our talk of 'genitals' and 'reproductive organs'). So, our biology is partly determinative of the significance of human sexual intercourse.[39] As Luke Gormally has written, a couple "negate that significance in setting out to render infertile any sexual activity which might otherwise be fertile. They do not negate its significance as generative (its "procreative significance") by having intercourse when they happen to be infertile, since fertility is not required for the act to be of the generative kind."[40]

Role of Sex in Marriage

Quite generally, we need a 'special' activity to mark a fundamental new role – just as pregnancy does this with already-achieved parenthood. Take, for example, surrogacy. The physical 'activity' of gestating a child seen as not one's own makes gestation no longer a unique relationship which marks a special bond between natural mother and child, a fundamental new role for the mother, and a new life and lifelong natural bond for the child. The surrogate intends not to adopt this role and does not, therefore, treat the state of pregnancy as bringing about a special role relating to a unique person, or enhancing a commitment to a spouse. Thus she dilutes the social meaning of pregnancy in an important and non-private way.[41]

But what of the unitive good of sex, bound up with the procreative? The unitive good is surely wholly dependent on the act being of a procreative type (or, as Pruss has it, one of 'bodily striving' for a procreative good even if that good is not in itself achievable).[42] This 'completed,' procreative good of new life is the primary good of both sex and marriage, but the primacy should be understood in terms of dependency. Just as procreative 'striving' is oriented to the 'completed' good of procreation, the same can be said of the unitive aspect of that procreative striving. The unitive good is 'dependent' on procreation, and in that sense secondary, but the term secondary should here carry no implication of 'inessential.'

If we talk abstractly about the immediate physical unity of the sexual act we are simply talking about procreative striving. We are talking about the *same thing*. However, if we are talking about the unitive in the richest and widest human sense, the unity experienced by a good spousal coupling, we are talking about something of which the purely physical procreative striving is a necessary aspect. This necessary aspect of the couple's unity, in the richer wider sense, is not necessarily superior to it even though this unity is dependent upon procreative physical striving. My body's overall good health is dependent upon the good health of my stomach, but it does not follow that my stomach is more important than my body's overall health.[43]

If we understand the procreative good of sex in the rich human sense, as something conducive to the 'completed' procreative good of bearing, rearing, and educating a child, then we are also talking about something identical to the unitive good in the rich sense (i.e. creating the right environment for child-rearing). So, the social function of the act, which is what we are discussing at this level, isn't something entirely relative to certain cultural practices, but is rather bound up with what is truly good for children – for the flourishing of new human beings.[44]

What then of the case of the sterile marriage where marital acts, though of a procreative kind, will never result in conception? People continue to argue why the commitment conditions for marriage exist in a case such this. However, following our earlier thought experiment, it would appear that if no marriage *ever* had a connection with children it would be difficult to make sense of the institution.

The sterile marriage is 'derivative' from the fertile marriage in the order of rationale – which is not to denigrate but merely to explain it. And in the sterile marriage, engaging in PS does nothing to override or thwart the meaning of the procreative act, which is the mark of marriage. The sterile couple are still engaged in PS and not SS and the rights of exclusivity they enjoy have an important social function as well as giving them security.

Substitutionary Sex and Society

Activities such as homosexual sex or condomistic sex[45] are per se inapt for procreation on this understanding, and therefore fall into the category of SS. Insofar as they do, what might be said of choices to engage in SS outside (or inside) of marriage? We saw earlier that marriage qua institution generates certain moral obligations. Insofar as SS becomes widely practised in a society whether outside or inside the institution it will inevitably become much harder for the moral obligations generated by marriage to be honoured in general. This is because of the close connection between SS and PS both in relation to pleasure and other emotions and in relation to bodily structure.

The couple engaging in SS are, on the view of inherent meanings put forward here, failing to respect the inherent meaning of a particular type of act, which meaning is the mark of a valuable and socially important institution. The enacted existence of SS thereby encourages PS to be seen in inappropriately subjectivist terms i.e. as though PS were not possessed of an inherent meaning, thereby weakening the ability to properly commit to PS. Failure to respect that significance causes clear problems for the good of an institution needed by society for the good and protection of children. For that reason SS acts can reasonably be held to be taboo, alongside normal fornication.

Such connections are hinted at by the journalist and supporter of gay liberation Matthew Parris, when he writes,

> No man is an island...There are ultimately no "private" acts. Everything we think, everything we say and do, however privately, shapes and influences us, our families and friends, and so touches the world outside. It is just fatuous to pretend that if a great many men are unashamedly making love to other men, however privately, that is without impact on the whole of society.... [46]

The effects on society of SS, whatever one may make of it, are surely undeniable. One striking aspect of the new social attitudes, promoting SS and subsequently a subjectivism with regard to sex and sexuality, is the uncoupling of personal identity from the subject's maleness or femaleness. David S. Crawford has observed that

> The identity of the person is no longer grounded in his or her masculinity or femininity; it is grounded in his or her "orientation." This shift effectively demotes the meaning of sexual difference – the inescapable correspondence of the male and female bodies as such – to a sub-personal and purely material significance… In effect, it has placed the body outside of the person as such. In this way, the sexualised body has been drained of its intrinsic meaning and relationship to the person him-or herself. The person as such has been rendered essentially androgynous... Sexual acts in fact rely on the sexualized body for their very possibility. But the body is only sexual insofar as it is a male body or a female body. Moreover, the fact that a body is either male or female depends on the correlation of the male and female. After all, the structures of the

male body would make little sense were it not for the concrete reality of the female body, and vice versa. The odd result is that under the liberal shift to orientations, sexual acts rely for their very being on that from which fully human and personal meaning has been drained by liberal androgyny. This paradox is particularly clear with regard to homosexual acts, which both depend on the facts of the body's sexual polarity for their very possibility and also effectively deny any deep anthropological significance of that polarity.[47]

It has moreover been recognized by defenders of sexual liberation that the increased practice of what I have called in this chapter substitutionary sex (including contracepted sex) has, as a matter of fact, undermined the traditional place in society held by procreative sex,[48] and subsequently its place in the minds of those who practise it. Crawford writes, making use of *The Invention of Heterosexuality*, the work of radical historian and admirer of Foucault, Jonathan Ned Katz,

> The strict division between what is heterosexual and what is homosexual becomes increasingly artificial as heterosexual patterns of behaviour begin to resemble those of homosexuals. In part this is due to the almost universal acceptance and use of birth control ('pleasure enhancers', as Katz calls them). But it is due also to the underlying systemization of pleasure on which the duality is based. As Katz astutely observes, 'The commercial stimulation of eroticism lifts the veil off the old sex mysteries. The marketing of pleasure-sex to all-comers with cash helps to demolish old rationales for heterosexual supremacy – even old rationales for the hetero-homo

difference. For, as pleasure pursuits, heterosexuality and homosexuality have little to distinguish them. Heterosexuals are more and more like homosexuals, except for the sex of their partners.[49]

Conclusion

This chapter has focussed on marriage as an institution which is crucial to the common good, teleologically-grounded and can be used as a paradigm for assessing the moral goodness or badness of certain kinds of sexual activity. However, sex is about many things, there are many and varied sexual phenomena, there are many different ways in which sexual desire is expressed and there are many questions raised about the role virtue and love play in both sexual activity and sexual willing. The chapters following, while continuing to analyse sex and marriage, will take us much further into the above-mentioned issues as a way of seeing just what sexual morality requires of us and why it is both special and important.

Chapter 4
Marital Willing

Set me as a seal upon your heart,
As a seal upon your arm;
For love is strong as death,
Passion fierce as the grave.

Song of Solomon

Corrupt nature. Man does not act according to the reason which
constitutes his being.

Pascal, Pensées

Conditional and Preparatory Intentions and the Good of Marriage

The *telos* of sex can be obstructed both in terms of the destruction of the social institution needed for people to flourish in this area and in the individual's pursuit of ends contrary to the *telos* which makes sex a rational and morally good activity. John Finnis, who has sought to give a philosophical justification for Catholic moral teaching on the basis of 'New Natural Law Theory' (see Chapters 1 and 2), aims to find a precise way of accounting for how it is that certain sex acts/intentions are 'against the good of marriage' and therefore irrational. His interesting argument rightly goes beyond references to what I have described as a generalised societal dilution of marriage and even beyond externally-visible sexual choices; for some of its conclusions, it also makes use of the notions of 'conditional' and 'preparatory' intentions.[1]

Finnis's account locates all sexual immorality as in some way involving offences against the good of marriage.[2] In a general paper, "Conditional Intentions and Preparatory Intentions," Finnis distinguishes, as he does in a later paper on sexual morality, between *conditional* intentions, in which the intention itself contains a qualifying condition ("I will do X only if Y") and what I will term 'contingent' intentions,[3] where no explicit condition has been made in the person's mind – i.e. the act is intended unconditionally at present, such that a change of mind would be required for it not to be performed.

It is not entirely clear whether Finnis means the 'contingent' intention to be contingent on its condition only by way of the subject's beliefs, or whether he is including causal preconditions which bypass the agent's explicit reasoning and instead help (or could in future help) give rise to an intention by way of, say, weakness of will or some other non-rational intention-formation process.

After discussion of conditional and contingent intentions Finnis moves on to discuss the related issue of preparatory intentions and applies such considerations to an example relevant to sexual ethics. He gives the following example:

> On getting married, someone says to himself that he will be a faithful husband, but decides to keep his address book of good-time girls just in case marriage fails to give him all the satisfactions he expects. By that decision, he is in his heart an adulterer, even though he has made no substantive decision to use the book, telephone a girl or make a sexual assignation… in so far as it is itself formed by adopting a proposal, the preparatory intention has, on the side of the subject, the unconditionality and

so the self-determining, character forming significance of all intentions.[4]

What should we say about such a man? In these kinds of discussion, we need always to be aware of the distinction between three different ways of expressing or recognising one's bad character: a) prediction of, without any kind of intention to enable, one's own likely bad behaviour, whatever attitude one takes to such behaviour, e.g. "I might well do bad thing x," as contrasted to b) a current intention to *make possible* a future choice to do something bad and c) a conditional intention to do that bad thing. It is important clearly to distinguish these three.

By describing the accomplished action of retaining the book as merely an "intention" Finnis risks inviting a confusion between the decision to keep the book and the future intentions which may yet arise – but which Finnis accepts have not at this point been adopted. The agent is leaving a future option open, even taking steps to facilitate a possible future course of conduct. The charge of 'adultery in the heart' may indeed be justified but requires more argument, as this is not the standard case of preparing for adultery one has already decided to commit in certain circumstances, nor is it even taking an adulterous pleasure in thoughts of the good-time girls, as the book retention may be done 'in cold blood' (though morally, it may be all the worse for that).[5] Compare a partially-reformed alcoholic who, knowing the frustration of being without alcohol when the urge is upon him and unsure whether he wishes to put his possible future self through that, for years keeps an un-opened bottle of whiskey on the sideboard.

Continuing, Finnis explains that the choice to keep the book is

> not yet the choice to do X, nor even the choice to *do X if C*. It is the definite intention not to exclude the option of

doing X from (further) deliberation, as a mere temptation, but rather to retain that option within one's deliber-
ations as still an *eligibilium*, as choiceworthy (choosable
by me). In that sense, one gives a real though as yet limited assent of will to that option (while not yet preferring
it to others by choosing to adopt it).[6]

This certainly seems right. A spouse, should she discover that
such a book had been retained, would not be happy – even if she
accepted that the book was not retained in pursuit of a firm plan to
betray, as opposed to a firm plan to make such a future plan possible. But, as with the alcoholic, this does not seem necessarily to
amount to a present 'assent of will' to the adultery itself – something which Finnis's terminology of "real though as yet limited assent of will" obscures. It is a case in which the husband recognises
that all his current good intentions may come to nothing, he may
face great temptation and decide to succumb to it, and if so he will
want his book – a firm plan to keep which he has formed. The initial description of the husband's decision, "just in case marriage
fails to give him all the satisfaction he expects" tends to suggest
a present conditional intention: to have sex with one of his "good
time girls" if satisfaction S is not forthcoming. And that is a present intention, even if it is conditional. It might even be expressed
"I will have sex with G unless I get satisfaction S." But the discussion shows that that is not what Finnis means. There is no such
present intention, and more needs to be said before concluding that
the husband has committed adultery 'in his heart.'

However, might it not be correct to say that the mere treating
this kind of option as choiceworthy is necessarily seriously morally
wrong, with all the character-forming consequences that entails?
Finnis appeals to Aquinas on this question and tells us,

St Thomas reserved a place for an act of will whereby one assents to a definite proposal for action yet without making a choice; he called this assent *consensus*. It is a sort of willing: one is minded, disposed, willing to treat some means, X, as acceptable. Very often some alternative option, Y, is also acceptable; one has not yet adopted (and may in fact never adopt) either X or Y in preference to the other. In this common case, *consensus* is distinct *re* as well as *ratione* from *electio*, choice. But in any case what makes the *consensus* is not simply the judgement that X (and Y) would be an effective way of securing some benefit in which one is interested, but the treating of X (and/or Y) as an acceptable option, the being interested in an option as one which I will keep in play as a live option notwithstanding that there remain incompatible alternatives in which I likewise remain interested.

Finnis then adds, "As a real disposition, consent can be mortally sinful acceptance of a possible option even though, not having chosen to do it, one does not intend, even conditionally, to do it. But Aquinas' formal account of consent uses the term *placet* for what I have called 'treating as acceptable,' and his later discussion of sinful *consensus* goes off on a particular type of case where one takes a kind of sensory pleasure, *delectatio*, in imagining and savouring some possible action."[7]

It does seem that "looking at a woman to lust after her," the phrase from Matthew 5:28 quoted by Finnis at ftn42, is not the only morally objectionable attitude in sexual matters: speculative preparation for a possible future desire or plan would also be morally objectionable.[8] The argument set out earlier in this paper concerning the relationship between non-marital and marital acts should suggest that there is a problem, even if we do not go as far as Finnis in describing this as "adultery of the heart."[9]

In a later paper, "The Good of Marriage and the Morality of Sexual Relations: Some Historical Observations"[10], which focuses very much on conditional intention and marital acts, Finnis widens the scope of his argument. In examining this paper we will make an attempt to draw out more precisely how a non-marital choice can be said to 'harm' or 'damage' the ability of human persons and societies to instantiate the good of marriage.

Without the possibility of *truly* marital intercourse the good of marriage is seriously impaired. Finnis, quoting Germain Grisez, supports the proposition that a choice such as the choice to engage in nonmarital sex, "damages the body's capacity for the marital act as an act of self-giving which constitutes a communion of bodily persons." Finnis then states that such damage

> is a damage to the person as an integrated acting being; it
> consists principally in that disposition of the will which
> is initiated by the choice to engage in an act of one or
> other of the kinds in question…to say "damages the
> body's capacity for self-giving" is, I think, elliptical for:
> that choice deforms one's will in such a way that unless
> one reverses one's choice (repents), it disables one – pre-
> cisely as a free, rational, sentient, *bodily* person – from
> engaging in a bodily act which would really express, ac-
> tualize, foster and enable one as a spouse to experience
> the good of marriage and one's own commitment (self-
> giving) in marriage.[11]

To argue his point Finnis introduces the notion earlier discussed of "conditional willing."[12] He describes cases of "obvious

violation" as ones in which "one or both of the spouses would be willing, or prefer, to be engaged in the act with someone else. Such a spouse is *conditionally willing* to engage in this sex act with someone not his or her spouse. That is, *if* such another person were available and all the other conditions were in place, this spouse *would* – unless he or she had a change of mind – have sex with another person." Finnis adds, "Let us call such a conditional willingness to engage in extra (i.e. non-) marital sex acts *consent* to nonmarital sex."[13]

There are problems with this exposition. "Prefer" is ambiguous: "they would prefer" suggests an occurrent desire, but might also indicate a counterfactual choice they might make in some other situation. And what of the important distinction Finnis doesn't make, namely that between possible future intentions (if intentions is even the right word – not if the option is seen as really counterfactual[14]) which the subject deliberately *entertains* (and thereby perhaps expresses and/or acknowledges his *akrasia*) and those he doesn't entertain. There is also the undiscussed issue of whether acknowledging such likely intentions also includes accepting them – in the counterfactual context. The final line quoted above amounts to a mere stipulation whereby "conditional willing" acts a bit like "suspected" or "alleged" as applied to terror suspects, i.e. encouraging the reader to take it as a mere modifying adjective adding extra detail, when in fact a suspected terrorist is not a kind of terrorist at all but a kind of suspect.

Given this, if one 'consents' (scare quotes required) to extramarital sex, one's choosing to engage in sex with one's spouse "cannot succeed in being an actualisation of *marriage*."[15] It seems that the only way to restore one's capacity to express marital self-giving is to negate/repent of one's 'consent' to any act of that kind (i.e. extra/non-marital sex).[16]

However, on Finnis's account it would seem that even counter-factual unacknowledged *liability* to give 'consent' would amount to a kind of stain which spoils all marital sex until removed. But that implies that there is some kind of 'staining' event – which isn't the case with a mere disposition. And does a mere change in one's liability remove the stain or must this involve repentance? And if the latter, how is one to repent of having a stain one is unaware of? In that case properly *marital* sex must remain an illusion.

To clarify some of these matters Finnis provides the reader with a number of examples, prefacing them thus:

> We have been considering the consent to nonmarital sex which may shape and divide the willingness of a married person, where the consent – conditional willingness – bears on that person's own actions in the (hypothetical) here and now.[17]

He moves to example A:

> I am so keen on having sex now that if an attractive woman were available (and my wife were not here), I would have sex with her, right now.[18]

This case is of a kind Finnis believes is relevant to Aquinas' discussions.[19] He cannot mean those cases discussed in his previous paper which were concerned with having sex merely for pleasure and thereby failing to connect with the good of marriage. True, thinking about having sex with another woman while having sex with your wife is an example of failed connection, but here 'conditional willingness' is just one form this can take. One might fail to connect maritally in all sorts of other ways. So, while in some cases the fact that one "would be willing"[20] to substitute another for one's spouse and even explicitly recognises this fact may be a sufficient indicator of a failure to connect in a truly marital way, it's not necessary for such a failure to connect, and is not the essential issue.

It might be argued that the fact that a spouse 'would' entertain adulterous thoughts, if they occurred to him, is evidence of a bad character likely to affect each 'marital' act, whether or not such thoughts do occur to him. However, Aquinas appears to be concerned with an actual identifiable defect in the actual sexual act, and doesn't need to consider 'possible worlds' in order to discover whether a given sex act is properly marital.

So, thinking A (and in this case, A's merely being objectively true) may (given normal psychological facts) be sufficient indicator of a failure to 'connect' in the Thomistic sense outlined, but it is only that. It's a sign of a defect which could perhaps be otherwise expressed. It establishes (fairly explicitly): "I'm so keen on having sex now" that I am only interested in the sex, and not in my wife.

Example B, "I'm not interested in having sex with anyone other than my husband right now, but if he goes off to war, I might well have sex with an attractive man"[21] doesn't have any implication that one is only interested in sex and not in one's husband. It is a contingency-prediction, and it also does not necessarily imply that one *approves* of the hypothetical course of action, whatever that amounts to. Though, as with all of the examples Finnis gives, the fact that it is in the first person and the idea that one might be thinking it occurrently while having sex with one's spouse gives an extra sense that it is an inappropriate thing to think.

Finnis's other examples of propositions expressing wrongful conditional willingness seem even less convincing. C is:

> While I'm married I'm not going to have extramarital
> sex, but if I weren't married, I'd try to have sex with
> someone attractive once a week, to keep fit.[22]

The inclusion of "to keep fit" seems redundant, not least because there's nothing so obviously wrong with having sex to keep fit provided that a proper 'marital' motive is also present. Otherwise the example seems as problematic as the first two.

Example D is: "While I'm married I'm not going to have extra-marital sex. But I think it's quite OK for people who want to have *extra-marital* sex to do it..."[23]

Example E is: "While I'm married I'm not going to have extramarital sex. But I think it's OK for unmarried people to get sexual satisfaction in any way they like, consistent with being fair to others..."[24]

The statement that the actor "thinks it's OK" sits uneasily with Finnis's rejection of a "legalistic morality of prohibitions and permissions."[25] That rejection allows Finnis to make the claim "it's OK" means "has some value."[26] But that is an assumption produced without argument. For it could equally be asserted that OK means simply OK, and not necessarily good or desirable. However, even if we accept Finnis's assumption, the preceding criticisms of A still apply *a fortiori* to B-E.

In relation to D and E, Finnis states, "the thought that it is permissible and OK for certain other people to get such satisfaction by nonmarital sex acts becomes deliberate approval, i.e. a thought of the form: "If I were in their situation, I would be willing to get sexual satisfaction by nonmarital sex acts.""[27]

At ftn107[28] Finnis glosses this by making it wholehearted approval of the core moral features of the action – and not their incidental or partly good effects. With that and what has been stated above kept in mind, to say "OK means has some value" establishes a thought of the form: "If I were in their situation I would be willing to get sexual satisfaction by nonmarital sex acts."

Yet this seems a leap, unless "in their situation" can be taken far enough (including, perhaps, changes in personality) to guarantee that result. Finnis continues, saying that the thought is "If I were then and there interested, I would under certain circumstances, and without having to violate or change any of my present moral beliefs, be prepared to choose to have nonmarital sex."[29] Note the phrase, "if I were then and there interested" – this can, of course, do the job of overcoming any loyalty to one's spouse (in case D) that might prevent one having the thought, and more importantly any such loyalty that might otherwise be contemplated as surviving in the counterfactual situation.

If we are to give a tight account of how nonmarital acts might be said to 'violate' marital goods then the approach here examined will need to be improved on. This is not to deny that, in general, the idea of 'keeping an option open' is problematic if the option is problematic, and in the next chapter I will examine questions relating to Christ's admonition at Matthew 5:28 which is, of course, relevant to the present discussion. In closing this section, I think it worth considering what might be the practical results of taking Finnis's concerns seriously.

If we accept (as someone influenced by Finnis's argument would accept) that someone who doesn't have a disposition to reject the idea of extramarital/nonmarital activity – or at least *tend strongly* to reject it – can't be engaged in *fides*-type activity, then this may have highly counterintuitive implications:

> (a) If a spouse is confused about what might be an OK structure for a sex act (e.g. he thinks that sexual intercourse with a perforated condom-style device to collect semen for fertility-tests is OK) and believes that such acts, in themselves, have 'some value' he can't engage in *fides*-type acts, assuming that he is, in fact, mistaken in that belief.[30] Does the spouse have to be an infallible moral expert, at least on sexual matters, in order to engage in *fides*-type acts? Does he have to be completely convinced about the right opinions?

> (b) A spouse may think that homosexual activity can be OK and has 'some value' while being emotionally horrified by it himself and therefore *very far* from either dwelling on it illicitly or saying that, if he were homosexually inclined, he'd have a civil partner – let alone that, if he ever does experience homosexual urges in the future, he will act on them.

> (c) a spouse may adhere to a moral philosophy sceptical of popular forms of consequentialism but eschewing moral absolutes (e.g. the kind of approach to ethics championed by Bernard Williams[31]) and may think that adultery is OK, i.e. 'has some value' (or *may perhaps* be OK) in desperate circumstances, while being *very far* from dwelling on it himself (e.g. taking deliberate pleasure, or any pleasure at all, in thinking about cases of adultery in concentration camps to save lives). Does such a judgement,

reached by the spouse last night, after watching a sad documentary regarding what someone *else* did mean that he can't have marital sex now? Or is it only if it flashes before his mind, however unwillingly, just before intercourse? Also, what if the man were an out-and-out consequentialist, but never connected that with his views about marriage?

(d) Imagine a voluntarist ("God could command adultery") or someone who thinks that polygamy is OK for biblical patriarchs. Can such a person not engage in *fides*-type sex?

(e) Imagine a coward who thinks "I would do anything to avoid death/torture – it's only human" (i.e. he's not just predicting his own weakness but mentally endorsing it in some way). Can he or anyone like him who is not prepared for martyrdom have marital sex? Finnis's arguments suggest a perfectionism which makes it hard to appreciate St Paul's admonition at 1 Corinthians 7:9 or Augustine's *De bono conjugale*. Seeing marriage as redemptive or curative assumes there are states of 'imperfection' that might be improved and chastened through marriage.

While we may accept that sometimes a strong disposition on the part of a spouse to make bad future choices or bad choices in counterfactual situations may suggest the absence of a good (enough) intention and/or disposition needed (a) to get married or (b) to engage in marital acts (these require a minimum of good will[32] which may be absent if a husband is disposed to betray/beat up/murder a wife at a moment's notice), such cases go way beyond the kind of cases Finnis wants to rule out.

Conditional willing of morally impermissible actions tells us something about the moral agent, as does the *liability* to will these actions in certain unrealised contingencies. Any effect on the validity of marriages or marital acts will depend on the moral weight one places on the relation of the agent to his pursuit/realisation of various 'basic goods.' But this need not (though it might) affect the moral permissibility of the act intended here and now. These two must not be conflated.[33]

Conclusion

Accounts of sexual wrongdoing will typically be concerned with concepts other than conditional intentions, namely lust and concupiscence. An account of ethical sex will therefore need to examine these concepts, and their opposites in terms of morally good desires and virtue, if it is to give this area of morality its due.

The attempt to account for major ethical principles in sexual ethics simply in terms of the relation of intentions to marital goods appears to be doomed to failure, not least because in capturing what seems plausible about anti-marital intentions the term 'intention' ends up being used to cover mental events which cannot be classified as such. In showing that this is the case here I hope to have shown that too blunt an instrument is being deployed and that an examination of the concepts mentioned above is required for a richer account of ethical sex. This means giving an account of the teleology of desire and an explanation of how that teleology relates to sexual virtue – an explanation that goes beyond a narrow examination of anti-marital intentions and 'background beliefs.'

Chapter 5

Sexual Desire

"Do I exhort you to chastity? With some chastity is a virtue, but with many it is almost a vice...Not a few who sought to drive out their devil entered into the swine themselves. Those to whom chastity is difficult should be dissuaded from it, lest it become the way to Hell – that is, to filth and lust of soul...Truly there are those who are chaste from the very heart: they are more gentle of heart and they laugh more often and more heartily than you."

Friedrich Nietzsche, Thus Spoke Zarathustra[1]

"You have heard that it was said to them of old: You shall not commit adultery. But I say to you, everyone that looks on a woman to lust for her, has already committed adultery with her in his heart."

Matthew 5:27-28.[2]

Setting the Heart

Contemporary liberal thinking on sexual ethics has tended to be dismissive of the kinds of arguments and concerns addressed by the Gospels and explored by Aquinas, let alone controversial takes on these of the kind discussed in the previous chapter. It is necessary to examine the Gospel passage cited above and what it might be taken to imply because the philosophical issues involved bear upon the place of virtue in ethics and especially sexual ethics. That we are concerned with biblical texts is not meant to imply that my arguments presuppose any particular view as to the authority of these texts. Rather, such analysis acknowledges the value that such texts can have in them enlightening philosophical arguments not reliant on theological presuppositions.[3]

Gareth Moore, a heterodox Catholic thinker, interprets Christ's admonition as meaning that,

> Setting your heart on another's man's wife will no doubt involve or even consist in wanting sexual intercourse with her. This does not, however, mean committing some special type of sexual sin, but preparing to infringe that man's property rights by taking what is his. It is setting in train a course of action that amounts to injustice against him...Jesus is not aiming to promote something that might be called 'inner purity,' if by that is meant a putative mental state divorced from any reference to activity. Neither is he merely wanting to stop particular thoughts and fantasies going through people's heads. He wants to stop people being unjust to each other... Thoughts and fantasies can indeed be very important... precisely because they can influence the way we behave.[4]

Moore later adds that it is simply a misconception to hold that "having something in your heart is the same as imagining doing it, or at least that if you imagine doing it that means you have it in your heart...this is not so...to have something in your heart is to set your desire on it, so that you may end up acting on it."[5]

Moore's emphasis is, then, on the formation of an actual plan to "set in train" a "course of action" toward a more or less specifically unjust act. Whereas Finnis was partly concerned with our relationship to the good of marriage seen in the light of conditional intentions and what we might call 'possible worlds,' Moore is only interested in desires directed toward specific courses of action (here, adulterous sex) that are themselves unjust (and not necessarily in a specifically sexual way).

Yet in order to 'set your desire' on an object (here, a course of action), such that you intend to act in a particular way you must, at least in general, have already desired the object, such that you find the object initially attractive and potentially to be intended by you. True, there are cases when we decide to desire in a rather abstract way (e.g. someone choosing to desire 'bloodlessly' as opposed to deliberately desire for purposes of immediate sexual arousal), but this is very far from the norm. Even in this case, we could see the 'desire to desire' as something that may well precede any choice to set in motion some way to achieve this.

In other words, when we 'set our desire' on a course of action involving another person this is because we have already desired it and often deliberately desired it, before any such further intention. And intentions help to form us, whether they are merely internal or externally expressed.

Bad Desires

The interpretation Moore places on Matthew 5:27-28 is unsustainable. As some biblical scholars point out, the Greek for "to lust after" uses the preposition of intimate connection (pros), and the aorist infinitive (epithumesai) to denote a man who looks upon a woman with express intent of lusting, and satisfies the intent in the act of staring.[6] Clearly, the verse is not referring to an inadvertent or involuntary glance at a woman. Nor is there anything in the text that supports Moore's presupposition that the lusting is not condemned if "divorced from any reference to activity." We can agree with Aurel Kolnai that "An unchaste wish is naturally a *lesser* thing than the unchaste deed which realises it; but, on the other hand, wallowing in unfulfilled sexual desires, the luxuriating of fantasy life, leads to *its own kind* of unchastity; here, solitary gratification and gratification through fantasies of the other begin to take on the form of 'something done', whereas, on the other hand, the 'saturation' of thinking and feeling with sexual dynamite and filth remains behind."[7]

Moreover, the term "heart" is used throughout the New Testament in a specific and important way. Karol Wojtyla, whose analysis is worth quoting at length, states that when Christ spoke of the man

who looks lustfully, he indicated not only the dimension of intentionality in looking, thus indicating lustful knowledge, the psychological dimension, but also the dimension of the intentionality of man's very existence. In the situation Christ described, that dimension passes unilaterally from the man, who is the subject, to the woman, who has become the object...she begins to exist intentionally as an object of the potential satisfaction of the sexual need inherent in his masculinity. Although the act is completely interior, hidden in the heart and expressed only by the look, there already occurs in him a change (subjectively unilateral) of the very intentionality of existence. If it were not so, if it were not a question of such a deep change, the following words of the same sentence: "has already committed adultery with her in his heart" (Matthew 5:28) would have no meaning. That change of intentionality of existence is carried out in the heart, since it is carried out in the will. By means of it, a certain woman begins to exist for a certain man not as a subject of call and personal attraction or as a subject of communion, but exclusively as an object for the potential satisfaction of sexual need. Cognitive intentionality itself does not yet mean enslavement of the heart. It can be said that desire has also gained possession of the heart only when the intentional reduction, illustrated previously, sweeps the will along into its narrow horizon. It brings forth the decision of a relationship with another human being (in our case, with the woman) according to the specific scale of the values of lust.[8]

These crucial considerations are entirely lacking in Moore's analysis which is not consistent with the Gospel idea that we are enjoined to love God with all our heart, and that is not possible when, in the words of Francis Watson, that "'heart' is filled with the fantasy of sexual intercourse with the object of the erotic gaze...The prohibition of the desire and the fantasy is intended to create space for *agape*."[9]

Augustine is clear that the tenth commandment summarises all of the law. According to him, the Apostle [Paul] "purposely selected this general precept , in which he included everything, as if this were the voice of the law prohibiting us from all sin, when he says, "Thou shalt not covet" [*non concupisces*]; for there is no sin committed except by evil concupiscence [*concupiscientia*]."[10] Watson observes with regard to this passage, "Here 'concupiscence' does not refer exclusively to sexual desire. But because desire for prohibited sexual objects is the paradigmatic form of the tenth commandment, Augustine elsewhere identifies concupiscence specifically with sexual desire."

Commenting on Paul's words to the Romans at 7:15, Augustine writes, "The law too wills not that which I also will not; for it wills not that I should have concupiscence, for it says: "Thou shalt not lust;" and I am no less unwilling to cherish so evil a desire" [*De nuptiis et concupiscentia* i.30].[11] In line with (or rather, inspiring) these pronouncements are Christ's words as recorded at Matthew 15:19, which take on an especial significance when we remember that it is the pure of heart who will see God. Moore's model conflicts most obviously with Christ's words at Mark 7:20-23, "It is what comes out of a person that defiles. For it is from within, from the human heart, that evil intentions come: fornication, theft, murder, adultery, avarice, wickedness, deceit, licentiousness, envy, slander, pride, folly. All these evil things come from within, and they defile a person." For to act or even think in the spirit of "pride" or "folly" need not be to have formed a specific plan for external action of the kind Moore requires the person to have in order for us to be able to talk of his 'setting his heart.' For example, a proud man might be doing *externally* just what a non-proud man would do but in a proud spirit.

Christ's words at Matthew 19:8 refer back to the "hardness of heart" of the Jews in the time of Moses, whose interior disposition distorted the law handed down to them. Moore's view misses out this rich seam of exegesis. Moreover, according to Moore's model there could be no condemnation, in the terms given by Christ, of someone indulging in sexual fantasy over a woman depicted in a pornographic magazine or indeed over any woman entirely unattainable to the fantasist (or over someone the lustful person has absolutely no desire to *actually* possess, even if attainable). For in such cases, the person knows that he will never act on the imagining or fantasy. Yet, in terms of intentionality and in terms of looking at others in a way that respects them *as persons*, these cases are morally problematic, for the reasons outlined above and below.[12]

Dynamic of Lust

One of the many weaknesses of Moore's account is its lack of attention to the dynamic of lust and certain necessary distinctions. Karol Wojtyla (later Pope John Paul II), in his early work *Love and Responsibility* writes:

> we must give proper weight to the fact that *in any normal man the lust of the body has its own dynamic*, of which his sensual reactions are a manifestation. We have drawn attention to their appetitive character. The sexual values connected with the body of the person become not only an object of interest but – quite easily – the object of interest of sensual desire. The source of this desire is the power of concupiscence (*appetitus concupiscibilis* as St. Thomas calls it), and so not the will. Concupiscence of the senses tends to become active 'wanting,' which is an act of will. The dividing line between the two is however clear. Concupiscence does not immediately aim at causing the will fully and actively to want the object of sexual desire: *passive acquiescence suffices* [my emphasis]. Here we stand at the threshold of sin, and we see that concupiscence, which seeks continually to induce the will to cross it, is rightly called the 'germ of sin.' As soon as the will consents it begins actively to want what is spontaneously 'happening' in the senses and the sensual appetites. From then onwards, this is not something merely 'happening' to a man, but something which he himself begins actively doing – at first only internally, for the will is in the first place, the source of interior acts, of interior 'deeds.' These deeds have a moral value, are good or evil, and if they are evil we call them sins.[13]

By ignoring this dynamic and locating 'sin' outside of interior 'deeds,' at least if these interior deeds are not already plans for action, Moore neglects the necessary role according to the Christian tradition of concupiscence in human action and in actually inclining us to inappropriate sexual desire in the first place. The act of will that consents to the 'wanting' is precisely that which enables the intention toward a particular end to be set which reinforces and impels the desire further. In order to make sense of the process one has to take account of the role of the interior deed, which as a human act is capable, in the last analysis, of being judged morally good or evil.

More radically (and outside of the Christian framework Moore sees himself as working within) the secular philosopher Thomas Nagel writes about the topic of 'sexual control.' He tells readers,

> Sex is the source of the most intense pleasure of which humans are capable, one of the few sources of human ecstasy. It is also the realm of adult life in which the defining and inhibiting structures of civilization are permitted to dissolve, and our deepest presocial animal, and infantile natures can be fully released and expressed, offering a form of physical and emotional completeness that is not available elsewhere. The case for toleration and an area of protected privacy in this domain is exceptionally strong.[14]

Nagel proceeds to make the bold statement:

> We do not inhabit a common sexual world in the sense – limited, to be sure – in which we inhabit a common natural, or economic, or educational, or even artistic world.[15]

He goes on to claim:

> If some men get their kicks...by watching depictions of
> gang rape or flogging or mutilation, this really should
> not give rise to a claim on anyone's part not to be sur-
> rounded by, or even included in, such fantasies. We have
> no right to be free of the fantasies of others, however
> much we may dislike them. If the division between the
> public and private means anything, sexual fantasies and
> means of sexual gratification belong firmly in the private
> domain. An awareness that things go on there which
> might disturb, disgust or frighten you, together with an
> unwillingness to regard this as providing any ground for
> interference whatever, should be a fundamental aspect of
> the kind of recognition of inviolability that makes up a
> commitment to human rights.[16]

Nagel concludes, in opposition to those "radical communitar-
ians" who would seek to protect the "dominant" values of society
by placing restrictions on "respect" for the privacy of "sexual
imagination," that "the only defence against them is an appeal
to the form of moral equality that accords each person a limited
sovereignty over the core of his personal and expressive life...this
sovereignty or inviolability is in itself, and not just for its consequences, the most distinctive value expressed by a morality of human rights."[17]

Nagel is concerned, in this paper, with confronting the problems of sexual morality in terms of rights disputes (e.g. what does
an individual have a 'political' right to engage in sexually, what
can a state legitimately outlaw in terms of sexual practices etc.)[18]
Such an approach largely sets aside concerns about virtuous and
vicious dispositions in relation to sex and human flourishing, and

in practice yields moral conclusions external to the subject matter of sexual morality per se.[19]

Felt Desire, Informed Desire: Desire, Choice and Cognition

In the light of the views of Moore and Nagel we need to ask: why is it important to take seriously from the moral point of view people's thoughts and imaginings, in this and other contexts? However, before exploring this question, we need to get clearer on what we mean by the term desire and some of its subdivisions such as felt desire, chosen desire, 'deep' desire, uninformed desire.

There is no reason to accept the once common idea, supposedly deriving from David Hume, that desires are always necessarily motivating states whereas belief requires desire if it is to motivate action. Jonathan Dancy, among others, has well explained that there are "*intrinsically* motivating states, which can be present without motivating but which when they do motivate do so in their own right. They can motivate in their own right, and so are not Humean beliefs; but they can be present without motivating, and so are not Humean desires."[20] Desires, *of themselves*, cannot be reasons for action at all (although they may be necessary preconditions for action). As Warren Quinn has pointed out, reasons have to be justificatory to show an action to be rational; they cannot be merely causal.[21] For Quinn,

> ...the primary job of practical reason is the correct evaluation of ends, actions, and qualities as good and bad in themselves. And what is it for something to be a reason for action follows from this. *On this view, a reason to act in a certain way is nothing more than something good in itself that it realizes or serves, or, short of that, something bad in itself that it avoids.* To the extent that one

realizes or serves some such good one acts well. To the
extent that one realizes or serves some such bad one acts
badly. An objectivist therefore sees moral obligation as
giving an agent reason to act only because, and only to
the extent that, the agent will act well in discharging it or
badly in neglecting it.[22]

Mere satisfaction of desire does not provide a reason for action, for it normally presupposes that such satisfaction is valuable in terms of what the desire is for. My simple urge is not enough to justify my action morally, even if one thinks this urge causes the action (and even if one thinks that there is *sometimes* some value to sheer desire satisfaction in the absence of countervailing considerations[23]). The desire may cause the action, but its reasonableness depends on the non-causal property of goodness. Values enter into reasons from the start (see Chapter 2 above).

It may seem, however, when we think about (or experience) something like that most overwhelming, urgent and intimate of desires, sexual lust (or indeed, morally good sexual desire) that some kind of motivated desire theory is more plausible. More will be said about this shortly. For now we can concur with Jonathan Dancy that,

> though desire is necessary for motivation, the occurrence
> of the desire is *the agent's being motivated* by that gap
> [between two representations, 'before' and 'after']...We
> could allow lust to be a non-cognitive state, since it is
> not a belief, but insist that what motivates the luster is
> not the lust but the combination of two representations,
> the 'before' and the 'after.' The lust is the agent's being
> strongly motivated by these representations.[24]

Willed and Unwilled Desire

The considerations above have not been explicitly concerned with the distinction between willed and unwilled desire. Instructive on this is the earlier quote from Wojtyla which ended by urging:

> As soon as the will consents it begins actively to want what is spontaneously 'happening' in the senses and the sensual appetites. From then onwards, this is not something merely 'happening' to a man, but something which he himself begins actively doing – at first only internally, for the will is in the first place, the source of interior acts, of interior 'deeds.' These deeds have a moral value, are good or evil, and if they are evil we call them sins.[25]

It is worth remembering here that even if unwilled desires are by definition unwilled at the time, they may be influenceable, for good or ill, by habits of behaviour. Ethics does not merely concern willed desires now (a kind of intention) but 'remote control' over future desires that may be unwilled at the time they are experienced. Virtue has been called the 'education of desire.'

Consideration of the morality of acts is necessarily focussed on human volitional states, including desires, and must involve consideration of human intentions or choices. All of these are particularly relevant to considerations in ethics and in sexual ethics.

Intentions and Evaluating Prospective Acts

However, there are certain approaches to ethics which downplay the importance and relevance of the concept of intention, at least insofar as it applies to the moral assessment of the permissibility or impermissibility of certain prospective human acts.

Jonathan Bennett, for example, holds that it is a mistake to think of that part of morality concerned with the guidance of deliberating agents as making any use of an evaluation of the deliberator's intentions in performing the act in question. For him, what provides moral guidance for conduct does also guide one's intentions, but not by instructing one as to what may or may not be intended.[26] For Bennett, intention is only relevant in guiding judgements on people in respect of past actions. Broadly speaking, intentions are relevant for the assessment of a *person* but not, ordinarily, of an act.

However, intention (or what TM Scanlon calls "intention in a narrower sense") is something more than volition and concerns what the agent's "aim was in doing it and what plan guided her action – how she saw the action as promoting her objective."[27] Attempting to treat intention in the narrow sense as having no relevance to the permissibility of future actions seems beset with difficulties. Separating out what counts towards assessing someone's moral character and what counts towards assessing an act that an individual chooses leads to a distorting view of morality. As JLA Garcia points out,

> We need not deny that to assess a person is one thing and to assess her behaviour is another. However, we morally evaluate actions precisely as exercises of agency, and the factors relevant and decisive to evaluating her conduct will be facts about her mind at the time of acting that will also be pertinent to evaluating her as a person when they are deep-seated and characteristic. The logical distinction between the two subjects of assessment is misunderstood and misapplied when it is thought to follow that it cannot be largely the same kind of fact that is decisive to both.[28]

This is surely right. If intentions or at least further intentions[29] are not to be involved in assessment of prospective acts (except, as some would allow, as 'external' phenomena to consider or factor in), it is hard to see how we are ever to 'improve ourselves' morally, say by making resolutions for future behaviour which necessarily will involve intentions whether further or immediate. Moral reasons for action invite us to intend particular acts, the adoption of which is an exercise of agency. One swallow does not make a summer (except perhaps in England), and one morally bad choice does not necessarily make a bad person; however, one bad act of a particular kind may do about as much as a single act of that type could do towards that bad result.

Irrespective of disagreements about prospective intentions as required for making moral choices, there is more widespread agreement about the moral undesirability of certain character traits which in turn will influence future actions. Above we referred to acts motivated by pride or folly and now we turn to examine internal acts – which, it must be remembered, are chosen acts as much as are external actions.

Hate Crimes: Bad Motivating Desires

To explore the significance of intention and underlying motivating attitudes, let us look at a rather different area – that of "hate crimes" as they are often called. Hate crimes, sometimes known as "bias-motivated" crimes, are standardly classified as crimes which occur when a perpetrator targets a victim because of his or her membership of a particular social group. The idea behind legislation regarding such crimes is that the motivation for the crime 'adds something bad' to the bad of similar crimes committed without such a motivation so that they need to be classified (and punished) accordingly.[30] I am not concerned here with the controversial question as to whether it is desirable for the criminal law to make such a distinction, but focus instead on what I think is relevant to judging the crime from a moral point of view.

The additional bad identified by speaking of "hate crimes" is of course, internal: an intention or motive. It does seem at least plausible that in the case of a "race hate" crime (say the racially-motivated lynching of a black man), the bad of the murder of an innocent person is added to by the bias motivation of targeting the person on account of his racial group. So, if we were to subtract the external act of killing we would be left with the bad attitude. And such an attitude is surely immoral in itself.

Someone might argue that the bad attitude is only bad when found in combination with the external act which it motivates. However, this seems unconvincing. Imagine the following: My neighbour wishes to murder me. He sets in place a plan to carry out this act. However, the plan is utterly ineffectual and I never even knew anything about it or about him. Clearly he has done something wrong here and wrong to me, something akin to murder even if he has been completely unsuccessful in his attempt. Now, if that is correct, we have to ask, why should the very attitude that formed the plan not be seen as bad in a similar way? Neither the attitude nor the plan was at all likely to cause me physical harm, we can imagine, but both seem wrong in themselves.

Alternatively, we can imagine a case where the attitude not only leads to a plan but causes actual harm which it was not un-likely to cause. We might imagine a rapist who, through exposure to huge amounts of violent pornography, has begun to regard women in certain ways – has formed a certain very bad attitude towards them which seems already morally evil. If he then goes out and rapes a woman it might be said that the actual rape is now expressive of this bad attitude in the most radical way (even if the vast majority of people with a similar bad attitude never go on to rape anyone). Aside from being highly plausible in itself, this story is confirmed by the actual testimony of, and studies on, rapists and murderers. Again, if a particular man was physically incapable of harming women, but nonetheless enjoyed visualising women being raped, such a man would surely have much in common attitudinally with the pornography user who eventually turned into an actual rapist.

In the case of spite, even of a trivial and/or dissipated kind, we accept that it is in the interests of people not to be the subject of spiteful as opposed to generous thoughts. This does not just apply to our friends and acquaintances, but applies to strangers. For example, if we are in a lift with strangers, we like to think there's some basic good will on their part towards us. Their role may be merely that of "fellow human being in a lift," but even that role has some duties.

Fantasy

Jeffrey Hershfield, in writing about the ethics of sexual fantasy, has argued that,

> a person's sexual fantasies function autonomously from
> his desires, beliefs, and intentions, a fact I attribute to
> their different forms of intentionality: the contents of
> sexual fantasies, unlike those of the latter, lack a direc-
> tion of fit and thus fail to express satisfaction condi-
> tions.[31]

We will return shortly to Hershfield's point about "fit" between mind and the world. Hershfield concedes that someone who harbours bad intent (or even a negative attitude) towards another is harbouring disrespectful thoughts about that person, but says it is far from clear that this applies to fantasies, sexual or otherwise.

One worry is that to be sexually aroused by fantasies of morally bad sex in particular is to fail to acknowledge fully the nature of that immoral behaviour. To this Hershfield responds that fantasies don't imply that you "desire" the *content* of the fantasy and therefore don't count as endorsement of the content of the fantasy as something valuable (note that it is not quite clear what Hershfield means by desires – whether he sees them as including only what you either plan to do or would do if you could). To this one might object that even if dwelling on and literally endorsing the content of the fantasy are not exactly the same thing, surely one who does the former cannot oppose to the same extent the moral disvalue depicted in the fantasy as someone who does not indulge in the fantasy.

Hershfield's autonomy thesis holds that endorsement is all about mind-to-world direction of fit and satisfaction conditions which are simply not present when it comes to (sexual) fantasy. On this picture, fantasies, unlike beliefs and desires,

> don't appear to be dependent on the actual world for their satisfaction. Whereas false beliefs and unfulfilled desires are deficient in an important sense, fantasies that go unrealized cannot for that reason be said to be defective.[32]

For Hershfield comparisons with emotions like *Schadenfreude* miss the point. In *Schadenfreude* the thought that real persons suffer genuine hardship is crucial to the experience itself, which would seem to go against the respect owed to others. Thus

Schadenfreude involves beliefs and desires or wishes involving a direction of fit – world to mind or mind to world – and "a functional role linked to a subject's central store of intentional states."[33]

Hershfield goes on to say that,

> Since our sexual fantasies are not indicative of what we are inclined to do, sexually or otherwise, they fall outside the traditional focus of virtue ethics.[34]

However, with regard to *Schadenfreude* it is worth considering the following. Imagine a case of *Schadenfreude* relating to an event which has not yet happened, whether or not it could still happen in the future. There are at least three possibilities here:

(a) I would like that person to slip on a banana and hurt and embarrass himself.

(b) I would like that person to slip on a banana even though I know that's impossible due to the absence of bananas (an attitude Hershfield may also classify as a 'desire').

(c) I wouldn't like them *actually* to slip on a banana but really enjoy vividly envisaging their embarrassment if they did.

In order for Hershfield's thesis to go through he is required to place a huge distance between (a) (and perhaps (b)), and in contrast (c). Yet (c) is not at all obviously so distant morally from (a) and certainly not from (b).

Indeed, sex itself has a 'direction of fit,' involving as it does a very intricate and delicate part of life, as this book has attempted to show. The treating of sexual fantasies as though they were not morally special or significant fails to recognise that direction of fit which allows for morally good or bad satisfaction conditions of sexual desires. Our minds should fit the world as it is and ought to be, in order to recognise real human capacities and to protect real, important human goods.

To this it might be objected that even if sex *itself* may have a 'direction of fit' and be dependent on the real world for its satisfaction, that doesn't apply to *imagining* sexual acts, any more than to imagining other enjoyable experiences (Hershfield mentions imagining enjoying a spa). However, in the case of sexual fantasy, there are certainly *some* satisfaction conditions, though bad ones: a real-world effect on the agent is still being sought which arguably does not reflect moral reality. Powerful socially important feelings or emotions are being harnessed which belong with other emotions like falling in love and true affection and commitment. Such feelings and emotions are very much more important than enjoying a spa as they power the institution of marriage and are concerned with couples bonding and the sense of irreplaceability appropriate to their subsequent fidelity, the generation of children and those children's subsequent welfare (see Chapter 3 and below). Emotions can be indulged which are not in line with what we might call the 'teleology of desire' and do not become integrated in a wider sexual project which makes sense as a whole, as we shall see. Similarly, the damaging nature of *sentimental* emotion for the moral life has been rightly noted by many.[35] Certain kinds of not-explicitly-sexual romantic imaginings too fervently indulged in may well distort or replace the very emotions needed by a person to honour the teleology of desire and relate to real human beings. (Conversely an adolescent might *benefit* from romantic imaginings of a more innocuous kind – saving a damsel in distress, say – as preparation for a later good romantic-sexual commitment. Indeed, 'falling in love' without *some* such imaginings is hard to imagine.)

Whatever we say about a direction of fit, if we focus on the imaginary sexual activity which is not actually 'desired' in Hershfield's sense, there certainly *is* direction of fit in the damaging co-opting of real sexual feelings that belong in a special social context: the moral demands of the real world are not being adequately met when an effect is deliberately produced which properly belongs to a different cause. Denial of that special status leads people like Hershfield into comparisons between surreptitiously browsing emails while talking to someone and thinking sexually of another woman while making love to one's spouse.[36]

Note that Hershfield saw it as important to remove from his argument about sexual fantasy considerations about desire (in what seems to be his restricted sense which excludes thinking about acts one does not wish to instantiate). Yet his argument, by ignoring the direction-of-fit that is the teleology of desire (understood as encompassing arousal and related phenomena) does not provide a plausible account of why we should exclude sexual fantasy from concerns about direction-of-fit. It is to that teleology which we now turn.

Teleology of Desire

Every desire is necessarily dependent on the desirer's understanding of its object and is therefore necessarily correctable (or so one might suppose) with an improvement of that understanding. If I eat a chocolate muffin, unaware that it contains human flesh, I have done what I desired (eaten a chocolate muffin) but not what I desired at a deeper level. Perhaps not all desires are so easily correctable, but in any case, desires and actions that are not based on the real truth about their objects are simply not deeply grounded responses of the desirers to those objects.[37] I will argue that this is certainly true in sexual ethics.

Even if desires are specific and even if we know what they are, some desires will change with certain factual information and some desires *should* change with such information (e.g. the girl you romantically pursued turns out to be 10 and not 18 or turns out to be 18 but not, as you thought she was, consenting to sexual activity). In Chapter 2 we saw the so-called fact/value distinction challenged and the close connections between value judgements and metaphysics examined. As we have seen and will see further, desires and their sexual expression can serve important social functions: functions largely denied by certain writers on sexual ethics.

Plain Sex

A popular view expressed by Igor Primoratz, loosely following Alan Goldman's "Plain Sex" (together with that of people like Wilhelm Reich and Alfred Kinsey) is that,

> Sexual activity can be defined as activity that tends to
> fulfil sexual desire, while sexual desire is sufficiently
> defined as the desire for bodily pleasures, period. This
> includes both sex with another person and solitary sex;
> the latter is not relegated beyond the pale, as some sort
> of imaginative substitute for, or deviation from, the for-
> mer.[38]

With regard to sexual desire, it is useful to resist the idea that 'desire' can be collapsed into mere 'wanting' to do something. The term 'desire' might indicate unusual psychological depth. It may also be more common or characteristic that desire, as contrasted

with mere wanting, lacks a specific focus (i.e. has some indeter-
minacy and vagueness in the intentional object or content of the
desire). The term 'want' sometimes indicates little more than that
someone would like to do or have something (we often ask and answer questions about a person's wants by talking about what they
would like). It is not clear that 'desiring' another person sexually
always relates to some envisioned future quite as clearly as this.

On the Primoratz account, sexuality cannot admit of imperfection or perversion as it is not that kind of thing, any more than
hunger is.[39] We saw in the Introduction that certain people think
that we cannot sensibly talk of sexual perversion unless we have
an idea that sex has some aim or goal. This point was made with
regard to sexual acts in the first place and their supposed natural
teleology. In Chapters 2 and 3, we addressed the question of natural teleology in terms of functions but not the teleology of desire.
There are however certain thinkers, for example Jean-Paul Sartre
and Thomas Nagel, who connect the notion of sexual perversity
not so much to sexual acts but to what they see as a diversion from
what I would call the *telos* of sexual desire. Those who are concerned with the perversion of desire itself need not also hold that
there are sexual perversions of a more biological/structural kind.
Moreover, they need not take sexual perversion to be something
necessarily morally wrong, as Nagel makes clear. Both Nagel and
Sartre, as well as the more conservative philosopher Roger Scruton in his classic study *Sexual Desire: A Philosophical Investigation*, maintain that sexual perversion is a real phenomenon. All are
agreed that, as Nagel puts it,

> We approach the sexual attitude toward the person
> through the features that we find attractive, but these fea-
> tures are not the objects of that attitude…Various people

may desire [an omelet] for different reasons...yet we do not enshrine the transcendental omelet as the true object of their affections...It is not similarly true that any person with the same flesh distribution and way of smoking can be substituted as object for a particular sexual desire that has been elicited by those characteristics. It may be that they would arouse attraction whenever they occur, but it will be a new sexual attraction with a particular object, not merely a transfer of the old desire to someone else.[40]

Similarly Scruton says that "desire proper" (as opposed to what he calls the desire to desire) focuses on a particular person – even in the case where a sailor is very much bent on having sex with someone just as soon as he gets into port.[41]

This is the context in which all three thinkers in their different ways agree that a variegated psychological reaction is involved in developed sexual attraction. All three agree that sexual desire cannot be reduced to desire for mere 'pleasure'.[42] Sartre, as we saw earlier, sees the paradigmatic case of sexual desire as one where, "the revelation of the Other's flesh is made through my own flesh; in desire and in the caress which expresses the desire. I incarnate myself in order to realize the incarnation of the Other. The caress by *realizing* the Other's incarnation reveals to me my own incarnation; that is I make myself flesh in order to impel the Other to realize for-herself and for me her own flesh...And so possession truly appears as a double reciprocal incarnation."[43] One does not have to share a belief in Sartre's existentialism or even his general approach to sex to appreciate that his assigning to sexual desire a 'goal' – namely the goal of eliciting in another sexual desire towards me – captures a truth about the special and uniquely embodied nature of that desire. Similarly Nagel's account of the self-consciousness of human sexuality and the mutual and reciprocal recognition of arousal in the other provides a positive model for assessing psychologically 'natural' sex and an argument against a 'sex is about pleasure' model. As Nagel puts it, "One's whole body does not become saturated with hunger as it can with desire. But the most characteristic feature of a specifically sexual immersion in the body is its ability to fit into the complex of mutual perceptions...physical possession must eventuate in creation of the sexual object in the image of one's desire, and not merely in the object's recognition of that desire or in his or her private arousal."[44]

However, the proponent of the 'sex is about pleasure' approach can ask the following questions. Firstly, do the accounts just given provide *moral* models for judging sexual behaviour and desire? Secondly, is there a 'sex is about pleasure' model which gives a better account of sexual phenomena and any related moral judgements?

Readers should recall that in Chapter 2 we showed that pleasure could not be seen as a 'basic good' in itself, although it may have a functional value in itself as promoting various goods. With that context in mind, recall too the point already made about human desire and the 'non-causal' property of goodness – a point which presumes that the desires in question are the desires of a rational being and not an animal.

Alan Soble,[45] a proponent of the virtues of masturbation, has argued for a 'sex is about pleasure' model (as outlined by Primoratz above, but without his insistence that sex has to be pleasurable in order to qualify *as sex*) – namely that sexual desire is about the rubbing of skin for the sake of pleasure relating to the sexual 'parts.' Soble has also argued for what he oddly calls a 'unitary' model (which would be better called 'solitary') which, he believes, gives the best account of paradigmatic sexual desire and in so doing avoids the kind of judgements seemingly demanded by other accounts (including even his fellow 'sex is about pleasure' advocate Alan Goldman who sees "binary" sex as paradigmatic as opposed to seeing solitary masturbation at the core of sexual desire and activity). On Soble's model the essence of sexuality is "unitary" so that paired intercourse is seen as masturbatory. In other words pairedness is not conceptually linked with sexual desire per se but is rather analogous to a particular kind of pasta sauce – something only linked contingently to the 'plain sex' that is the pasta.[46] For Soble, then, as for Primoratz, masturbation is absolutely not 'substitionary' for something else or a truncated form of some 'binary' paradigm.[47] Neither writer tries to explain why various terms for masturbator (e.g. 'wanker') are still regarded as deeply insulting and demeaning across cultures and continents and have been for hundreds if not thousands of years.[48]

One of the many problems with these kinds of account are that they end up suggesting (by analogy) that e.g. eating is to be accounted for essentially in terms of achieving a feeling of unhungriness – as well as relying on deeply flawed and unargued-for notions of desire and the good. If we are interested in a phenomenological description of sexual desire, then we have to accept that the experience of sexual values simply cannot be accounted for in such a manner. As the phenomenologist Aurel Kolnai points out, building on some of Thomas Aquinas's observations,[49] solitary or frustrated sex shares a basic feature of lack of completeness, involving as it does what he calls "a certain kind of *intensification of the surrender to excitement as such*, a heaving lust for sexual gratification with no objective end in view..."[50] And of course, masturbation is generally done instead of something else and often by those who would prefer to do something else and are, in fact, instrumentally using a part of the body to achieve some approximation of the more holistic experience of that other thing.[51]

There is, of course, a difference between something being sub-optimal, what the promoters of masturbation might think of as eating plain pasta, and its being morally wrong. We move now from phenomenology (admittedly concerned with the experience of value) and forms of desire to the more strictly ethical and social matters that are the overall concern of this book.

Functionality Again

In Chapter 3 we explored the social function of sexual acts and attempted to show that the institution of marriage can be undermined by certain sexual practices (what we called "substitionary sex") at a societal and 'common good' level, and that such practices therefore require strong taboos due to the fundamental nature of the good or goods they undermine.[52] Interestingly, Rudolph Allers has said of solitary sex that it constitutes "the most extreme denial of community."[53] So what might consideration of the common good tell us about what good and fruitful sexual desire (and activity) is and why certain deviations from it might be sexually perverse – and perverse in a sense which makes them immoral?

Sartre and Nagel attempted to provide a description of the form of sexual desire, but without a great deal of content in terms of what might be called bodily meaning. Perhaps considerations of sexual morality will help us to understand more about sexual desire and its perversions, providing a framework allowing us to make sense of what most fundamentally fulfils sexual desire – a desire which cannot be reduced to mere animal wanting.

If masturbation is functionless pleasure for its own sake, it appears as a truncation of sexual desire and its 'achievement' – a significant withdrawal from the whole personal world of sexual desire (which would even be the case with a widower who engaged in it thinking of a deceased spouse, for it could not be fully personal).

When speaking of functions (as we did in Chapter 2) we need to remember that masturbation which causes ejaculation and pleasurable sensation is *evidence of* functionality even if on that particular occasion it doesn't serve the wider function of the sub-function used (i.e. procreative-type union in an appropriate social context). It is 'functionless' in the light of that consideration, even though the pleasure experienced has a function of sorts. Alexander Pruss, in exploring the issue of sexual desire's function, makes a valuable point which emphasises the specifically human nature of that desire:

> Desire...does not *directly* strive for intercourse, and so the couple does not go against sexual desire in refraining from intercourse. Desire strives merely to incline the will in the direction of intercourse... If we identify the proper functioning of desire with desire's striving for its goal, then we will see the goal of desire not as the final action as such, but as either informing or inclining an act of choice in a particular direction. Consequently, one is not acting directly against the nature of sexual desire when one chooses to abstain or even when one takes measures to reduce sexual desire...in fact, in such a case, one is acting in support of sexual desire's function of *influencing a rational choice*, by ensuring that a rational choice actually occurs.[54]

Pruss is clear that by function he does not just mean mere libido. What he perhaps doesn't spell out is that the sexual inclination present in human beings to ensure that rational activity of certain kinds occurs is not going to be 'doing the same thing' for the committed celibate as for the non-committed celibate or the non-celibate. The good at stake in possible choices is best seen, as previous chapters have argued, in terms of social functionality, which the next chapter will address. Certain religious traditions place the consecrated celibate life ('for the sake of the Kingdom') above the married life in terms of the honour in which it is held, though it is beyond the philosophical remit of this book to explore this question.

Conclusion

In examining the *telos* of sexual desire we have shown that approaches which ignore the irreducibly interpersonal direction of that desire have profound problems. Focus on the *telos* and function of desire raises questions regarding the 'internal' acts which are morally relevant to assessing the importance of sexual dispositions and activity. That assessment can only be made in light of the fulfilment of interpersonal desire in love, and it is to this concept that we now turn.

Chapter 6
Love, Virtue and Vice

Let me not to the marriage of true minds
Admit impediments. Love is not love
Which alters when it alteration finds,
Or bends with the remover to remove:
O no; it is an ever-fixed mark,
That looks on tempests, and is never shaken;
It is the star to every wandering bark,
Whose worth's unknown, although his height be taken.
Love's not Time's fool, though rosy lips and cheeks
Within his bending sickle's compass come;
Love alters not with his brief hours and weeks,
But bears it out even to the edge of doom.

If this be error and upon me proved,
I never writ, nor no man ever loved.

William Shakespeare, Sonnet 116

Man is so profoundly ordained towards losing himself, towards surrendering to beings endowed with intrinsic value, that he will never become happy except when he conforms to beings not for his sake only but for their sake.

Josef Seifert, True Love

Love

The term social functionality may sound a rather cold term – and one rather distant from the term 'love,' a term often associated in one way or another with sexual desire. In Chapter 3, we said a little about interpersonal union, the unitive and the procreative and marriage and commitment as the proper context for the expression of sexual desire. Yet some of the great thinkers in the history of philosophy, not to mention literature and drama, have seen a conflict between sexual desire and at least some forms of love. They have seen sexual desire not as something necessarily ordered to expressions of love, but rather as an obstacle or likely obstacle or at best only a discardable beginning to such expressions which ultimately relate to a uniting with transcendent beauty, as suggested in Plato's *Symposium*, for example.

In opposition to this, certain thinkers in the Christian tradition see married sexual love, though belonging to the non-heavenly stage of human existence,[1] as important and valuable enough to be a fitting symbol of Christ's relationship with His Church. Alternately, there are those like Richard Wagner who, at least in *Der Ring des Nibelungen,* if not in *Parsifal*, see human (and therefore mortal) sexual union as the highest form of love.

A not-uncommon view put forward by Anders Nygren[2] sees *agape/caritas* as a love owed to God and neighbour – a choice involving intellect and will (and only in that minimal sense, if at all for Nygren, desire): it is almost entirely unselfish and certainly has nothing to do with anything like (sexual) desire. It is spontaneous and creative of value and without motive. *Eros* directly contrasts with *agape*, on this view, insofar as it is determined by its object. It is about satisfaction of human need and seeks as we have seen reciprocity: it is according to Nygren love of a desirous, egocentric kind. However, Nygren's apparent assumption – surely grounded in one kind of Protestant (especially Lutheran) theological world-view – that desire, including sexual desire, is necessarily egocentric is not supported by any plausible argument for an action theory nor does it provide a metaphysical foundation for such a view and it is difficult to make sense of how *agape* could be, in effect, essentially 'motiveless.'

Unsurprisingly, a target of Nygren is Thomas Aquinas whose metaphysical system is a standing refutation of his approach, not least because of the way it relates desire to 'the good' (an approach for which this book argues in Chapter 2). Nygren believed that Aquinas had attempted the impossible in trying to integrate *eros* and *agape*.

Affirmation of Beloved's Existence

Aquinas's discussion of love sees it in terms of a fundamental affirmation of the goodness of the beloved's very existence. In speaking of the love of God (and indeed God's love of us)[3] the question arises as to whether *eros*, including sexual desire, is something that is simply part of *agape* or whether it is something separate from it. For Aquinas, all kinds of love are grounded in will (including desire), which provides the initial framework for seeing different forms of love as integrated. Note that this view of love sees it as something that can be reasonable and not as an uncontrollable or merely involuntary emotion. Even as an emotion, love has an object; it can often be controlled, and even uncontrollable love can be entirely reasonable. The ethicist is particularly interested in the notion of love as an act of will that is (or is not) reasonable and as such can be fostered or refined directly or indirectly.

For Aquinas the approval expressed in the statement "it's good that you exist" is an expression of will, something which the Thomist Josef Pieper says "signifies the opposite of aloof, purely "theoretical" neutrality."[4] Pieper notes that there is

> a form of willing that does not aim at doing something still undone and thus acting in the future to change the present state of affairs. Rather, in addition to willing-to-do, there is also a purely affirmative assent to what already is, and assent is likewise without "future tension..."[5]

It is necessary then before loving a person[6] to have a movement of will by which we perceive it as 'good' that the beloved person exist. In contrast when we *like* a person, we may also see it as good that the person exist but the focus is more on their capacities, which of course can change.

Unconditional Love

The *unconditionality* often associated with love should not be understood to mean that one is confident that this aspiration will be realised in oneself.[7] It is rather that the goodness of every human person's existence *should* give rise to a commitment to appreciating the inherent goodness of that existence.[8] If the goodness is inherent (if it is good i.e. virtuous to desire that someone exist) then the response to that goodness should be unconditional – simply in virtue of the goodness – and may involve a stronger commitment in the case of certain forms of love such as spousal or parental love.[9] However, as Josef Pieper notes,

> to find lovable and to love are two different matters... the step from the one to the other need not necessarily

be taken. If it is actually taken, that happens out of the spontaneity of volition; or, to say it another way: out of freedom. At any rate, love is in no way a logical conclusion that we can be compelled to draw... "To believe someone" and "to love someone"...these are spontaneous acts in which...freedom certainly plays a part.[10]

So if the goodness is inherent, then the response to that goodness should be unconditional and may involve stronger willed commitment for particular forms of love, such as love between a husband and a wife. In the words of Alexander Pruss, who links human lovability to basic features such as personhood and being a creature of God,

Once we see that the momentous question whether or not to love someone at all does not ride on his or her qualities, but should always be answered affirmatively, we have much more freedom to allow various ingredients such as our own choice, chance, providential circumstance, and the endearing qualities of the beloved to enter into the justification of the form of love, and to provide additional reasons for the love. The wife can say that she loves her husband for his wit, meaning that because of his wit she loves him in the particular way that she does, and maybe also that his wit constitutes an additional reason for love. The exact role played by the qualities of the beloved depends on the form of love in question, and may also differ from case to case. At the same time, the qualities that determine the form of love may pale in importance when compared to personhood or being a creature of God, the quality that justifies our loving the beloved at all.[11]

Of the commitment in particular, a major focus of his impressive work on sexual love, Pruss says that

> while uttering one's marriage vows, one is both generating the unconditional obligation of future love and accepting that obligation. Of course, if Christianity is right that one always owes love to everyone, then even in marriage, the obligation precedes the acceptance. However, even so, the marriage vows generate an *additional* duty to love the spouse, and this additional duty is closely tied with its acceptance.

Note the importance in this account of distinguishing between forms of love, and choosing the right form for the particular loved one. As Pruss says,

> The dynamism of love is like the dynamism in our beliefs. Our beliefs answer to reality. So long as there is any possibility that reality might not be as we think it to be, we need a commitment to change our beliefs to fit reality. Love likewise should respond to the reality of the beloved.

Pruss notes that

> each of [love's] forms is in some way the same, and yet the forms are different. Moreover, love becomes distorted when we get the form wrong – for instance, by standing in a relation of *eros* to one's parent.[12]

Three Aspects of Love

Pruss argues that there are three essential aspects of love: willing the good of the beloved for the beloved's sake, appreciating the beloved,[13] and seeking union, and that these aspects are necessarily intertwined. He notes that love is experienced as one thing, for we cannot have love where any one of these elements is missing. Following Aquinas' notion of 'formal union' Pruss notes that one's will is united with the beloved's in willing the beloved's good.[14] That said, there is a union that is had simply in virtue of loving. In recognising the beloved as a *person*, "one recognizes that the beloved *has* a point of view, and by recognizing the beloved as a *human*, one realizes what certain aspects of this point of view must be."[15]

However, formal union, which is a necessary part of love, can impel us to 'real union' – a union which is a way of being together, not just in mind and will, but externally and cooperatively. And love doesn't seek just any old real union, but one expressive of the form of love in question. What primarily differentiates the forms of love is not the benevolent or appreciative aspects, not the formal union part of the unitive aspect, but the kind of real union that the relationship calls for. For Pruss it appears that some kinds of real union are paradigmatic and consummatory of a particular form of love.

Procreative Union

Pruss considers forms of love and focuses on specifically erotic love as one that seeks a real union of two persons as one organism in loving, lifelong commitment through a personally integrated reproductive striving (lifelong, so the brief act of intercourse can be stretched through time by an act of commitment allowing for sexual union as a fully personal union of *one body*). This might explain why lovers are so prone to make undying promises to one another, which they fully intend to keep. Returning to the themes of Chapter 3 of this book, Pruss argues that the 'real union' of the activity of sexual intercourse involves a set of organs functionally matched and striving towards a momentous (non-trivial) end. This organic unity, necessarily involving two persons embodying a single procreative function, is unique and, on the understanding of the bodily nature of persons defended in Chapter 2, directly unites two persons and in a way in which other physical contacts which lack the unitive function cannot.

Pruss considers and rejects alternative suggestions for what unites the couple, for example pleasure and psychological union. The latter is in no way exclusive to *sexual* relationships and so cannot be what defines the kind of union specifically striven for: there must be some kind of sexual 'colouring.' Sexual pleasure, even as a specific kind of pleasure, cannot be what unifies couples as it is irreducibly separate for them: couples experience pleasure differently and often at different times and in any case, can only directly experience it for themselves. Karol Wojtyla rightly says that,

> Pleasure is, of its nature, a good for the moment and only for a particular subject, it is not a supra-subjective or trans-subjective good. And so, as long as that good is recognised as the entire basis of the moral norm, there can be no possibility of my transcending the bounds of that which is good for me alone...Love will be no more, in either of the persons or between them, it will not be an objective reality, for there is no objective good to ensure its existence.[16]

None of this is to deny that, as with other important pleasures, sexual pleasures can have social as well as biological functions and/or effects.[17] Indeed some kinds of pursuit of sexual pleasure can unintentionally lead to intimacy and to love – one need only observe how some people have to go to some effort to prevent intimacy and love interfering with their narrow sexual projects. Even as formidable a sexual conquistador as Vicomte de Valmont in *Les Liaisons Dangereuses* ultimately fails to prevent himself from loving his conquest.

Staying with Valmont, it might be said that his seduction of the virtuous Madame de Tourvel is very much connected with pleasure of a different kind – the pleasure of conquest and the manipulation and humiliation of the other, in this case the conquest of the hitherto impressive chastity of his target, together with her eventual knowing and willing her own corruption. If sexual pleasure is what can justify sexual activity, why cannot the pleasure of conquest, or the pleasure of moving toward a 'reward' be reason enough for sexual activity? In this case it is Valmont alone who is pursuing these pleasures, but what if the two were united by willing similar pleasures of conquest or rewards involving money or power or manipulation? They could be very honest with each other about their motives (something one could easily imagine occurring between Valmont and the very far from virtuous Marquise de Merteuil). Would the mutual pleasures involved here be justificatory of the act and give it some important kind of unity? And if such pleasures can't do that work then how is it that *sexual* pleasure can?

One Flesh: Instrumental to Procreation?

We have looked in previous chapters of this book at notions of human flourishing. We asked in speaking of human functions and the 'overall' function of human beings what might be the social, not merely biological, function of sex and marriage. The reader may or may not have found this trajectory convincing. Either way, in referring to the specific kind of union found in sex and marriage, the question arises whether love is extraneous to this model. Does it not sound as if sexual love is merely instrumental towards what Pruss calls a "non-trivial end" and somehow not good or valuable *in itself*? Indeed, isn't there a danger of making the capacity for love sound like some kind of useful evolutionary adaptation only valuable insofar as it can aid the child-centred social-biological function of marriage and procreation?[18]

However, in discussing love in the current chapter, our focus has been on union of *many* kinds, not only union of a spousal, procreative-oriented kind. In noting the essential uniting common to all kinds of love, together with the very evident striving for union to be found in sexual desire, it should have been clear that when exploring sexual love in particular 'from the inside,' we are brought face to face with an idea of union that has much in common with other forms of love – and cannot therefore be merely instrumental to the procreation and rearing of children, even if it remains oriented towards this. The broad existential importance of affirming the goodness of others is obvious to many of us, and if this is an important aspect of *any* love, that certainly includes spousal love. (Of course, quite generally something can be valuable in itself while still aiming at something beyond itself – such as the virtue of benevolence which certainly benefits the agent while being focused on the person benefited.)[19]

One way spousal love differs from many forms of love is in being not only lifelong but exclusive in a particularly strong one-to-one sense (see Chapter 3). The additional duty created by the marriage vow grounds the idea that we are dealing with an institution based upon treating persons as irreplaceable,[20] a crucial truth appreciation of which is essential for the flourishing of children as they grow up. And just as sex loses its value and character if seen as purely instrumental to pleasure,[21] if marriage is seen as only a means to an end – the procreation and rearing of children – then it loses its character and its very ability to foster parental projects. It is good for neither children nor parents (or potential parents) for couples to treat each other as merely instrumental to the child-rearing project. On the contrary, through their own relationship and their genuine interest in and focus on each other the couple should teach their children how to relate to peers and eventually other adults.[22] The opposite failing is when couples are too focused on each other rather than on any joint projects such as parenthood – we might think of Tristan and Isolde radically losing their identities, away from the hated world of Day, with an erotic love that has non-existence as its secret,[23] or of Paolo and Francesca forever tragically entwined together in Dante's *Inferno*. As the saying goes, "Love is not two people looking at each other but two people looking in the same direction."

Objectification

Early in this book, in discussing rape, I suggested that our sexuality is, in the words of David Archard, "at the centre or core of the space that metaphorically defines the self" or, in other words, something central to who we are. The notion that sex is at the core of our being or occupies some special place in our lives is one held by people with widely differing views about sexual morality. In the course of this book, I have given various arguments which support this proposition about centrality. If sex is truly central, it would seem that violations of respect for our sexuality may be deeply morally problematic, involving a serious failure in love, at least in the sense of missing the true good of the other at which love aims.

Some of the writers I have been considering have talked as though paradigmatic sexual desires or practices involve only one actual person. As JLA Garcia puts it, for such writers,

> Sex is the private domain: it occupies the inner life, it consists primarily in desires, feelings, and fantasy, and it matters in that someone cares about it. There is no hint here that sex is normally oriented toward another person (preferably not just in thought) and always raises questions of charity, respect, justice for that person as well as for others who may be affected by what happens between those sexually involved.[24]

We have also seen that we can relate wrongly towards others through our attitudes, desires, and intentions even when these are 'private' and that this is true in non-sexual areas such as the harbouring of hateful thoughts. Even externally 'good' activities can be accompanied by bad motivations such that we may need to purify our inner lives to meet the full demands of morality, in sexual as in non-sexual areas.

A common worry amongst traditional sexual moralists, feminists, and indeed certain kinds of liberal is the worry that sexual desires may lead to or even involve an 'objectification' of other persons: something inherently unjust and certainly incompatible with consistent love. Immanuel Kant formulated the following fundamental principle of the moral order in his Categorical Imperative: "Act always in such a way that the other person is the end and not merely the instrument [means] of your action." Sex is a particular problem for Kant, since despite recognising that sex is needed to reproduce the species he sees it as essentially objectifying to make someone the 'fungible' object of one's sexual desire or to allow oneself to be such an object. It is striking that the fundamental principle seems to come into greatest conflict with the sexual appetites, something which undoubtedly makes them 'special' even if in a negative sense when things go wrong.

Sexual desire for Kant cannot be a form of love because it aims at the use of another's sexual organs for pleasure, and marriage itself is, as Kant notes elsewhere, "the union of two persons of different sexes for lifelong possession of each other's sexual attributes." As Allen W. Wood summarizes his position, Kant does concede "that sexual appetite can be combined with human love and thus carry with it the aims of love, but he thinks this combination is [due to the powerful nature of sexual pleasure] always contingent and unstable."[25]

Kant's concerns with objectification have been hugely influential and this is hardly surprising given most people's experiences of the sometimes overwhelming and irrational and self-seeking nature of sexual passion. Any remotely honest history of human sexual activity will acknowledge the damage done by those who treat sex as though it were outside the moral realm or a matter of no special moral import.

Kant's account of sex, then, seems to hold that in fact sexual pleasure and the drive toward it are so intense that these sensations banish the possibility of respecting other persons and therefore violate the Categorical Imperative. Kant does, however, hold that marriage is the solution to this problem (thereby also assuming that outside of the marriage contract all sexual activity reduces human beings to mere things for another's use).

How does this work – in other words how is the relative 'poison' of sex, in Kant's view, nullified through marriage? As Martha Nussbaum notes, this can happen,

> only if sexual relations are restricted to a relationship
> that is structured institutionally in ways that promote
> and, at least legally if not morally, guarantee mutual re-
> spect and regard. If the two parties are bound to support
> one another in various ways, this ensures a certain kind
> of respect for personhood which will persist undestroyed
> by the ardors of lovemaking, though it is apparently
> Kant's view that this respect and "practical love" can
> never color or infuse the lovemaking itself.[26]

So, marriage is a 'container' of the inherently objectifying activity that is sex. While no-one can doubt that sexual desire and activity *can* be morally evil, Kant's position seems extraordinary. Already we have seen in this book that sexual desire is essentially interpersonal and aims at some form of uniting. Moreover, as Joshua Schulz points out, in discussing Kant on sexual desire,

> To get the moral *problem* in question started...we must
> say that the intentional object of sexual desire includes
> the quality of personhood. Deny this and the moral prob-
> lem disappears. The fault in Kant's definition of sexual
> desire is just his leaving out this aspect of personhood
> in the object desired, since to begin with a deficient no-
> tion of the object of sexual desire and then to argue that
> sexual desire is immoral because it desires a person defi-
> ciently is simply a *petitio principii*.[27]

One can certainly also make a case, working in broadly Kantian terms, that if certain marital conditions *are* met there is no reason to see sex as objectifying or depersonalising in itself. Joshua Schulz rightly criticises Kant's overall approach here by noting that while one can reject Kant's presumption about sexual desire and its fixing upon bodies and organs rather than the bodies or organs *of persons* (or rather, bodily persons themselves) one can also show that marriage brings with it *teleological* criteria which encourage the pursuit of ethical sex – in line with the Categorical Imperative in its second formulation. These criteria are lifelong monogamy in marriage (this limits possible objects of objectification and makes the sexual partner non-fungible[28]); sharing a household, enjoining responsibility for the consequences of sexual intercourse upon the agents especially as a precondition of the sexual act itself; and dedication of each partner in the relationship to the mutual sanctification of the other, including responsibility for the procreation and education of children. If all of the above encourage ethical sex – a sex of respect if you like – then, as Schulz says,

> the pursuit of these ends constitute...the most (morally) suitable context for the pursuit of sexual goods ...within the context of a marriage...these ends constitute what is meant by respecting another person while at the same time sexually desiring her. They provide criteria for evaluating what *counts* as using one's sexual partner as a source of bodily enjoyment *at the same time* as respecting her as a person.[29]

Interestingly, in order to make sense of Kant it seems that we have had to appeal to some form of teleological argument, not something always associated with Kant's general philosophy. His defences of traditional sexual morality when it comes to unnatural sex (e.g. masturbation) are heavily reliant on natural teleology[30] and considerations of the common good,[31] something Kant scholars such as Allen W. Wood see as in tension with Kantian ethics generally (Wood argues that Kant's discussion of the 'fig leaf' means that for Kant sex is something transcending the 'merely incidental' fact of sex's reproductive nature – a dualistic view which sits uneasily with Kant's use of natural teleology).

Certainly Kant's dualistic tendencies are evident in the following passage from his *Lectures on Ethics*, which suggest that maleness and femaleness are not seen (as in fact they almost always *are* seen) as deeply personal, [32]

> Since the sexual impulse is not an inclination that one has for another *qua* human but an inclination for their sex, it is therefore a *principium* of the debasement of humanity, a source of preferring of one sex over the other, and dishonouring of that sex by satisfying that inclination. The desire of a man for a woman is not directed to her as a human being; on the contrary, the woman's humanity is of no concern to him, and the only object of his desire is her sex. So humanity here is set aside. [33]

However, even if we reject Kant's view about 'inherent objectification' in sexual desire and activity we can still ask a) is objectification, loosely defined, always wrong and b) how we are to understand the nature of any wrongness that it has?

Recall our discussion of love and its unconditional nature, especially as it relates to persons (who possess their own value): that in love the most important focus was on the essence of the person as opposed to any accidental features he or she possesses. And recall also that we have taken and argued for a non-dualist conception of the human person throughout.

Objectification In and Outside the Sexual Arena

With this in mind we can start with a definition of objectification offered by the Thomist Edward Feser, namely that it occurs

> when the mind transforms a substance into something reduced, closed and dead to be analyzed or used. Its concrete, mind-independent existence is ignored.[34]

We are here concerned with the substantial form that is a human person. This view could be expanded to include other possible signs of objectification such as the previously mentioned fungibility as well as (for example) enslavement. Clearly objectification, which will always be a matter of degree, must be opposed insofar as it contrasts with love understood in its most complete sense of identifying with and wishing the loved one the right goods in the right way. Such a love will, or should, be also unconditional because related to an essence good in itself and therefore calling for indefeasible appreciation (what is supposed to defeat this morally?)[35]

Clearly there are many ways in which human beings can be objectified, in Feser's sense of the term. Workers can be treated as tools by factory owners (as in Charlie Chaplin's *Modern Times*), wives can be treated as little more than trophies or slaves, children can be treated as designer accessories, IVF embryos can be treated (for example, quality-controlled) as though they were products. Some philosophers such as Jeff McMahan even propose that newborn babies could be used as 'donors' of vital organs.[36] Of course none of this means that those doing the objectifying necessarily treat their victims *literally* as objects. Valmont certainly relates to Madame de Tourvel not as he would relate to an inanimate sex

185

doll, for example, but precisely as someone with human responses and thoughts – in fact, a highly complex virtuous rational woman whom he sees as potentially lovable, but whom he sets out not to love or respect in any way. Nevertheless, all of the above people are to various degrees failing to value the person they exploit as one who exists for his or her own sake.

In the sexual arena, Karol Wojtyla notes the following:

> *Man, alas, is not such a perfect being that the sight of the body of another person, especially a person of the other sex, can arouse in him merely a disinterested liking which develops into an innocent affection.* In practice it also arouses concupiscence, or a wish to enjoy concentrated on sexual values with no regard to the value of the person.[37]

Wojtyla goes on to say,

> The human body is not in itself shameful, nor for the same reasons are sensual reactions, and human sensuality in general. Shamelessness (just like shame and modesty) is a function of the interior person, and specifically of the will, which too easily accepts the sensual reaction and reduces another person, because of the person's 'body and sex,' to the role of an object of enjoyment.[38]

What are some examples in the sexual arena of attitudes which do *not* objectify? Certainly, the apparent Kantian reluctance to see gender as personal has a dualist tone to it and fails to do justice to what is at stake in sex between embodied persons of complementary type. Sexual desire and activity and indeed sexual bodily polarity are already inherently personal. As this book has argued throughout, the body is integral to what we are: we are unified bodily beings and the sexual aspect particularly calls for a specific concern not raised by other aspects of our person. So it cannot be objectifying simply to appreciate or be aroused by the bodily features of (in particular) one's spouse, which surely constitute the valuable sexual attributes of an inherently valuable person in a marital unit geared towards the couple's social and biological fulfilment. In fact it would be odd in the context of such an embodied one-flesh act if one were *not* aroused by those very sexual values and attributes but only by, say, mental excellence.[39] Just as with other biological functions it is appropriate for these to be achieved, where possible, without bypassing relevant sub-functions, the same would appear to be true in the case of physical characteristics some of which appropriately arouse.

This is not to deny that a married couple might not objectify each other by treating each other as fungible, as seen in some of the examples discussed in Chapter 4. However, the *telos* of sex and marriage involving a lifelong unitive and procreative bond is of a kind which militates against objectification. To say this is to recognise that the *telos* of sex itself, as essentially marital, is what is at issue here in talk of objectification – which thus means something rather different from objectification in non-sexual areas of behaviour which do not so obviously involve an inherent personal and bodily teleology specific to themselves. Recall that in Chapter 2 we spoke of the 'overall function' of the human being. All lack of respect or objectification is anti-teleological in nature, though in sex this is much more obvious than in, say, property crime.

Sexual Arousal and Sexual Interest

In the previous chapter we briefly examined the concept of what are known as "hate-crimes" in terms of the motivations, attitudes, and intentions they involve. When assessing sexual desires it must be remembered that these, like hateful thoughts, can remain purely internal and indeed quite 'low-level' yet be still an appropriate object of moral criticism (or praise). There is no reason why bad attitudes, thoughts, and intentions in the sexual realm which, say, objectify others by placing them in demeaning fantasies should not be the subject of moral censure any more than attitudes of hate.

It could be argued that 'sexual arousal' can properly be construed quite narrowly to refer to such physiological states as penile tumescence, vaginal lubrication, the flushing and sensitization of other erogenous zones, etc. So, the moral exclusion of deliberate sexual arousal outside marriage (as taught by, e.g. the Catholic Church) might be taken to say nothing directly about what *mental* states may licitly be stimulated, even intentionally.

With regard to sexual arousal itself, the contention of this book is that non-marital arousal is condemnable insofar as it is deliberately invited (or insufficiently guarded against). Insofar as it is invited, the prior images (or sensory stimulation) that are sought with arousal in mind are morally problematic if sought in a particular way (i.e. with arousal unrelated to marital activity in mind or related only contingently to marital activity, e.g. looking at other women to prepare for marital activity). If these images/sensations are sought in a way that relates them to one's own libido it seems that they are sought in a way not merely appreciative of their aesthetic value or even their erotic value in some detached, generic sense, but in a way intended to arouse or help arouse oneself (for is that not a function of libido)? If virtue (to be discussed below) is the good functioning of the human psyche, such functioning will be thwarted if our vision of the things which are worthwhile in themselves is distorted, or if our ability to achieve this vision is some way damaged (as it surely can be by exposure to certain imagery apt to arouse).

A separate point is that one can welcome and want sexual desire at some low level while not wanting or even morally objecting to 'arousal,' i.e. sexual desire at a much higher level. And such a low-level desire, while it may well be a form of lust, will not be the kind of overpowering felt desire of the kind described so well in Chapter 3 of *War and Peace* in relation to the character Pierre and his feelings for Helene.

The whole notion of impurity of thought and consent to it raises a number of problems. Which thoughts are impure and why? Which are wrong in themselves and which only to the extent that they raise an excessive danger of committing (other) wrongful choices in the sexual domain?

How is consenting to a genuinely 'impure' thought distinguished from simply appreciating what's good and what's bad? In determining excessive risk are the ugliness, destructiveness, and evils of a fearful, crabbed, negative response to the erotic adequately appreciated? Even a fairly conservative moralist might argue that certain kinds of sexual imagining might keep oneself sexually interested, alive, and open to stimulation (something that might be particularly important for a married person) in a way that might sometimes be warranted – even when inappropriate, though perhaps low-level, physical arousal may be an unintended side-effect.[40] Such a moralist might argue that glimpsing/imagining the 'sexy' could sometimes be positive in that it helps one to appreciate some of the wonders of Creation even if doing so carries with it certain risks and negative elements. Even if such imaginings relate to sexually bad actions from the past, it is surely not morally required of anyone that they are to feel guilty (again) every time they recall a past wrong action – in this or any other area of life – nor that they excoriate negative social trends each time they appreciate a good aspect of the world. Is this not scrupulosity?

What might we say about this relatively permissive approach to sexual imagining and the sexual gaze? I hope to show that a thorough understanding of virtue, and of the 'specialness' of sex reveals a way in which sexual ethics can be rational and balanced within an overall framework of human flourishing. In investigating borderline cases, it is perhaps useful to begin with a case which almost everyone would agree is morally dubious, and then ask ourselves to what extent the principles we apply in this case are also applicable to those cases which appear less clear *prima facie*.[41]

Morally Problematic Low-level Desires

What might be an example of a lower-level, but nonetheless morally problematic sexual desire? We might think of a prurient, snooping neighbour, a 'curtain-twitcher', who takes an excessive interest in the male visitors of the lady next door. He is not sexually aroused by this interest nor does he aim to be; nevertheless, his attitude can hardly be described as a 'pro' attitude with regard to his neighbour's sexual value as a person. If sex is something core to her very being, and indeed to everyone else's, then the objection arises that he is not relating to her holistically and yet is taking an interest in a core value in a detached and latent way. Nothing about the role in which he stands towards her (he is not her spouse or boyfriend nor even, we can imagine, potential boyfriend) legitimises even a more holistic sexual interest in her (of a still low-level kind). Nor is he a sibling or parent who would be entitled to special concern for her (though hopefully not of a sexual nature, however low-level).

In contrast, imagine an elderly heterosexual man who enjoys travelling to work on the underground and being surrounded by pretty women. Imagine that this man barely has any libido at this particular point of his life. One might still say that his attitude to these women is nuanced by his sexuality – i.e. his appreciation of them and behaviour towards them (including chivalrous behaviour) differs from his responses to those of his own sex. Sexuality nuances his behaviour towards them, and in a perfectly good way (he may for example be reminded of a former love without having what could fairly be described as lustful thoughts with regard to either the woman or his remembered love).

Now imagine that, for some extraordinary reason, the girl is naked in front of the man. It would seem quite wrong to view her only as a trigger to pleasant past memories without also adopting a particular protective attitude toward her. And the likelihood of adopting the correct attitude to her as she sits naked before him is perhaps unlikely. Even if the man is not lustfully focused on her, some morally good focus of concern seems appropriate here since the girl is a human person who is obviously vulnerable and not just a source of pleasant memories. People should be holistically viewed and the subject of the right kind of focus for one's role and the situation.

Is it possible to be too strict in this area? Aristotelians in particular should be aware that avoiding sins of excess is not at all sufficient for virtue in any area, not least because one may slip into the *opposite* sin of 'excess,' i.e. deficiency of some kind. Certainly it can be argued (returning to a theme of the Introduction) that, particularly in some Christian circles, the virtue of chastity has been seen too much as a mere sub-species of the virtue of temperance (see below) and thus too much as a virtue solely concerned with the control of sexual appetite. However, if we take the virtue of chastity to be one concerned with respecting the good of marriage and therefore the transmission of life and the nurture and education of children this will help to guide us through otherwise difficult dilemmas in the sexual area.

Appreciating Erotic Goods

Before looking at the principles we can use for discriminating between cases, it may be worth briefly mentioning, if only to reject, one argument which has been put forward in defence of the permissibility of some sexual imagining. The argument runs as follows:

> In light of the close logical connection among (i) judging
> X to be good, (ii) wanting X, and (iii) taking pleasure
> in the thought of X, how can someone fully appreciate
> erotic goods, even contextual ones, without at least some
> level of wanting them (even if not being possessed by
> strong 'desire') and taking some pleasure in their con-
> templation? What does 'consent' add to what seems to
> be an entailment?

As regards the connections between (i) and (ii), this thought can be resisted, for it seems that one can judge that X is good without 'wanting' it oneself. I can desire a happy marriage for a couple of friends of mine – a very different happy marriage from the one I might desire to have myself. Similarly I can judge the goodness of mathematical truths and desire them for mathematicians without particularly desiring them for myself or even knowing what they consist in. True, I might desire that others desire the good that is X in a way that helps them to pursue and appreciate it – but in any case this is very different from desiring these goods for myself.

The Primacy of the Virtuous

Throughout this book, I have repeatedly described 'the good' as that which it is virtuous to desire; and in doing so have adopted an approach which treats virtues as fundamental; that is, a theory where, in the words of JLA Garcia, "the importance or understanding of the desirable, of duty, and of rights is based on that of the virtues."[42]

Such an approach to ethics and axiology has many advantages, even aside from the often unconvincing nature of its rivals. This theory sets the moral agent, a role-occupying person, at the heart not just of the moral endeavour but of value itself. So, for example, the approach supports our moral intuition whereby states of affairs which consist in intentional killing with regard to innocent person X are worse than states of affairs where X simply dies. The first state of affairs is worse (morally more undesirable) in that a personal desire for that state of affairs would be a worse one morally than would be a desire for the latter state of affairs.[43] Value becomes not an arbitrary or mysterious phenomenon; rather, in the words of Garcia,

> 'normativity' is not a surprising *explicandum* but a predicable and necessary part of the familiar world. Indeed,

moral virtues and many other valuable things are rooted in our desires for actual and current but also non-actual, future occupants of certain role-relationships.[44]

The fundamental position of virtue is further clarified by Garcia, who argues that,

> ...statements that are normally taken to be ascriptions of intrinsic goodness or badness to states of affairs should instead be understood as *moral* evaluations of certain human attitudes towards those states of affairs and the latter must be defined in terms of the former ...moral value is more basic than the value of states of affairs and the latter must be defined in terms of the former. Since this definitional move is antithetical to that often made in consequentialist systems, the account of value judgements developed here raises serious doubts about all such ethical theories. [45]

This input-driven virtues-based understanding of the moral life is especially important when it comes to understanding sexual ethics, not least because of the important nature of the kinds of roles we hold towards another in this area. So, for example, it is much more important for a husband to wish the good of his wife than it is for him to wish the good of his neighbour, all else being equal.

What are Virtues?

In order to understand more fully the importance of roles both in moral thinking generally and in sexual ethics, it will be necessary to say something about the virtues and particularly the virtue of chastity. Aurel Kolnai gives a definition as good as any, and in line with broadly Aristotelian and Thomistic conceptions:

> When we refer to a person's customary and lasting
> 'disposition' in the fulfilment of the moral demands of
> a particular sphere of value, we talk about the relevant
> 'virtue.' A man has the virtue of chastity when, inter alia,
> he normally refrains from certain kinds of sin, and when
> he considers and deals with questions of sex with the se-
> riousness they deserve. [46]

Traditional thinking on virtues names four 'cardinal' virtues;
that is, prudence, justice, temperance and fortitude.[47] These are the
virtues on which all the others 'hinge' (*cardo*) and there are strong
reasons for believing that there must be in some sense a unity of
the virtues.[48]

In St. Thomas Aquinas's discussion of the virtues, the virtue of
chastity is linked with the cardinal virtue of temperance. Temperance is concerned with selfless self-preservation and "has its immediate subject in man's concupiscence (*appetitus concupiscipilis*), to
which it attaches itself in order to restrain the instinctive appetites
for various material and bodily goods which force themselves upon
the senses. Sensual reactions (*erga bonum sensibile*) (with regard
to a good apprehended by the senses) must be subordinated to reason: this is the function of moderation [temperance]."[49]

This defence of the inner order of man should not be understood as a purely negative break with the world beyond oneself but
rather as a virtue aimed at corresponding with the natural order and
truth of this world. However as Karol Wojtyla asks, should we look
for the essence of chastity in moderation [temperance]? For Wojtyla reflecting our earlier discussion about love,

> *Chastity can only be thought of in association with the*
> *virtue of love...*To be chaste means to have a 'transpar-

ent' attitude to a person of the other sex – *chastity means just that – the interior 'transparency'* without which love cannot be itself, for it cannot be itself until the desire to 'enjoy' is subordinated to a readiness to show loving kindness in every situation…The objection that chastity is merely negative is then incorrect. The very fact that it is bound up with the virtue of moderation (*temperentia*) means that it cannot be so. For by 'moderating' the feelings and actions connected with the sexual values we serve the values of the person and of love…It [chastity] does not lead to disdain of the body, but it does involve a certain humility of the body. Humility is the proper attitudes towards all true greatness, including ones own greatness as a human being, but above all towards the greatness which is beyond one's self.[50]

In thinking of interior 'transparency,' we tend to think of radical openness to the other, free from distracting egotism and fantasy: a clear-eyed view of the person to whom we are relating properly involved in the unconditional love and affirmation which we discussed earlier. Such unconditional love is the only appropriate recognition of the great value of the other human being who is a personal subject like ourselves. Although, of course, chastity applies to everyone and not merely to spouses, in the case of spouses it paves the way for any real (not merely formal) erotic union of the kind discussed. Through such transparency, we unconditionally appreciate the value of another person and can form a real bodily union which makes us 'one body' and is truly appreciative of sexual values.

Sexual Virtue and the Common Good

It is, I think, no accident that use of the word 'virtue' historically has often been, rightly or wrongly, associated primarily with
sexual virtue and especially the sexual virtue of women.[51] This is
not a work of history or sociology, but it is also noteworthy that the
term chastity (or at least 'purity') has also been one used at certain
points in history as a term interchangeable with the general term
virtue. These curious phenomena may tell us something about the
virtue of chastity which helps to explain its importance: they may
not be entirely misguided and may highlight some truths, albeit
with some exaggerations.

Recall that Thomas Nagel was quoted in Chapter 5 as saying
that the case for an area of protected privacy in the sexual realm is
exceptionally strong, and that

> We do not inhabit a common sexual world in the sense –
> limited, to be sure – in which we inhabit a common natu-
> ral, or economic, or educational, or even artistic world.[52]

While of course sexual experience – like all experience – is private, and, as we shall see, we especially value in the sexual realm
the privacy that makes room for real intimacy, there is a very real
sense in which we *do* share a common sexual world. As we have
seen above, an earlier version of Nagel sees sexual desire as essentially *interpersonal*[53] – in a way that I have argued is concerned
with morally very important features of human beings, thus placing sexual desire outside the realm of purely private concern and
within the realm of social virtues: virtues which hold a special importance for the common good.

For Thomas Aquinas, it is obvious that a virtue like justice concerns the good of the multitude to a greater extent than does temperance which is more about the moderation of "only the desires
and delights of those things which pertain to man himself."[54] From
here, it is easy to see why someone could conclude that chastity is
an even more 'private' virtue, dealing as it does with areas of life
which most of us prefer to keep out of the public eye. However,
as Patrick Riley has pointed out, justice, undoubtedly a part of the
'common good' or shared, social human flourishing, plays a powerful role in chastity (in fact we could go further and claim that
chastity and justice partly constitute each other):

> Justice concerns dealings with another, and in the act
> of genital congress three persons are present and af-
> fected: the two actors and, potentially yet really, the
> child. Where the man and woman are not married, they
> deal unjustly with one another. Where one is married to
> someone else, or where both are so married, they also
> do an injustice to the spouse or spouses. The child too
> is dealt with unjustly: he is brought into the world by
> parents who are not married to one another and conse-
> quently cannot provide him with the home necessary to
> his proper nourishment, his comfort, and above all his
> education. Moreover they are more likely to destroy him
> before birth.[55]

One important role of marriage, where faithfully adhered to,
is giving children a secure sense of identity by reliably identifying
fathers and giving them a recognised stake in the child's life. More
generally, secure married families give both spouses and children a
sense of irreplaceability, of a kind basic to love. Although this book
focuses less on reproductive ethics than on more broadly sexual

ethics, it should be stressed that these considerations apply even more strongly to judging cases of artificial reproduction. [56]

The Common Good

St. Thomas says,

> The common good is the end of individual persons living in a community, as the good of the whole is the end of each and every part.[57]

As Riley puts it,

> As with the whole and the parts, the well-being of society redounds to the well-being of each member. In fact the well-being of each depends on the society, civil and familial, in which all live. Because the good of the part is necessary to the good of the whole, every member of a society is able to refer his own good to the good common to all the members. Hence all members of a society can refer the good of another member to their own good. All share in the individual member's good, and each individual member shares in the good common to all. The existence of the society enables each and all to do both.[58]

The family is a form of friendship and as such is a part – in fact, an absolutely crucial constituent – of society. The family is a natural or fundamental 'group unit': the *very first* human society. It is often referred to as something more fundamentally human than civil society, insofar as it is seen as the foundation for society. It is in this sense 'pre-political' and is grounded in basic human needs – which is not to say that it does not also refer to wider social groupings for which children are being prepared.

David Crawford rightly notes that

> the family reveals the identity and nature of the person
> who is the subject and the doer of justice. The family is
> an ordering principle of justice…in the sense that it is in-
> scribed in the identity and structure of the human person,
> who precisely as *corpore et anima unus* is the "subject"
> of moral action and virtue [*Veritatis Splendor* #48]. It is
> on this basis that the family is an ordering principle of
> political and legal institutions that codify and instanti-
> ate legal justice. If juridical forms and civil institutions
> are not to be alienating and fragmenting, they need to
> anticipate and support the concrete person as he really
> is, rather than a hypothetical and denatured person…The
> family is the "foundation of justice" and is antecedently
> organic to society in the sense that it informs the nature
> of the person who is or should be presupposed by those
> institutions.[59]

This is not to prioritise in some facile way the status of the family. The family is part of a much larger network of relationships and of course the family must respect the just requirements of civil society – which should, however, be built around respect for its fundamental group unit. On this subject it is worth noting that, as Crawford points out, citing the *Compendium of the Social Doctrine of the Church*, the family "should serve as a model for society, since it avoids the extremes of both individualism and collectivism through its attention to the person."[60] And it is particularly apt as a model, because the experience of a child is one that is naturally deeply rooted in the love of parents. Thus,

...love declares to the child that even before his existence, as a subject of love in his own right, his presence was implied and somehow at least tacitly acknowledged in the hope and mystery of the parents' own love. It is therefore the ground in which familial love as a whole can spread its roots. The experience of being someone's child gives us the "prehistory" necessary to see life...as fundamentally "good" and even destined to exceed the finite bounds of the original family.[61]

Unsurprisingly, political theorists have attempted to reshape the family according to their own notions, not least when they assume that free rational individuals are the people around whom a voluntarist, non-teleological political order must be founded. The move to reimagine the family in individualised terms and reshape marriage in terms of dissoluble contracts reveals how political theory for hundreds of years now has seen the family as a problem: something to be demystified and, in its traditional form, undermined. The idea that the family is the natural unit of society to which other human associations are added has largely given way in political theory to the idea of the family as a contractual relationship of free rational beings which occupies no special position in a modern liberal society.[62]

It is notable that the political theories referred to above have a marked tendency to privatise the traditional virtues and to downgrade their role in public life. Chastity has perhaps suffered more than other virtues in this gradual downgrading, not least because of modern views of the family but also because of a general association of chastity with superstition.[63]

Chastity and Roles

Chastity is a virtue that, like the other virtues, is supposed to free us for and encourage us towards good thoughts and actions in society. There are some roles which are clearly defined by sex, such as those of husband and wife and mother and father. One thing that should be obvious is that these roles are absolutely fundamental – much more so than almost any other role in people's lives – and owe their very existence to a sexual act. As described above, it is crucial for the marital relationship and for children's protection that husbands and wives be loyal to each other and treat each other as irreplaceable, in both thought and deed. This is the shape that chastity will take with regard to these central roles. If sex is the very gateway to and rationale for these roles, it is no surprise that the virtue governing such acts has an importance corresponding to the importance of the roles themselves. These are the roles that most people will identify as forming their core identity. To prepare children for these roles, which many if not all will wish to fill when they are older, is a large part of the task of parenthood.

Those hoping to fill such roles should avoid relationships which are 'doomed' in some way: where, for example, the partner is married to someone else[64] or where the object of erotic love is of the same sex, and therefore cannot be someone to whom one is teleologically inclined, as opposed to simply attracted. That also applies to flirting with those who are not maritally available: such interactions are going nowhere (or nowhere they should go). Flirting, like foreplay, cannot be said to be chaste if it has no marital direction: it will not free people for non-sexually charged friendships of a kind that can be very valuable – or indeed for everyday human interaction focusing on other things.[65] In contrast, being playful and engaging socially in ways that appreciate the maleness or femaleness of one's companions is part of normal social life and something that should generally be encouraged. It also serves as a remote preparation for courtship, for those who are (or will soon be) maritally available.

The need for the 'education of desire' that is virtue is evident insofar as it relates to the protection of a variety of social roles. Part of that education must include modesty, which the *Catechism of the Catholic Church* has defined as something which,

> protects the intimate core of the person. It means the re-
> fusal to unveil what should remain hidden. It is ordered
> to chastity to whose sensitivity it bears witness. It guides
> how one looks at others and behaves towards them in
> conformity with the dignity of persons and their solidar-
> ity.[66]

In talking of the common good and the nature of chastity we have in no way wished to endorse the false idea that this area of life should not be protected or kept private. To complain of the 'privatisation' of sex is something very different from believing that sex, as something by nature both precious and precarious, is in need of protection that privacy affords. Indeed, we can agree with Thomas Nagel when he says that

> We need privacy in order not to have to integrate our
> sexuality in its fullest expression with the controlled
> surface we present to the world. And in general we need
> privacy to be allowed to conduct ourselves in extremis
> in a way that serves purely individual demands, the de-
> mands of strong personal emotion…But intimacy also
> plays an important part in the development of an articu-

late inner life, because it permits one to explore unpublic
feelings in something other than solitude, and to learn
about the comparable feelings of one's intimates, including to a degree their feelings toward oneself... [67]

The defender of modesty as defined above, something which
presupposes that sex is a special sphere of life, can fully accept
these sentiments and further point out that the nature of the core
aspect of the person modesty seeks to protect is crucial to the con-
tinuance of civilisation and a matter of legitimate concern – even
if the nature of that which is protected needs protections of various kinds not all of which Nagel would endorse. And a society
that refuses to endorse and create space for modesty is one which
undermines its own members in their ability to live out the most
fundamental roles of the foundational unit of the society or live out
other roles which respect that unit. The 'privatisation' of sex has
brought with it a saturation of the public square with prurience and
with sexual imagery which undermine the privacy needed to experience what sex truly is.[68] This is not paradoxical if one remembers
that treating sex respectfully, and taking account of its nature, is to
treat it as marital and to do that is to make it public and publicly
related to fundamental goods, while at the same time not the subject of unhealthy focus but visible in discreet and 'dispersed' ways
through the presence in society of marriage, family life, pregnancy,
and childbirth. In a world of 'free rational agents' engaging in sex
without reference beyond the 'private' we would expect, as in fact
we get, a world full of explicit images embodying a truncated view
of sex not enriched in any way by concerns about the family and
common good and therefore what it is to be human. And as DH
Lawrence rightly observed,

It is marriage, perhaps, which has given man the best
of his freedom, given him his little kingdom of his own
within the big kingdom of the State, given him his foot-
hold of independence on which to stand and resist an
unjust State. Man and wife, a king and queen with one or
two subjects, and a few square yards of territory of their
own: this, really, is marriage. It is true freedom because
it is a true fulfilment, for man, woman, and children.[69]

Conclusion

We began by noting the interesting phenomenon of the 'specialness' of sex and the failure of reductive arguments to explain
away this phenomenon. A natural law account of ethics, making
use of concepts such as 'basic goods' and 'human flourishing' al-
lowed us to explore teleological explanations of human sexual
functions and overall flourishing in a way that recognised their
importance. That importance can only be fully appreciated within
a social setting, and the social value of sexual functions can be
understood through an argument as to what would be the best 'designed' institution to protect the goods at stake. We argued that
'marriage' was exactly the kind of institution best suited to the
good of children and parents, and that the distinctive mark of that
institution is the sexual act which is at once procreative and unitive. One of the ways in which sex's specialness shows up is in the
fact that sexual acts which deviate from the unitive-procreative
marital act radically affect appreciation of the good of marriage.
There are different ways of accounting for why the marital act is
paradigmatically good. Another approach is our own experience of
sexual desire and love, the examination of which gives us strong
reason to see the marital act not only as safeguarding the interests
of children and the common good but as paradigmatically fulfilling

of our sexual desires and expressive of a particular kind of love. The interpersonal nature of sexual desire which should involve valuing the good of the other is tied to a particular form of love which is valuable and which expresses itself unconditionally, i.e. in a way adequate to the value of the object of desire. The examination of sexual desire and love supports through a different route the idea that marriage is the appropriate institution for the expression of this kind of desire. Reflection on the virtue of chastity and the common good underlines the importance of roles in identifying the requirements of sexual ethics for human and societal flourishing, such that sexual wrongdoing involves a departure from the *telos* of our sexual capacities and normative desires in a way undermining of crucial societal roles related to sex.

In his book *The Origins of Sex: A History of the First Sexual Revolution*, Faramerz Dabhoiwala reminds readers that effective calls for 'sexual freedom' arose largely as a consequence of Enlightenment arguments over religious liberty – another great subject of controversy.[70] To many, not least Dabhoiwala, both these freedoms are cause for celebration, but I hope to have given readers at least some reason to doubt whether the current arrangements of our society treat sex seriously, let alone ethically.[71] For 'ethical sex' ultimately is not about a series of hurled-down laws external to a fluid subject matter, but is rather about something called marriage, something written on our hearts, hearts made for love. As Herbert McCabe puts it, in words which could partially serve as a conclusion to this book:

> Just as the urge to possess depends for its meaning on
> the institution of legitimate ownership, so the human
> sexual desire depends for its meaning on the institution
> of marriage. And just as robbery is imitation ownership

and would be meaningless without ownership, so sex
without marriage is just imitation marriage. It is defec-
tive marriage, something is lacking to it...sexual desire
in man is a matter of sexual *love* and if we are to criticize
some forms that the satisfaction of this desire takes, it
is criticizing their relevance to love. Love is not added
to sex; sex without love, or sex with bogus or imitation
love, is distorted in itself, one of its essential elements is
missing.[72]

That message, despite the ever-increasing propaganda put out
by self-styled sexual revolutionaries, is the one that remains for
those who still have ears to hear.

Philosophical speculation on sex does almost nothing to improve people's sexual behaviour: other sources are needed for that.
But experience of the sexual realm, the joys, the miseries, the sins,
and the consolations, involves distinctive confrontations with value
of a directness and vividness seldom felt elsewhere. Many of us
will have both joyful experiences in this area and bitter regrets of
one kind or another which are longer lasting and more 'present' to
us than many other things in our lives. That this is so is perhaps a
curious tribute to the distinctive value of that good activity that is
ethical – which is to say marital – sex.

Appendix

Unintended Morally Determinative Aspects (UMDAs): Moral Absolutes, Moral Acts, and Physical Features in Reproductive and Sexual Ethics[1]

If people know one thing about Catholic moral teaching, then it is that it contains a number of exceptionless moral norms in the area of sexual ethics - more, in fact, of such exceptionless norms than are found in any other area of ethics. And it is these norms in this specific area which cause, in this highly sexualised age, the greatest outrage amongst people both within and without the Church.

Why might this be? Following Max Scheler, Karol Wojtyla notes the phenomenon of "resentment" which he defines as

> a lack of objectivity in judgement and evaluation [that] has its origins in weakness of will.

Wojtyla explains that

> attaining or realizing a higher value demands a greater effort of will. So in order to spare ourselves the effort, to excuse our failure to obtain this value, we minimize its significance, deny it the respect which it deserves, even see it as in some way evil, although objectivity requires us to recognize that it is good.

He continues:

> Chastity, more than any other, seems to be the virtue which resentment has tended to outlaw from the soul,

the will and the heart of man...chastity and sexual conti-
nence are seen above all as dangerous enemies of love.[2]

The special significance of sex has been recognised by the
greatest philosophers, artists and social historians, in opposition to
those living in the wake of the sexual revolution who would claim
(at least in public) that this area of morality is in no way special
or unique.[3] And it is no coincidence that the theory propounded
within the Catholic Church rejecting 'moral absolutes',[4] namely
'proportionalism', arose because of the Church's reaffirmation of
Her teaching that contraceptive acts are inherently morally wrong
regardless of the circumstances in which they are performed. For
proportionalism rejected the exceptionless moral norm regarding
contraceptive acts and in doing so proposed a system that - like
similar consequentialist systems - rejected the possibility of *all* exceptionless moral norms.[5]

Veritatis Splendor sounded the death knell for at least the 'proportionalist' kind of opposition to moral absolutes. Again, it is no
coincidence that Karol Wojtyla, an important thinker in his own
right on sexual ethics, was also the man who, as Pope, was to con-
front the proportionalist theories - theories which grew up around
a rejection of traditional teaching on sex. That confrontation was
particularly important because those Catholics practising and
defending contraception were, necessarily, choosing to defy the
Church, and not merely surrendering to episodic weakness of will
in the face of unplanned and urgent sexual passions. The combined
rejection of the authority of the Church and denial of the possibility
of exceptionless moral norms came primarily in relation to sexual
issues. These issues, perhaps more than any others, are bound up
exceptionally closely with our bodily nature and its profound, intrinsic moral meaning.[6]

Veritatis Splendor

VS #74 tells us that 'proportionalism' holds:

> The criteria for evaluating the moral rightness of an ac-
> tion are drawn from *weighing of the non-moral or pre-*
> *moral goods* to be gained and the corresponding non-
> moral or pre-moral values to be respected. For some,
> concrete behaviour would be right or wrong according as
> whether or not it is capable of producing a better state of
> affairs for all concerned.

VS, in condemning such a view, does not, of course, claim that
the consequences of an action cannot be relevant in appraising its
moral goodness or badness – merely that such consequences are
not necessarily a decisive criterion when such an appraisal is made.

VS #48 explains what the proportionalist means by 'pre-moral'
goods, in the context of considerations of the place of the body in
questions concerning natural law:

> A freedom which claims to be absolute ends up treating
> the human body as a raw datum, devoid of any meaning and
> moral values until freedom has shaped it in accordance with
> its design. Consequently, human nature and the body appear
> as *presuppositions or preambles,* materially *necessary* for
> freedom to make its choice, yet extrinsic to the person, the
> subject and the human act. Their functions would not be able
> to constitute reference points for moral decisions, because
> the finalities of these inclinations would be merely *"physi-*
> *cal"* goods, called by some "pre-moral." To refer to them, in
> order to find in them rational indications with regard to the
> order of morality, would be to expose oneself to the accusa-
> tion of physicalism or biologism.[7]

Bearing all of this in mind then, what might be more central criteria for moral assessment – criteria that allow for the possibility of exceptionless moral norms? *VS#78* states, referring to St. Thomas Aquinas's discussion of human action at *Summa Theologiae* I-II, q.18, a.6:

> *The morality of the human act depends primarily and*
> *fundamentally on the "object" rationally chosen by the*
> *deliberate will...*In order to be able to grasp the object
> of an act which specifies that act morally, it is therefore
> necessary to place oneself *in the perspective of the act-*
> *ing person.* The object of the act of willing is in fact a
> freely chosen kind of behaviour. To the extent that it is in
> conformity with the order of reason, it is the cause of the
> goodness of the will; it perfects us morally, and disposes
> us to recognize our ultimate end in the perfect good,
> primordial love. By the object of a given moral act, then,
> one cannot mean a process or an event of the merely
> physical order, to be assessed on the basis of its ability to
> bring about a given state of affairs in the outside world.
> Rather, that object is the proximate end of a deliberate
> decision which determines the act of willing on the part
> of the acting person.

VS#78 goes on to explain:

> The reason why a good intention is not itself sufficient,
> but a correct choice of actions is also needed, is that the
> human act depends on its object, whether that object is
> *capable or not of being ordered* to God, to the One who
> "alone is good," and thus brings about the perfection of
> the person.

This crucial passage tells us some significant things. Clearly the moral object of the human act needs to be understood in terms of how the agent deliberately chooses to locate him or herself in relation to an end, a choosing of which sets his/her will in a way which has an intransitive significance[8] which has a relation to reason and necessarily to our final end.

Stephen Brock, in an important paper,[9] has noted that *VS#78* by talking of the "merely physical order" makes clear that it rejects the proportionalist view that a "proximate end" (i.e. that which we immediately intend, regardless of our *further* end) can be reduced to a 'pre-moral' state of affairs or event. Rather, *VS#78* insists that the proximate end cannot be reduced in this way insofar as it has a moral object of its own – a target relating to the order of reason, no less than any further end the person may have. In contrast, if exceptionless moral norms can only apply to the moral object of a human act and if there are no determinative moral objects for human acts then there can be no exceptionless moral norms covering determinative moral objects.[10]

I take it that proportionalism is, ultimately, an incoherent philosophical theory, as many critics have strongly argued.[11] However, one approach to critiquing proportionalism in the name of moral absolutes has contained – alongside genuine insights, not least on the scope and significance of intention - other aspects which are, I believe, harmful to Catholic moral thinking, not least because this critique presents itself as in full harmony with what is stated in *VS*.

This approach holds that the moral object of the act for the acting person just *is* the intentional structure of the proximate end and nothing more. Proponents of this view, most famously proponents in the 'New Natural Law' tradition, will often justify it by saying that those who would argue that a physical nature can play a formal role in specifying the moral nature of the object even where a relevant aspect of that physical nature (say, the non-procreative character of its structure) is not intended *as such* are somehow understanding by the object the very 'merely physical' object/event that *VS* was concerned to exclude in rejecting proportionalism.

In contrast, other writers argue that a physical nature *can* enter formally into the constitution of a moral act and its object even where the agent does not intend precisely that aspect of the physical that ultimately makes the agent's choice morally wrong. An agent may choose to act for an object formally described (intended), but in doing so brings about certain material events or features of those events, which he need not have intended but may have foreseen. The New Natural Law approach to action theory, best expressed in an influential paper co-authored by John Finnis, Germain Grisez and Joseph Boyle,[12] must deny that certain unintended side-effects can have a central and morally conclusive role in the description of certain kinds of act.

Stephen Brock has suggested that if the physical *can't* play this role then we consign "everything physical about what we do to the domain of the praeter-intentional, and so ultimately to the 'merely premoral' domain." That said, Brock also stresses that "if indeed a physical nature can play a role, it will only be insofar as the role is conferred upon it by reason. Reason is the *first* formal principle of human acts. All others depend on it."[13]

New Natural Lawyers can, however, rebut Brock's statement regarding consignment of the physical to the pre-moral domain, given that *some* physical features may, after all, be intended by the agent. For New Natural Lawyers hold that physical nature *can and does* play a role for every *intended means and end* included in the agent's proposal – in particular, every physical structure and causality from which the agent thinks that he can benefit. Moreover, they can also hold that such physical structures are the normally overwhelmingly intra-intentional structure of the human act, and dominate its moral assessment accordingly. For these writers, reason is the first formal principle of human acts, yet they hold that this precludes physical structures playing a role outside the structure of the proposal shaped by reason and adopted by choice.

However, it is surely a mistake for the New Natural Lawyers to assume that certain physical 'side-effects' cannot have a morally conclusive role in the description of certain kinds of act. I prefer to call these 'side-effects' by another term – Unintended Morally Determinative Aspects (UMDAs) - since the term 'side-effect' may confuse as denoting both side-effects which are morally determinative of the act through entering into its moral object and side-effects which play no such morally determinative role in themselves.

Even where New Natural Lawyers see certain chosen physical structures as morally conclusive, the question still arises what it is about those structures – something that may not itself be part of the agent's intentions – that *makes* them morally conclusive. For example, if certain sexual structures are seen as morally wrong to choose because they are non-procreative in kind, their wrongness need not rest on their being intended *qua* non-procreative (an issue to which we will return). To choose the structure itself is not necessarily to choose the fact that the structure is non-procreative, even if one knows not only that it is non-procreative but that this makes it wrong to choose.

Importantly *VS* says only that the object of choice cannot belong *solely* to the physical order: a trivially true statement. And it should hardly surprise us that Wojtyla, who more than anyone else in the world is associated with phrases like 'the nuptial meaning of the body', did *not*, as Pope, rule out as merely pre-moral that which can in fact play a formal role in the constitution of the moral act and its object.

Nowhere does this become more obvious than in the area of sexual ethics. The Catholic Church has always held that certain sexual acts are *contra naturam* (e.g. sodomy, masturbation, use of barrier contraception). What makes these acts wrong is the way they involve the use of sexual capacities in a sense quite different from acts of normal uncontracepted heterosexual intercourse. For with the acts first mentioned, it is enough to know that a particular physical structure has been chosen: that is, the physical kind deliberately targeted determines the moral kind as well. These acts relate to reason differently from an act of normal heterosexual intercourse, about which we need to ask further questions to see if it is morally right or wrong, such as whether the couple are validly married. This last issue is an example of a *non*-physical UMDA in relation to someone engaged in sexual relations with another. If the couple are not married, then this aspect of what they are doing is enough to make their act morally wrong even though the couple are not precisely intending (as opposed to foreseeing) that their sexual relations will be non-marital. Interestingly, use of non-barrier 'contraception' such as the Pill, since it does not affect the structure of intercourse itself, is also something about which we need to ask further questions, such as whether contraception as opposed to some other physical effect is intended, or whether the motive in taking the Pill is, in fact, non-contraceptive.

An example in sexual ethics of the dangers of ignoring the formal role a physical kind can play in determining a moral object can be found in the work of Germain Grisez, who writes:

While self-stimulation to obtain a semen sample is physically the same as any other masturbation, it is morally
different [i.e. because the aim is not to obtain orgasm].

Grisez adds, however, that

obtaining a semen sample in this way is a grave matter,
for it is a proximate occasion of grave sin (the more or
less probable sexual fantasy and willing of the experienced sexual satisfaction).[14]

This passage makes clear that Grisez does not locate the
wrongness of certain kinds of solitary sexual activity in physical
structures intended by the agent (whatever the *further* intention of
the agent) but rather in what he presumes to be the likely willed
experience of certain sexual fantasies and pleasures. Detaching this
condemnation from any clear account of what is wrong in 'the act
itself' makes it hard to see why anyone should accept the condemnation: if it is wrong to seek the function of sexual pleasure outside its proper holistic context, why would it not be wrong to seek
another sexual function such as ejaculation outside this context?
In contrast, locating the wrong in the misuse of a natural faculty,
though one of unique social importance, helps explain why taking
deliberate pleasure in solitary activity might be part of the wrong
of such 'truncated' activity, as well as accounting for the wrongness of sexual acts which have no accompanying pleasure or fantasy, but nonetheless share functional features in common with acts
which do.[15] And it should come as no surprise that Pope Pius XII
twice confirmed masturbation as morally illicit in all circumstances
precisely on the grounds of its misuse of a natural faculty, regardless of the agent's further intention.[16]

Grisez's approach to this question, and his influential approach to action theory in general, makes it hard to see why, for

example, the use of condoms solely to prevent the transmission of HIV through sexual intercourse is absolutely morally excluded, as many have argued[17] and as Grisez and his collaborator John Finnis believe. Grisez and others from the New Natural Law perspective might argue that to intend the physical blockage is already to intend something wrong: something which is contrary to the good of marriage because the act has been rendered non-procreative/non-unitive in kind. And yet, an agent blocking the sexual act in such a way that it cannot constitute an act of a procreative/unitive kind (a necessary condition for it being a morally good sexual act) may agree he is intending a blockage - albeit for prevention of HIV transmission - but say that this is a mere 'physical structure' and that he is not intending against any basic good, such as marriage or procreation. So, although Grisez does in fact oppose the use of condoms to prevent HIV transmission, it is hard to see how he can do this without conceding that a physical kind not intended precisely qua non-procreative *can* play a formal role in determining the moral object of the act. And it is particularly noteworthy when it comes to sexual ethics that it is here, par excellence, that (intended) physical structures do generate exceptionless moral norms. This should not be surprising if we take the moral meaning of the body and of bodily acts seriously.

Ignoring the importance of the body in this way is fatal for sexual ethics: if masturbation, for example, is sometimes permissible, traditional Catholic sexual ethics can have no coherence whatsoever. It is also fatal for other areas of ethics. New Natural Lawyers and others, most recently Martin Rhonheimer, have defended certain practices in obstetrics which the Church has several times condemned.[18] These include craniotomy (the crushing and emptying of a baby's skull, often done in the past when the baby is trapped in the birth canal) and the bodily invasion and forcible removal of pre-viable babies - again in order to save the life of the mother. Admittedly, the baby's death need not be intended as such in these cases; however, even if the doctor does not intend to kill the baby, he does intend a bodily invasion of the unborn child, of a kind which is in fact lethal. And isn't such an act unjust to the child? After all, his/her bodily integrity is grossly violated and he/she is deliberately deprived of what he/she relies on[19] to continue to exist. The baby's skull is indeed, as David Crawford has pointed out, 'the person' and not a mere part.[20] And that person is violated by a deliberate invasion of his/her body of a lethal kind. Similarly a doctor operating on a dying, unconscious person in order to extract a vital organ to give it to someone else might not be intending to kill or even harm the person by lethally cutting into him/her – but is necessarily committing a gross lethal bodily violation of the person of a kind that cannot be anything other than unjust. There is a state of affairs – an 'object' - which is illicitly targeted here, even if not all morally determinative aspects of that state of affairs are intended as such.

In other words (and to conclude): we must not forget the meaning of the body: the physical has a crucial role to play, both in and outside of sexual ethics. Only by artificially denuding the physical world – or at least some aspects of the physical world - of meaning are we tempted to think that certain intended structures are inconclusive, so long as we do not intend an aspect of these structures seen as uniquely problematic. Many harmful things, after all, are not intended precisely qua harmful, but are intrinsically wrong for all that. And the sexual capacity in particular has a profound relation to reason, or, as Brock neatly puts it, "it has its own nature and it is part of human nature. It cannot but have a moral meaning."[21]

Notes

Introduction: pp. 10-33

[1] Williams (1985), 140-141.

[2] Thomas (2006), 147. I leave to one side whether such a society has ever existed or could have existed.

[3] Singer (1993), 2. It seems that a certain kind of environmentalist is particularly prone to minimising the importance and specialness of sexual ethics. Some general examples of rejections of the specialness of sex include Goldman (1980); Soble (1980); Primoratz (1999) and Webber (2009). I use the term 'Singerite' to denote someone who broadly agrees with Singer on the lack of 'specialness' of sex, as opposed to his radical consequentialism or justification of infanticide or his view that bestiality should cease "to be an offence to our status and dignity as human beings." Singer (2001).

[4] Adler (1970), 327-328. Adler presumably changed his views later in life as he died a Catholic.

[5] See Benn (1999), 236-237. A recent example of a virtue ethicist who sees sex as, at least minimally, 'special' while defending sexual permissiveness is Halwani (2003).

[6] See Reich (1972); Freud (2004); Marcuse (1969). Marcuse also rejects Freud's view of the infantile and narcissistic nature of non-procreative-type sex, and seeks to undermine 'genital supremacy' (and with it the institution of the monogamous family) as a way of eroticising our life and work in order to achieve a utopia very different from the Freudian view of the requirements of civilisation. With regard to Reich especially, compare someone who holds that breathing is an area of life that doesn't require a 'special' ethic – yet does not deny that stopping vast numbers

of people from breathing would have an enormously negative (or at least dramatic) impact on society. All three authors cited put a huge premium on the importance of sexual matters in our culture. It is worth noting here that Immanuel Kant saw sex as crucially related to the birth of reason in human history: "The *figleaf* (Genesis 3.7) was...the product of a far greater manifestation of reason than that which it had demonstrated in the first stage of its development. For to make any inclination more inward and enduring by withdrawing its object from the senses, shows already the consciousness of some dominion of reason over impulse and not merely, as in the first step, a faculty for doing service to those impulses within a lesser or greater extension." (*Conjectural Beginning of Human History*, cited in the analysis of this passage in Wood (2008), 230-234.)

[7] As opposed to faulted for their understanding of love and its appropriate forms.

[8] See the Book of Kings. Some Jewish commentators hold that those Israelites attracted to these sexual practices knew that there was nothing profound in them but found them to be a good excuse for sexual hedonism. Whatever the case, for the Hebrew Prophets the danger of men following false gods by, among other things, taking part in sacrilegious sex rituals was obvious. In temple prostitution they saw grossly evil yet very pleasurable acts raised to the level of sublime religious ritual – a potent mixture that might lead a Hebrew to depart his people forever.

[9] Jonathan Webber (2009), 12.

[10] See for example the French classic epistolary novel by Pierre Choderlos de Laclos *Les Liaisons Dangereuses*.

[11] Webber (2009), 7.

[12] Priest (1997), 371.

[13] An obvious case is that of Jean-Paul Sartre who appears to hold that all sexual activity is necessarily perverse, a view that makes sense especially if sexual desire is held to be something that can be fulfilled, which is not at all clear from Sartre's account. He states in his central work, "Thus, the revelation of the Other's flesh is made through my own flesh; in de-

sire and in the caress which expresses desire, I incarnate myself in order to realize the incarnation of the Other. The caress by *realizing* the Other's incarnation reveals to me my own incarnation; that is, I make myself flesh in order to impel the Other to realize *for-herself* and for me her own flesh, and my caresses cause my flesh to be born for me in so far as it is for the *Other flesh causing her to be born as flesh*. And so possession truly appears as a *double reciprocal incarnation*." Sartre (2003), 412-413. For Sartre, sexual activity is doomed to rupture the 'double reciprocal incarnation'. Whether he also held the view that sexual *desire* is necessarily perverse is a matter of some controversy – sexual desire itself may or may not be 'perverse' in the light of Sartre's ontology. Either way, the concept of perversity is central to Sartre's analysis of sexual desire and activity and may indeed describe all instances of both, while not being a concept the use of which necessitates a 'sexual paradigm' comparator as opposed to a non-sexual ideal of reciprocity. Sartre's famous discussion occurs in *Being and Nothingness*. For differing accounts see Scruton (2006), Nagel (1979), and Oaklander (1980), the last of whom argues that Sartre held that sexual desire is not necessarily perverse. It is also worth considering what we might say to someone who held all existence to be 'perverse' (something that seems to be suggested in the work of people like EM Cioran) and therefore saw sexual activity as 'perverse' without having any notion of 'good' sexual activity (for none could exist on this view). The Cioran-style thinker may have a deep sense that the whole world is perverse before getting a clear idea on the goodness of nothingness!

[14] A liberal (by which I mean one who broadly holds that participant consent is sufficient to render a sexual act morally acceptable) might hold that there is nothing special, as opposed to important, about rape as a sexual violation: it's just that consent is particularly important because sex is important (as are other things – perhaps the liberal can imagine other, non-sexually motivated non-consensual bodily invasions which would be equally wrong, because non-consensual, although not necessarily physically harmful).

[15] Goldman (1980), 131.

[16] Goldman (1980), 120.

[17] Halwani (2003), 172.

[18] Hewson (2013), a barrister, notes that "[b]efore the Sexual Offences Act 2003 was passed, the UK Home Office produced a document on reforming sexual offences law called 'Setting the Boundaries'...I was struck by the incongruous use of the phrase 'a fate worse than death' at paragraph 2.10.8 of this official document - seemingly without irony - to describe rape." It should also be noted that even as brilliant a defender of 'traditional' sexual ethics as the phenomenologist Aurel Kolnai can be condemned by Jenny Teichman on the grounds of not seeing rape as essentially sexual wrongdoing:

"Writing in phenomonological mode he says that sexual sin is not a sin against another but a sin with another. He has not forgotten about rape but thinks its badness is not essentially sexual, because it is possible to violate people in many other ways. Surely here he has confused badness that is unique to a certain sphere of action with badness that is essential to that sphere. One could equally well infer that the badness of robbery with violence is not essentially theft on the grounds that rape too is a violation. Secondly sinning with does not rule out sinning against; a man who persuades another to carry a bribe to a politician sins against that other as well as with him." Teichman (2008), 410. Teichman is perhaps unfair here, for Kolnai also states, in the passage under consideration, "Certainly there are sins, or components of sins, like 'violation,' 'destruction of a good name,' 'infection with disease,' which may depend on sexual activity, but these are not sexual sins in the proper and certain sense. There is also the theory that, especially in loveless sexual congress, the formal element of 'using a person as means to satisfy one's own lust' is what really matters. But this element would also be a component of eating people, or simply ill-treating them (in order to work off our feelings), or perhaps even when we offer them employment; there is clearly some utterly different essential component in sexual abuse...I shall hold to the contrast...between the phenomenon of 'immorality presenting itself primarily as dirt' and 'immorality presenting itself primarily as interference, prevention, or injury.'" Sexual abuse surely includes rape. Kolnai (2005), 12.

222

[19] Williams (2008), 78.

[20] Denyer (2003). It should be noted that, in light of ideas about sexual violation being something that brings with it an especial dishonour, alleged rape victims (and other victims of sexual offences) are exceptionally granted a legal right to anonymity in British courts to this day - see Sexual Offences (Amendment) Act (1976) and Sexual Offences Act (2003). In James Dickey's novel *Deliverance* the narrator Ed witnesses the brutal rape of his companion Bobby and later reflects on the aftermath, "None of this was his fault, but he felt tainted to me. I remembered how he had looked…how willing to let anything be done to him."

[21] It should be borne in mind that succumbing to seduction, i.e. by having one's consent won rather than coerced, would for the Romans be more shameful still, for the woman would have been complicit in her own dishonour by deliberately choosing to commit adultery. In Shakespeare's *Measure for Measure* Isabella, a novice nun, refuses to give coerced consent (consent will save her brother from execution) to fornication viewing such consent as involving a violation of her chastity and therefore obviously absolutely wrong.

[22] Such thinking with regard to 'shame' and the involuntary is not at all confined to the West. We learn in Buddhism (my thanks to Geoff Hunt),

"At the Second Council, there was disagreement between the Theravaada and Mahayana Schools...According to the Theravaada version, the venerable elders called for the assembly because many monks had become lax concerning ten points of discipline. The reprehensible practices were considered as accepting money in lieu of alms-food, eating afternoon, following improper procedures at meetings, etc. According to the Mahayana version, the liberal monk Mahaadeva initiated the Second Council with five criticisms against the conservative arhats who dominated the Buddhism of the time by virtue of their supposed enlightenment. The five criticisms are that those who claimed to be arhats had not fully conquered passion as they still had wet dreams, were not omniscient because they often had to ask for directions, etc, were still subjected to doubts, had gained their knowledge through others rather than through their own experience, and would be making verbal exclamations during meditation." KR Paramahamsa, *Buddhism in Scripture and Practice*, (Friendswood, Texas: TotalRecall Publications, Inc., 2007). http://www.vedamu.org/Veda/KRP-Sir%5C4.%20Buddhism%20eBook.pdf, 6.

[23] St. Augustine, *City of God*, Book I, Chapter 19. It is noticeable that in Shakespeare's *Titus Andronicus*, set in pagan times, Lavinia's chastity, something her father believes is to be valued "more dear than hands or tongue," is said to be robbed through forcible rape. It is a robbery which Titus believes warrants his execution of innocent Lavinia during which he declaims, "Die, die, Lavinia and thy shame with thee [Kills Lavinia]; And with thy shame, thy father's sorrow die!" 'Honour killings' which may involve victims of coerced sex are sadly still prevalent within certain cultures around the world.

[24] Williams (2008), 93.

[25] Williams (2008), 90.

[26] See Bergoffen (2006).

[27] Though these aspects may make one particular instance of sexual assault worse than another.

[28] Some authors, such as Burgess-Jackson (1999), have attempted to define rape purely in terms of coercion in a worthy attempt to capture a wider range of sexual acts that should fall under the term "rape." But this approach, strictly interpreted, can preclude categorising a sexual act on an unconscious person as rape, making it mere battery. As this seems counterintuitive I will hold to the more traditional definition. In the UK, section 1 of the Sexual Offences Act 1956 makes rape an offence, and states that a man commits rape if, inter alia, he "has sexual intercourse with a person (vaginal or anal) who at the time of intercourse does not consent to it" (section 1 (2) (a)); or "induces a married woman to have sexual intercourse with him by impersonating her husband" (section 1(3)). The last is certainly rape, though not under consideration here.

[29] These examples are mentioned in Pruss (2013), 72-73. The thrust of the analogy highlighting the differences between theft and rape is surely

right, although Pruss does not consider complications such as that expropriations might be viewed in terms of loss of entitlements, so that there need not be even a *prima facie* requirments for consent.

[30] Archard (2007), 383-384.

[31] Archard (2007), 386.

[32] Archard (2007), 388 and 390. At an Oxford conference I attended, held in honour of the philosopher GEM Anscombe, an elderly Catholic philosopher, Christopher Coope, appeared to cast doubt on whether paedophilia did any meaningful harm to children who were not aware of what was happening to them. His subsequent quips about the late Sir Jimmy Savile (an infamous alleged paedophile) suggested that his thoughts on the matter were not as developed as they might be.

[33] Pope John Paul II (1981), 178.

[34] Kolnai (2005), 13.

[35] Kolnai (2005), 12.

[36] von Hildebrand (2010), 13.

[37] Scruton (2006), 186-187. What might make certain kinds of wrongdoing especially bad in themselves need not, of course, mean that those who commit such wrongdoing are especially bad people. After all, the passions people are prone to in what appears to be a unique area may be uniquely (or at least especially) powerful, which may lessen the culpability of those who succumb to them.

Chapter 1: pp. 34-65

[1] Cited in Grisez, Boyle, Finnis, and May (1988), 366. The quote has appended to it the following footnote (2): ""*Decret. Greg IX*, lib. V, tit. 12, cap. v; *Corpus iuris canonici*, ed. AL Richter and A. Freidberg (Leipzig: Tauchnitz, 1881), 2, 794: "Si aliquis causa explendae libidinis vel odii meditatione homini aut mulieri aliquid fecerit, vel ad potandum dederit, ut non possit generare, aut concipere, vel nasci soboles, ut homicida teneatur." Some translate "causa explendae libidinis," which is broad

enough to cover all motivation by sexual impulse, "to satisfy lust," which unnecessarily limits the motive to habitual vice."

Such texts are philosophically interesting, although it is worth recalling here that this book is a work of philosophy and does not rely on the authority of religious texts/teachings for its conclusions.

[2] Reprinted in Ford, Grisez, Boyle, Finnis and May (1988), 35-116. All further references to this text in this book (referred to henceforth as GBFM (1988)) will be to this source. This paper has subsequently been further defended/amended by Grisez (1993), 506-516 and by Grisez and Boyle (1998), 228-232.

[3] For more on the arguments focusing on contraception's contralife character within the Church's tradition see Noonan (1986) and the relevant references in GBFM (1988) 37 fn.2 & 38 fn.3.

[4] Grisez (1993), 513 fn. 104 states: "An argument against contraception grounded in its opposition to the good of life can be articulated without articulating the general theory of basic goods and modes of responsibility"; he refers to the *Thomist* article (reprinted in GBFM (1988)) as such an argument. However, to make sense of the idea of willing against the good of life does require some kind of foundational ethical theory and it is unclear which account GBFM can be appealing to other than the basic goods theory. Moreover, the appeal GBFM make to the incommensurability of future goods apparently assumes such a theory (see GBFM (1988) p.52 footnotes 8 & 9).

[5] In addition to the contralife argument, other writings of John Finnis in particular have developed theories on sexual ethics involving marital goods which could be applied to contraception – see Finnis (1997). In this paper Finnis refers to the good of marriage as "one of the basic human goods to which human choice and action are directed by the first principles of practical reason" p.97. See also Grisez (1993), 567.

[6] I refer here specifically to John Finnis, Germain Grisez and Joseph Boyle, who have developed their theory in a number of works including: Grisez (1983), Grisez (1993), Finnis (1980), Finnis (1983), Grisez and Boyle (1979), Grisez, Boyle, Finnis (1988).

[7] *Summa Theologica*, I-II, q.94, a.2.

[8] Grisez (1983), 121.

[9] Finnis (1991), 42.

[10] Chappell (2005), 29.

[11] Finnis (1980), ch.4.

[12] Finnis (1980), 100-133 where Finnis adumbrates 9 basic requirements. Grisez generally refers to these requirements as 'Modes of Responsibility'.

[13] Finnis (1980), 101-102.

[14] Finnis (1980), 120-121. For more on respecting basic goods see Finnis (1983) 124-127.

[15] See for example *Catechism of the Catholic Church* (1994), #2266. For criticism of Finnis's understanding of how to respect the basic good of life see Lamont (2002).

[16] GBFM (1988), 54. Of course, couples may have other motives for contracepting or abstaining from potentially fertile intercourse, such as that they feel too fragile psychologically to conceive now, and recoil from the psychological burden without assuming that a possible future with a child would be a 'worse' possible future. In such cases the decision need not involve the kind of comparison of long-term futures that GBFM envisage. Moreover, a couple deciding to delay for two months bringing a new child into the world, so as to avoid the woman being heavily pregnant during a predictably hot summer, may be making their decision not on the basis of two long-term unknowable futures, but rather on the basis of a short–term concern. They may not focus at all on comparing the long-term futures, or they may assume that the good of the lives of the two possible children would cancel each other out so that only short-term considerations are relevant.

[17] GBFM (1988) appear to adopt two lines of argument. One concerns the incommensurability of basic goods such that commensurating calculation between them is practically impossible. The choice to contracept is, on their grounds, contralife and therefore contrary to a reason (not directly

to will against the good of life) that cannot be rationally outweighed. The other line of argument concerns our lack of knowledge of the future, even when any commensuration might be done in terms of just one basic good.

Consider a case where a couple make a decision about when to conceive with reference only to the good of life. A couple that choose, via contraception, not to bring about a child at t1 might be taking into account all sorts of reasons not to bring about a child at this time. Those reasons might well relate to 'respecting' the good of life, in that bringing about a child at t1, although instantiating life, is not thought to be an act sufficiently respectful of life (due to, for example, the inappropriateness of the situation for receiving a child). Contraception may indeed be an inappropriate way by which to avoid bringing a child into the world, but this argument about commensuration does nothing to prove this. What would need to be established would be the 'contralife' character of contraceptive acts as distinct from the practice of abstinence.

A further question is whether GBFM are committed to the view that, *ceteris paribus*, if a couple were to have a choice between conceiving twins or a single child, they should aim at conceiving two, for example if they are receiving fertility enhancement. Presumably they would have to answer yes, particularly given their position regarding the pilot example (see main text below). But surely in this case, the couple cannot know, at least on the GBFM view, that two is better than one as concerns the long-term future – in which case why would it be necessarily better to choose two?

[18] GBFM (1988), 55. GBFM might reply that three lives as opposed to one life is the kind comparison that *can* rationally be made. However, imagine if you knew that the three people in field 2 all had one second to live, regardless of whether you crashed the plane into them or not – whereas the one person in field 1 had many years to live. Would this not affect what the pilot should do? If so, we are implicitly acknowledging that numbers are relevant only other things being equal (such as potential victims having equal expectations of future life). And if this is the case, then cannot a couple, in delaying conception for two months for, say,

the health of the mother, be recognising that by doing this they achieve life + health with conception in month 3, which outweighs life + lack of health with conception in month 1? If the pilot's decision cannot be rationally faulted on grounds of incommensurability, then neither can the contracepting couple's (of course, this is not to deny that the choice to delay conception via contraception may be irrational/immoral for other reasons).

[19] GBFM (1988), 56 offer another example of the conditions required for rational decision-making. Here a house-hunter is deliberating between two houses, one of which has all the value-and-more of another, in terms of price, size and proximity to the school (the exclusive criteria for choosing in this example). The house with all the value-and-more than the other, say GBFM, provides one with an unchallenged reason to buy it. However, this immediately suggests another example where house (a) which far outweighs house (b) in terms of two of the set criteria but underweighs it a tiny bit in the remaining one criterion (e.g. size) cannot be 'rationally' chosen over the other house (assuming that there is no priority amongst the three criteria). If house (a) is chosen over house (b) here, the size (i.e. specific spatial area) of the house rejected is 'lost', but it might be argued that this is not a very important loss, and does not change the outcome of commensuration. To anyone who objects that the fact of a particular choice means that one is, in this case, commensurating by rating the criteria in some way the question remains why, at the general level, commensuration should be thought to be impossible. Moreover it is unclear whether GBFM think that one can commensurate even at the level of particular instantiations of goods.

In the pilot example the loss of V's life clearly is, at least, an important loss. But what reason is there to dismiss the idea that the choice of house (a) over house (b) is simply more rationally fulfilling of the chooser in that almost nothing will be lost in comparison with what is gained?

[20] GBFM (1988), 57-58.

[21] GBFM (1988), 42.

[22] See Smith (1992), 340-370 and Anscombe (1972).

[23] For a representative statement as to what the Grisez-Finnis school takes to be the defining feature of an action see Grisez (1983), 233. For a more recent account of what constitutes the moral object of an act see Finnis, Grisez, and Boyle (2001).

[24] Smith (1992), 360-361.

[25] I do not here propose to give a full exposition of the 'contraceptive sex act' or an account of how sexual acts ought to relate to marital goods; these are subjects for later chapters. GBFM recognise this different approach to the question of contraception, which they see as compatible with the contralife approach, observing that "recent Church teaching focuses almost entirely on contraception's wrongness in relation to other values, especially chastity, marital love, and the sacred character of virtuous sexual activity in marriage." GBFM (1988), 38.

[26] The Catholic Church holds that use of contraception prevents sex in marriage from being what it holds it should be: an act of *marital intercourse*: complete bodily and personal self-giving. For the same reason, it holds that sex between unmarried people falls short of what it should be (again: marital intercourse) on yet another ground, hence "further distanced."

Self-giving, the giving of a gift, would also be violated by a couple who after sex used a spermicide out of fear of pregnancy. Perhaps rather similarly, for the Catholic Church, attempting to cancel your marriage vows doesn't nullify those vows but does radically disrespect them. The effects of those vows continue over time and are open-ended and have implications for the couple's life.

Sex and contraception are 'separable' as they are in any case of non-barrier contraception (a person forgets they took the pill or had an implant 3 months ago). Nevertheless, for the Catholic Church the distortion of self-giving is clear if we see the giving as being potentially prolonged in effect over a period of time even if the nature of the gift may not be fully known.

[27] It is unclear what the term 'impede' is meant to encompass in GBFM's paper. If they mean by 'impede' any action undertaken with the intention

of preventing the completion of a causal process which could otherwise lead to the creation of a new life, an argument needs to be made as to why the impeding of such a causal process is always wrong. Such an argument would, presumably, have to take into account the significance of the teleology of sexual activity (see later chapters in this book) and of any objective meanings such activity embodied, as well as explore why it might be morally wrong to have a dual intention of performing and thwarting an act that could give rise to the causal process leading to conception.

Suffice it to say here that I do not believe GBFM have given any satisfactory account of why 'impeding' is wrong in this context, nor have they sufficiently defined what they mean by 'impede' so as to rule out those actions which they would accept as morally licit. Is the thought that there is some general principle of the type: It is always impermissible to impede a process that is under way that might lead to a good, because to choose to do something to stop that process involves willing that that good not be?

This cannot be a general principle. For example do I have a duty not to impede the recovery from illness of someone who is a threat to the common good? Do I have a general duty not to impede someone about to make a true but dangerous communication to a third party? It seems clear that these are not moral duties even though my choice that someone not recover now or learn something now is surely against the good of health and knowledge respectively.

By using the term 'impede' GBFM are indicating that there is more to their contralife argument than mere 'willing against life'. Given that some 'impeding' of processes under way that might lead to a good appears to be morally justifiable, the term is used in too wide a sense.

None of this is to deny that 'impeding' can indeed be morally significant and even morally conclusive in view of what is being 'impeded' and how, in the context of chosen sexual activity. But if 'impeding' must take a particular form in this particular area to be morally conclusive, then we are dealing with a substantively different issue from the mere possession of a contralife will.

[28] Masek (2011).

[29] GBFM (1988), 44.

[30] Finnis (1993), 189 states: "…contracepted intercourse has, objectively, the masturbatory feature that it simulates an aspect of the conjugal good that has in fact and in intention been excluded from it by an act which affects the reality of sexual activity (*qua* chosen) itself."

[31] A woman taking a pill and subsequently repenting of, or at least regretting, her decision, who proceeds to have intercourse which has been rendered sterile by the pill she took, is not, in having that intercourse, confirming the intention embodied in the former pill-taking act. It is a more complex question whether a woman who takes a pill and is later completely indifferent as to whether her intercourse is rendered infertile by the pill is having intentionally contraceptive sex. It is worth noting that a woman could take a pill *in case* she chooses to have intercourse (which she is hoping to resist as immoral or unwise), not with the *intention* to have intercourse. See the discussion in Chapter 4 of conditional intentions.

[32] GBFM (1988), 43. This statement has since been amended by Grisez and Boyle (1998), 231 to "contraceptors necessarily foresee that a baby might come to be, they want that foreseen baby not to come to be, and they choose to do something in order to make it less likely that he or she will come to be."

[33] GBFM (1988), 36.

[34] GBFM (1988), 43.

[35] GBFM (1988), 44.

[36] GBFM (1988), 46. It is not clear whether the 'practical love' of a possible person is even possible. Even God surely doesn't create out of love as opposed to creating a real person though a willingness to share love with him/her.

[37] GBFM (1988), 45.

[38] GBFM (1988), 46-47.

[39] The moral object of such a will – the deprivation of life – is what defines the nature of such a will.

[40] On this point see also Bayles (1976), 298-299. It should be clear that 'harm' and 'benefit' are not being used in their ordinary senses when relating to non-existent possible persons. A couple may bring about future benefits, including the benefit of existence, but cannot be said to be benefiting pre-existing persons. Possible persons may be specifiable only in the sense of exactly the person who *is* conceived as it happens.

[41] By "essential" condition I presume GBFM mean something at least as strong as "necessary" condition.

[42] Defining contraceptive acts in terms of a will that is necessarily contralife would also have the result that a couple using a condom to prevent the transmission of an infection was not contracepting in any sense. I think that GBFM are correct not to characterise such activity as necessarily contraceptive as opposed to wrong for non-contraceptive reasons.

However, the GBFM account of the wrongness of contraception would appear to make the following case, suggested to me by Edward Feser, wrong and for contraceptive reasons: Suppose someone creates a drug which guarantees that every act of sexual intercourse will result in pregnancy, and indeed will result in twins, triplets, or quadruplets. Now suppose he tells me that he has put it into the water I just drank and that unless I vomit it up within five minutes it will take permanent effect. Do I act immorally if I induce vomiting, and if I induce it precisely because I don't want 50 or 100 children? Would this mean I have a 'contralife will' or 'hate' these babies? On the GBFM account the answer would appear to be 'yes'. This example at least shows that the answer requires much thought before 'yes' could be accepted as reasonable (one might ask, though, of Feser whether in a case of ovarian hyperstimulation someone could destroy excess ova for avoidance of multiple conceptions and not be said to be contracepting).

An example of activity that many would consider contraceptive but would not be deemed so on the GBFM model would be the following (again from Feser): Suppose someone develops a drug/device which ensures that after conception takes place, the fertilized ovum (zygote) is put into suspended animation for a year, or five years, or whatever, within the woman's body, and that after this period the pregnancy will resume as normal. And suppose further either (a) that after this happens the woman cannot get pregnant again until the existing child is born, or (b) that other children may be conceived, but they will go into suspended animation too so that a 'backlog' is built up and the woman will give birth to multiple children later on.

Now, in either case – and whatever moral differences there are between (a) and (b) – we can imagine that people might use this device precisely to enjoy sex as long as possible without children. But they are not (especially in case (b)) acting with a 'contralife will,' at least if we imagine that they are perfectly willing to have the child(ren) when the time comes.

Such an action does seem to have many of the earmarks of contraception many people find objectionable. If GBFM's account of what contraception consists in is lacking (see the discussion of NFP in this chapter), then we need to find an independent way of judging the morality of such acts, as opposed to the type of acts GBFM are concerned with. Whatever one thinks of Feser's example (and one might object that a couple *could* reasonably delay childbirth in this way for serious reasons, not involving contraception or a 'contraceptive mentality' but relating to the mother's or children's health), the example does raise questions for the GBFM approach.

[43] Moore (1992) held that it is difficult even to make sense of the notion of a specific possible person, not least because only actual human persons are truly individuated. As he puts it, "babies not yet conceived are not particulars." p.167. See also Bayles (1976), 298-300. But this is too radical a claim, for we can certainly make sense of a proposition that conditions a, b, c (etc.) for conception z were such that only specifiable person X, and no-one else, could have resulted. As Hare (1975), 220 put it, such a potential person is "identifiable in the sense that identifying reference can be made to him," although clearly he is not identifiable with some already existing person. On a Kripkean model a possible particu-

lar must be individuated by some connection with the real world - and on Kripke's scientific essentialist view, this would involve identifying the gametes which 'would have' combined. We can make sense of that proposition (assuming determinism at the relevant ontological level – i.e. only one sperm could have 'won'). However, we'd need to know the intimate details of the course of the sexual act in question (body positions etc) – and it would have to be a possible alternative course in which contraception was not used. But, arguably (depending on one's view of so-called externalist theories of meaning) even having a theoretical criterion for identifying the possible person doesn't help much *if* we are talking about the couple having a pre-existing identifying reference to that person which is accessible to their minds. For the best they are likely to be able to manage is 'the person that could result from this sexual act' – which is not a unique description of possible persons – certainly not from their epistemic position, anyway. For an argument about how we can harm future people see Carter (2001).

[44] We do not have to accept Frege's description theory of reference. Even on Saul Kripke's New Theory of Reference, there would appear to be an analogous problem with possible persons.

[45] GBFM (1988) refer to the couple not wanting "*that* possible baby to begin to live" p.46 emphasis added.

[46] I know from personal communication that Finnis agrees with this revision. I am unaware of the position May has taken with regard to the revision.

[47] GBFM (1988), 66.

[48] GBFM (1988), 81.

[49] Grisez and Boyle (1998), 232 now deny that a couple could carry out a contraceptive choice via NFP. As they put it, "The choice to practice natural family planning is a choice to abstain from acts in which a baby would become a real possibility; the choice to contracept, presupposing the intention to engage in such acts, is a choice to try to prevent the baby who might result from them."

[50] GBFM (1988), 84-85.

[51] Ibid.

[52] GBFM (1988), 86.

[53] Obviously some baby side-effects might be avoided by other means, such as employing an army of nannies. But here we are only interested in the couple's plan to avoid baby side-effects by preventing the baby's coming-to-be.

[54] GBFM might make the claim that the baby's not-coming-to-be is to function as a *causal* means to the end of avoiding baby burdens, but is not a means *chosen* by the couple. But, insofar as a couple know that the causal means functions in this way, it is likely they are choosing this very causal path as part of their plan to achieve their end.

It is of course quite possible to choose an end y without knowing that means x is a necessary causal precondition of end y. In such cases there is present a false belief that an imagined particular pathway is all that is necessary to bring about y. But such is not the case with the NFP couple, whose plan for end y includes a plan of chosen means x, insofar as the couple is aware of this causal relation. The incoherence of any other position on their part is logical and not merely psychologically improbable in adoption (Vacek (1998), 62-63 appears to believe it is only psychologically improbable).

[55] Compare GBFM's argument to GBF's statement : "an action is intentional if it is part of the plan on which one freely acts. That is to say, what one tries to bring about, whether it be the goal one seeks to realise or the means one chooses to realise that goal, is intended." p.79.

[56] Masek (2011), 93.

[57] Kamm (2007).

[58] I take it that bringing about deliberate constipation, while in this case morally wrong as unfair on the baby, does not fall under any absolute prohibition of the kind that applies to contraceptive use in the view of Masek and the Catholic Church.

[59] Not merely "do not intend to."

[60] *Humanae Vitae* (16), to which GBFM are committed, states, with regard to a contracepting couple and a couple practising NFP: "In reality, these two cases are completely different. In the former married couples rightly use a faculty provided them by nature. In the latter they obstruct the natural development of the generative process. It cannot be denied that in each case married couples, for acceptable reasons, *are both perfectly clear in their intention to avoid children and mean to make sure that none will be born.*" (my emphasis). A couple charting their fertility are 'avoiding' rather than 'preventing' children coming to be. A couple don't chart in order to have knowledge regarding the promotion of other goods. They promote other goods via the non-conception of a new child. Here abstaining is something the couple 'do' (just as they might choose to be silent).

[61] Patrick Lee has suggested to me in correspondence that the claim that a couple are intending by omission that a new child not come to be is groundless, and that a couple making a choice to use NFP is analogous to a man choosing not to write a book because of the burdens involved in undertaking such a task. However, the analogy is not exact. The proper analogy with the NFP case would be a man choosing not to write a book because of the burdens that would come about *if the book were produced* (e.g. getting into trouble with the government). In this case the man *does* choose specifically against the proposed book in the same way that the NFP couple choose against the proposed baby.

[62] See for example Grisez and Boyle (1979); Finnis (1995).

[63] See endnote 55 above for GBF's statement on what counts as an intentional action, which is consistent with their views expressed in later work.

[64] Rhonheimer (1989).

[65] Joint Committee on Bioethical Issues of Bishops' Conferences of Scotland, Ireland, England and Wales (1986); Joint Committee on Bioethical Issues of the Bishops' Conference of Great Britain and Ireland (1986); Pennsylvania Catholic Conference, "Guidelines for Catholic Hospitals Treating Victims of Sexual Assault" (1993). It remains an open

question in Catholic moral theology whether such evacuation of sperm is morally permissible (though almost all writers would accept this), as well as whether other methods such as suppression of ovulation may be used. The feasibility of suppressing ovulation without unduly risking the life of any newly conceived human is a subject of intense debate.

[66] GBFM (1988), 69.

[67] Grisez (1993), 512. May (2000), 140-142 observes that: "...the moral object specifying the rape victim's (or potential rape victim's) human act is *not* to prevent the conception of a new human person but rather to prevent ultimate completion of an unjust act of sexual violence." He later states, with regard to acts undertaken to prevent the rapist's sperm from making his victim pregnant: " Such acts are not acts of contraception because the *object* freely chosen and morally specifying them is *not* the impeding of a new human life that could begin through a freely chosen genital act (=definition of contraception) but is rather the *protecting of the raped woman from further violence by the rapist*."

[68] It might be argued that a rape victim *does* have a *prima facie* duty to remove the rapist's sperm from her body prior to any possible conception on the grounds that the sexual act has not been freely chosen and this an inappropriate way for a child to be brought into the world. This argument would depend on an idea of parental duty to the future child, and would not apply in a case where the woman knew that the act was in any case infertile. It seems that Grisez would have to accept, if the presence of sperm is truly seen as part of the act even after its apparent completion, that a woman has a duty to have the sperm removed as soon as feasible *even if she knows the act is already infertile.* This seems particularly unreasonable.

[69] Grisez (1993), 512. See also Grisez (1997), 251-255.

[70] In GBFM (1988), 36 it is stated that the distinction between seeking to prevent conception and seeking to impede the beginning of the life of a possible person is a merely conceptual distinction.

[71] GBFM (1988), 97: "Since contraception is always wrong and since producing babies is always wrong, the only morally acceptable way to

engage either in lovemaking or life giving is by engaging in sexual intercourse that is open to new life."

Chapter 2: pp. 66-100

[1] See Grisez, Boyle, Finnis, and May (1988), 99: "moral norms cannot be derived logically from entirely theoretical premises." The following statements are also suggestive of a denial of "ethical naturalism": "one's primary understanding of the human good…is attained when one is considering what it would be good, worthwhile to do, to get, to have and to be – i.e., by definition, when one is thinking practically." Finnis (1983); see also Finnis (1998), 90-94. As Grisez, Boyle, and Finnis (1987) observe (p.113), "the moral ought cannot be derived from the is of theoretical truth – for example, of metaphysics and or philosophical anthropology." See also George (1998), p.vii. Accordingly, no theoretical insight into human nature and its inclinations can provide grounds for knowing which basic moral goods we ought to pursue. Grisez has said more recently that while the primary principles of practical reason cannot be derived from antecedent knowledge, one way in which people come to know the basic goods is through theoretical reflection on human action. Grisez (2001), 8-9.

[2] In choosing to act, an agent may bring about events which he did not intend but may have foreseen. It seems that an account such as GBFM's needs to be qualified in order to take account of certain cases of side-effects which, while remaining unintended, can have a central role in the description of certain kinds of act. This point is explored in the Appendix. See also Watt (2004).

[3] More precisely, in Alexander Pruss's (unpublished) formulation: "acting with and through one's faculty F at t in a way that per se makes F be incapable of exercising at t any of its natural functions." See later discussion.

[4] See Oderberg (2010). The traditional formulation of St Thomas Aquinas (*Summa Theologica* I, q.91, a.2 ad I) is that Natural Law is the participation in the Eternal Law of the rational creature (which would include an-

gels). However, it might be argued that Natural Law is about more than practical rationality, but doesn't include things that are in the domain of the latter, such as choices about actions that are morally indifferent – though it has things to say about how morally indifferent acts might be identified and how they might be embedded in a wider moral context, as in the Principle of Double Effect. Nevertheless, a question remains as to whether it is Natural Law that has things to say about identifying such actions, or whether they call for mere physical scientific description. When I describe a carefree movement of my arm (i.e. a movement seemingly unconcerned with practical rationality) am I not describing something according to scientific laws? And these descriptive 'laws' seem only like moral laws in an analogous sense (just as the movement of the planets seems a very different thing from a rationally motivated action).

[5] Murphy (2001), 2-3. The following analysis is much influenced by Murphy's work.

[6] On these terms, see, amongst many others, Bourke (1974) and Lee (1997). As the definition presented here should make clear I am *not* referring to 'naturalist' in the sense of a thesis holding that there exists nothing supernatural but only inanimate or animate bodies, with animate bodies being either intelligent organisms or non-intelligent organisms. See Smith (2001).

[7] Such an account of values is disputed by those who see no logical problem in deducing 'ought-judgements' from 'is-judgements' or who regard the is/ought distinction as problematic. Recent examples of arguments against the validity of the so-called naturalistic fallacy can be found in Lisska (1996); Garcia (2001); Martin (2004).

[8] Oderberg (2010).

[9] By which is meant a foundational category which picks out a group of individuals as being of a specific kind. The group is defined by the properties which make up its essence. We can pick out these properties (as opposed to accidents) through the application of general rules. Those properties which persist in a variety of contexts can be recognised even before knowing the essence of a thing. Moreover we have an ability

to recognise similarities between things sharing essences and can look for instances of the same kind that persist across a variety of contexts. In grasping that particular properties flow from the essence, we simply grasp properties that make up the essence of a thing (this is not, of course, to say that we grasp *all* the properties that make up the essence). For a detailed examination of these matters see Oderberg (2007). It should be noted that the terms essence and natural kind are closely related but not interchangeable. It could conceivably be held that there are essences but not substantial forms, and vice versa. However, the Naturalists I am here discussing do hold that there is a close relation between substantial forms and essences.`

Such conceptions of entities in nature are not materialist but hylomorphic. That is to say, they treat a concrete substance as a composite of matter and form. The substantial form of an object – what makes it the kind of object it is – is the specific aspect of a substance's organisational structure; the matter is that which is given organisational structure by the form. On this picture the idea of a substantial form is abstract and universal, irreducible to any particular material thing or to any aspect of our classificatory practices. For a modern account of this metaphysical view and a series of arguments as to its plausibility and explanatory power see Oderberg (2005).

[10] A property with a fundamental 'tending towards' built into its very nature. In the terms of one author, Lisska (2003), a disposition is in itself an incomplete property. It tends towards its 'completion' (or 'actualisation'). Such properties are not 'accidents' but flow from the essence of the object. The dispositional properties of the essence make up the 'formal cause' of the entity in question. I use the term dispositional property interchangeably with the term inclination – though see below for different types of inclinations. See also Oderberg (2007).

[11] Finality meaning 'having an end' – tending in a definite direction toward an end, carrying an 'order' toward one thing and away from what is opposed to it.

[12] Lisska (1996), 199.

[13] Lisska (2003). It should be noted, however, contra the apparent claims of some naturalists, that the concept 'good' is in one sense not strictly 'derived' from the concept of nature on a Thomist account. The concept of good i.e. 'final cause' presupposes formal and efficient cause and *adds* the notion of desirability. As Aquinas says: "every existence and good is considered through some form" (*Summa Theologica* I-II, q.85, a4). As with existence, every good is proportioned to some nature, while also transcending it. The idea of something being an 'end of a natural process' / 'according to nature' is, on this view, contained in the concept of good (not vice versa). However, Aquinas claims that 'according to nature' is so formally contained in the nature of the good, that he judges it impossible to will what does not seem somehow to suit one's nature (*Summa Theologica* I-II, q.6, a.4, ; cf I-II, q.19 a.10). It is important to note that for Aquinas it is the intellect that bears upon the abstract concept of the good and not merely concrete goods as desired (which the will bears upon). It is for this reason that the concept of the good is what gives intellect an act that is formal, constitutive, for any act of will (i.e. Aquinas does not hold that the concept of the good is nothing more than what we experience as good – that which is experienced in willing as willing's own object). See later comments in this chapter on the good as virtuous to desire. See also the discussion in the Appendix of the New Natural Law Interpretation of Aquinas and the illuminating paper by Brock (2005).

[14] Naturalists will often refer to *Summa Theologica* I-II, q.94, a.2 in support of their position, although this famous text is referred to by anti-naturalists and interpreted differently. For the naturalist, knowledge of our nature is presupposed in any work of practical reason because "…the intellect apprehends primarily being itself; secondly, it apprehends that it understands being; and thirdly, it apprehends that it desires being. Hence the idea of being is first, that of truth second, and the idea of good third, though good is in things." (*Summa Theologica* I, q.16, a.2).

[15] Or might all reason be in some sense practical? Once you have substantial theoretical (i.e., disinterested, as opposed to action-oriented) knowledge that something is of a certain kind, what that kind of thing is for, and how it is to achieve its goal, and thus also know (some of)

what counts as its being a good exemplar of that kind of thing, then you know enough to make some claims not only about (i) what it ought to do (how it ought to operate) and be (like) but also about (ii) what you or I ought (conditionally, of course) to do with it, for it, etc. The last group of 'ought'-judgments (#ii) should certainly count as 'practical', even if one insists on withholding that classification from the earlier group (#i, re what the thing itself ought to do and be like). As a matter of fact, 'theoretical' knowledge that I'm a physician, say, provides grounds for your or my inferring (at least, some of) what I ought as a physician to do. If the above is correct it is hard to see what the 'is-ought' problem is supposed to be. I owe this line of thinking to some comments of JLA Garcia.

[16] A necessary condition, on this account, of grasping the self-evident basic good is that one have the data of one's 'felt inclinations' and that such inclinations direct us towards the differing goods, though such inclinations are not part of the criteria used to judge what is and is not good. See Finnis (1980), 34 and 402.

[17] See also Finnis (1983), 34.

[18] Grisez (2001), 9-10. See also Garcia (2001).

[19] How a child moves from mere liking/attraction to practical experience of a benefit is a question beyond the scope of this chapter. However, it is uncontroversial that practical experience helps us to understand what is beneficial. But it is also the case that we can understand many things as being beneficial without experiencing them ourselves. The point is not that there need be a conceptual connection always, but rather that experience of benefit of some kind gives us a type of knowledge seemingly unachievable from theoretical reflection only. Experience of benefit comes naturally and 'pre-rationally'– and becomes incorporated into our understanding of goods which creates our natural (rational) inclinations for new goods.

Such a position might be challenged by those who would make the following type of argument: God asserts a proposition. The proposition states a first principle of natural law. We know therefore, from theoretical premises, that this first principle of natural law is true. Here the inference is theoretical and there is no logical gap. Such arguments, whatever we might make of them, suggest at least that more work needs to be done to make clear what kind of 'gap' is supposed to hold which prevents inference from theoretical to practical knowledge.

[20] Theoretical *at least* in the sense referred to earlier.

[21] Compare debates concerning qualia in philosophy of mind.

[22] Lisska (1996) 161. George (1999a) has argued that practical reason grasps a basic good (an epistemological mode of analysis) and that working backwards, an ontological phenomenon can be discovered. But the connection between the two remains unclear.

[23] It is worth focussing on the general role of natural inclinations and the apprehension of goods. Thomas Aquinas at *Summa Theologica* I-II, q.94, a.2 says the following: "Since… good has the nature of an end, and evil, the nature of a contrary, hence it is that all those things to which man has a natural inclination, are naturally apprehended by reason as being good, and consequently as objects of pursuit, and their contraries as evil, and objects of avoidance." The inclinations referred here to are not 'pre-rational' it would seem (see Brock (2005) to which this account is heavily indebted). Rather, they are, as is the apprehension of good, *rational* and follow on from the apprehension. Only on this understanding can we make sense of the idea that "reason naturally apprehends as good all the things to which man is naturally inclined." Those things to which man has a natural inclination (i.e. one contained in man's fundamental dispositional properties) reason naturally apprehends as good, and it apprehends consequently that such a thing is to be pursued through action. As Brock puts it, "both the inclinations and the precepts follow upon the understanding of the objects as good." p.65. At *Summa Theologica* I, q.80, a.1, ad 3 Aquinas states that one thing is the inclination of each faculty toward its proper object, and another is the appetite that follows on apprehension; by the latter, he says, something is desired, not because it suits the act of this or that faculty, but because it suits the whole animal. Humans, as rational animals, grasp the proportion between themselves and the things that suit them – and some of this understanding comes 'naturally,' even if it takes time to develop.

244

However, I think this should be contrasted with the inclinations of, say, a baby. A baby has a pre-rational inclination toward the end of knowledge, contrasted with the self-conscious and rational inclination toward knowledge. In a way their objects are the same – they are the same 'thing' but under different 'rationes'. What the baby has is just a direct impulse toward knowledge; the 'rational' inclination (the inclination of the will) is toward knowledge understood as a particular human good. The latter is still natural, but it naturally 'flows from,' and is regulated according to the will's primary inclination, which is toward the human good as a whole. The baby's inclination is 'natural,' but it is not natural inclination in the properly 'human' mode, the mode of reason and will – rather he/she has a pre-rational and pre self-conscious inclination, ie an inclination not derived from knowledge of the object's goodness (though different from entirely unconscious inclinations such as the inclination of a heart to pump blood).

The point is that there are rational inclinations that are results of human understanding which are not pre-rational. If we view inclinations, as Anti-Naturalists cited appear to view them, as merely pre-rational impulses – things felt – it becomes hard to see how such an impulse becomes a rational grasping of a value i.e. how a pre-rational inclination becomes a rational one. On Brock's understanding of the cited (first) text from Aquinas, that explanation is given by accounting for "natural inclinations" as proceeding from an understanding of the good – these natural inclinations are "neither physical dispositions, nor spontaneous feelings, nor elements of man's very essence…they must be movements of man's rational appetite, inclinations of the human will. But if so, they must be inclinations that derive from reason's apprehension of their objects as good. The will is not moved toward anything except what reason – practical reason – apprehends as good and desirable" p.62. The baby's inclinations whilst 'natural' are not natural inclinations in the properly human mode of reason and will.

[24] Murphy (2001), 17.

[25] Haldane (2000).

26 By saying "constitutive" I am making only the minimal claim that one set can at the very least be said to be constitutive of the other. Murphy (2001) makes the following claim with regard to the two sets of judgements: "there is a set of truths, knowable by theoretical reason, that both affirms the existence of such a thing as human flourishing and states what aspects of human flourishing there are; and second that there are strong reasons to suppose that any state of affairs that theoretical reason correctly grasps as 'x is an aspect of human flourishing' would be correctly grasped by 'x is a good worth having', and vice versa." p.19.

Leaving aside the controversial point as to whether there can be a non-practical 'theoretical grasp' of human flourishing per se, Haldane's general point re facts about human nature and human goods worth having is plausible and helpful to remember. Although it is beyond the scope of this book to examine the possibility of tightly linking the two sets of judgements with reference to specific basic goods, Murphy (2001) Chapter 3 provides a clear account of why what he terms the "Real Identity Thesis" is plausible. One way to understand the link is to follow Aquinas (*Summa Theologica* I, q.16 a.4) in seeing that while the true regards being absolutely and immediately the true is more closely related to being than is good. For, as he says, "the true regards being itself simply and immediately; while the nature of good follows being in so far as being is in some way perfect; for thus it is desirable." So if good enters the mind later than true its nature includes the nature of perfect. By perfect is meant something like 'fullness of being' – and what determines this is, as we saw, the form of the being. The nature of 'a good' adds something new to 'fullness of being according to its nature' – it adds the relations of desire – final causality. This does not mean that our original apprehension of the good is not practical – for, as Brock (2005), in a brilliant analysis of Aquinas, points out: "grasping "the nature of a being" is needed for grasping what a good or a final cause is. It is needed as a principle of grasping perfection, "fullness of being." But the mind need not yet be seeing "the nature of being" as an effect of goodness…it need not be judging that a thing's perfection is what the thing is *aimed* at by nature, the *purpose* of its being what it is.…the first thing our mind apprehends as an effect of goodness, the effect tied to its initial grasp of "what a good is," is its own desire" p.74. And its own desire is apprehended in a practical way. So the perfect is fit to desire or we might say, virtuous to desire – and desirability is the note of the good (it might be added here that insofar as the good is virtuous to desire it is, in some thin sense, already practical).

[27] I do not here mean to imply that this is not also a metaphysical worldview adopted by Anti-Naturalists. It is, however, noticeable that thinkers such as Germain Grisez and John Finnis are deeply distrustful of function-type moral concerns usually associated with such a worldview (e.g. Grisez (1993), 646, fn.184, Finnis (1980), 48). Given this distrust Anti-Naturalist thinkers will not use arguments in sexual ethics that are reliant on 'function-type' arguments (see e.g. the arguments in GBFM (1988) as discussed in Chapter 1 of this book). See also Appendix on George (1999), 181 fn.2 and the 'perverted faculty' argument.

[28] Brock (1998), 96.

[29] Ibid.

[30] This is not to say that mechanistic processes do not form part of an explanation for a (more macro) process, merely that there is an irreducibly teleological framework into which they fit.

The attempt to eliminate from explanation the whole idea of directedness (e.g. Darwinian accounts which attempt to do away with talk of natural purposes/ends) becomes question-begging if we remember that such accounts do not deny the intentionality of mental acts, nor have made any progress towards accounting for them. It is also useful to remember that Darwinian evolution as such does not *define* function. Darwinian evolution is merely descriptive whereas facts about function are necessarily normative.

[31] Of course when we speak of rational action we are talking of a mind directing volitional acts. However, talk of final ends need not begin with (though it may end with) reference to a guiding intelligence. See Brock (1998), 98-99.

[32] See especially *A Treatise of Human Nature* book I, part III.

[33] Taylor (1980), 10-17.

[34] Brock (1998), 108.

[35] Ibid.

[36] A strict Darwinian has an additional reason to assert the functionality/parthood connection. For presumably he holds that it is the organ's performing a particular activity that helps the organism of which it is a part, and that it is this contribution that explains how this organ got to and stays where it is. See Levin (2005).

[37] This does not mean, as Murphy (2001) makes clear, that "there is some function y to which all of those parts of y must contribute. It means only that a condition of their being parts of the same object on account of their functions is that each of them contributes to at least one of the functions of the object." p.25.

[38] Aristotle, *Nicomachean Ethics,* 1097b24-1098a3. The argument is not, of course, a deductive one. Rather, the thought is that we need to identify a first principle which makes intelligible certain phenomena (the functioning of organs). That first principle is that the human being himself must have a function.

[39] See for example Wright (1973) and subsequent responses to his article. I owe much in this section to the discussion of functions in Murphy (2001).

[40] Levin (2005), 174.

[41] Healthy functioning is not defined by statistical normalcy in this respect. A malfunctioning heart is not defined as malfunctioning with regard to statistical normalcy.

[42] That is, propositions which contain constituent terms which are of equal scope as universal predicates. See Aristotle, *Posterior Analytics* I, 2, 72a6-19; I, 33, 88b30-89a4; II, 19.

[43] Garcia (1986), 242-245.

[44] Garcia (2010). However, the state of affairs and the (or a) person reacting need to be thought of simultaneously, as with beauty and the beholder.

[45] Garcia (1986) and (2010). See also references in Chapter 6.

[46] Garcia does not say, but it seems important to add, that the virtuous person would desire to take pleasure/enjoyment in the value, all things being equal.

[47] Our knowledge of 'rat flourishing' is not purely theoretical precisely because in order to understand the term flourishing it is necessary for us to have experienced benefit ourselves. Our knowledge of flourishing is practical in the sense of referring to this necessary input. However to talk of 'rat flourishing' as good does not necessarily commit us to any idea that that judgement need be action-guiding (if by action-guiding we mean something over-and-above the thought that this is, in the abstract, virtuous-to-desire).

[48] If we accept the idea of function at the organic level (leaving questions of inorganic teleology to one side) it seems that we must be committed to some notion of the good – not just good in the sense of contributing to something else but good forming part of the explanation of why organisms and organs do what they do. On a natural selection model of teleology, such as Mark Bedau's, it is unclear that we can even say that the heart pumps blood *because* it contributes to an organism's survival. Oderberg (2008), 263-264 fn.15 points out that we can't even say that the heart pumps blood because it contributes to the organism's survival "if it doesn't do so because survival is good (which itself implies…that it is the *organism* which is using its heart *for* its own survival)." For, as Oderberg later says with reference to Bedau's natural selection account of functions, if nature is thought to work blindly, i.e. "not only with no good end states in view, but with *nothing* in view, not even a contribution by anything to anything," then there can be no such thing as a teleology of the form: x performs a function y *because* the function y contributes to some result and the result *happens* to be good. Such a view of the good, implicit in any teleological explanation, is entirely compatible with the

idea that good states are those which it is virtuous to desire. For they are good states relative to an idealised rational perceiver. For a general defence of the possibility of functional explanations see Cohen (1978), 249-278.

[49] Function understood as function of organism or organ – and as the end realised through a particular casual pathway (*successful* functioning). The context of use should make clear the distinction to be made between a 'functioning' (or 'working') of a body part (e.g. a function of a mouth is eating) and the purpose served by that operation (e.g. the function of eating is nutrition). I will allude to where this distinction is relevant for my argument at appropriate points in the text.

[50] Of course there are functions and sub-functions in hierarchical order. An example relevant to this book would be: the function of a man's penis is sexual intercourse, allowing the deposit of semen in a woman's vagina, allowing for reproduction to take place. But from a wider perspective the function of such acts is the creation of new human life within a nurturing and educative marital context. So at a biological level a non-married couple would be exercising a reproductive function but would be thwarting the overall social function of such acts (assuming my later arguments are correct).

[51] This point is crucial to remember. Of course by not using certain functions we can diminish our flourishing (if I never exercise I damage my health). But this is a different matter from what is being discussed here, which is the active deliberate thwarting of functions by uses contrary to the goals of the function. GBFM (1988) in their discussion of contraception by not referring to the disvalue of function-thwarting, i.e. something that it is *prima facie* not virtuous-to-desire, are open to the criticism that their theory (as discussed in Chapter 1) pays insufficient attention to the contraceptive act itself: they attribute the evil of contraception to a contralife will – a will defined in terms of an end state.

In contrast, Smith (1991) writes: "…what one intends to do (the external act) is defined as good or bad independently of any act of the will. Thus contraception is an unnatural act that one can either choose or not choose to do. If one knowingly chooses to do something bad, one sins…" p.355. The term 'exterior' (or 'external') act is used in the literature in one of three ways. It may mean either, the exterior thing about which an exterior act concerns itself; the exterior act itself; or the physical/natural species of the exterior act. By using the term "external act" here Smith presumably means behaviour disentangled from any action-moulding intention. If this is what she means, and if we understand good/bad in terms of 'virtuous-to-desire' then it seems we can make some sense of this statement. However, we will still need to consider cases where a state of affairs that contains an inherent disvalue (e.g. a woman about to be raped brings about a state of temporary sterility – sterility being a 'health disvalue') might nevertheless be licitly brought about for overriding reasons, given that we are not here concerned with the thwarting of a chosen sexual act, which is arguably something else entirely. Similarly certain animal behaviours or states even though they have a *prima facie* disvalue can be brought about licitly for a good reason.

[52] Levin (2005), 173. Note that the teeth example is of permanent disabling, so an analogy in the sexual realm might be with a gender reassignment operation or a sterilisation.

[53] I leave to one side more controversial cases such as taking drugs as part of a drug trial which may give one false beliefs of a comparatively trivial nature in order for some medical goal to be advanced. Here an argument might be made for allowing a temporary thwarting, but not, I think, a permanent thwarting.

[54] And the differing importance can apply to the same organ.

[55] I am grateful to Edward Feser for suggesting this example and for illuminating discussions about these matters in general.

[56] Watt (2007), 544. See also Braine (1994).

[57] Braine (1994a), 227.

[58] Braine (1988), 6.

[59] It is important to note that enjoyment/pleasure itself does not constitute a 'basic good' – even if it can be a part of successful functioning. This is

primarily because there is no 'faculty' of pleasure as such. See Oderberg (2004). As Oderberg says: "the point about pleasure…is that it can accompany bad activity, and this in the sense that it can be bad *because of its very content*." Pleasure is virtuous to desire qua outcome of successful functioning. And pleasure is good if it is pleasure taken in successful functioning. But pleasure can be taken in activity that is immoral. To take pleasure in deliberately killing an innocent would be to take pleasure in something bad in its very content (basic goods are not like this – their content cannot be 'bad' in itself – only put to bad uses). While pleasure might be taken in the successful physical functioning of my arm's movement, and to *that* extent have a good content, this minimal good is an odd thing to take pleasure in given the harm I am doing in killing another person.

Pleasure, while not a 'basic good', is linked to functioning. And the virtuous person will prefer to take pleasure in those activities that he rationally prefers (i.e. good activities). None of this is to deny that pleasure can be a function of some activity. Sexual activity is pleasurable and a function of the pleasure might be to encourage further sexual activity – but whether that sexual activity is good (morally) will determine whether the pleasure is useful qua function at the social as well as the biological level. If the pleasure is separated from the good activity which naturally generates the pleasure then the pleasure is empty and does not serve a valuable function overall.

As the search for pleasures shows, not everything we find desirable is an intelligible/basic good. We are often (too often!) moved by concupiscence so that what we desire seems good merely because it is desired, and not, as would happen with the intellectual appetite, desired because it seems good in itself (although, as earlier stated, there might be *some* sense in which a wrongly desired thing is good in itself). As Brock (2005) points out, citing Aquinas on things that are good in themselves, "Neither reason's judgement that they are good, nor the will's resulting desire of them, supposes any prior appetitive response such as pleasure." p.66 (though see earlier distinctions between natural pre-rational and natural rational inclinations). Pleasure taken in genuine goods presupposes the judgement that they are good. And goods to which sense-appetite extends can, as we saw earlier, be understood before any urge is felt towards those goods. But, as Aquinas explains: "…what is desired according to concupiscence seems good because it is desired. For concupiscence perverts the judgement of reason, such that what is pleasant seems good to it. But what is desired with intellectual appetite is desired because it seems good in itself." p.66.

[60] According to Aristotelian/Thomist metaphysics, a substantial form permeates the entirety of the substance that possesses it, such that each part is fully human insofar as it is fully harnessed to the operations of the organism in which it exists. For more on this see Oderberg (2005).

[61] This is not to say that there might not be dispute as to what constitutes an 'attack'. But permanently disabling a healthy function must surely count as an attack on health if anything does (and is much more obviously an attack than a temporary suppression of a function). Thomas Pink has asked what we might make of an operation that meant my eyes functioned permanently as though I was wearing sun-glasses. The example is interesting but involves a relatively minor adaptation of a function rather than its complete disabling. Indeed nearly all the 'mini-functions' of the eyes are preserved here and the operation does not radically damage the essential function of the eyes. So such thought-experiments do not tell against my central thesis.

[62] Someone over-eating is not serving the overall flourishing of the organism, though there is a (micro?) value to the successful functioning of his jaws and so on.

[63] It should be remembered that, according to Aristotelian/Thomist metaphysics, it is rationality, and not so-called 'animal' features, that is the form of specifically human life. As the classic formulation has it: The rational soul is the substantial form of the body. In other words, this is what gives being to the whole human individual. Amerio (1996) makes this point, referring to man's sensitive, nutritive and respiratory faculties and whether they 'inform' man's life in the same way as rationality, stating: "They do not; his life is composed of these various things each having

its own value, but what informs the whole and makes man is his rationality." p.223 ftn55. This is not, however, to deny that man's 'animal-side' is fully permeated by the substantial form (a rational form) that makes him a human being.

[64] Acquired knowledge is also, according to Thomas Aquinas, a kind of knowledge which Christ possessed as a necessary consequence of the reality and completeness of His human nature.

[65] This is not to deny that it also has other functions (e.g. a urinary one). As pointed out in the brain case, different organs may have a multiplicity of functions, some with a more 'rational' and some with a more 'animal' nature. When discussing function-thwarting we are interested in thwarting in the sense of using e.g. an organ in a manner contrary to its purpose (and not merely using it for something other than its purpose/purposes). Nothing in this formulation requires that an organ should have only one function, or that its various functions are equally important. There can be a hierarchy of importance in the functions of a particular organ such that the thwarting of a particular function is a more serious matter than the thwarting of another function. And that hierarchy will be dictated, in the final analysis, by those functions which play a greater role in the achievement of overall human flourishing. In the case of reproductive activity we can talk of the immediate biological function and the further social function (the begetting and educating of children in a morally suitable environment). I am grateful to Edward Feser for many valuable discussions of these questions.

[66] And whether we accept an Intelligent Designer or natural selection account of how these organs came to be there is still a sense in which we can say the penis has a particular function. The strict proponent of purely natural selection still appears to need to talk in terms of adaptiveness and function, although such proponents need not be committed (and it would seem ultimately cannot be) to the idea of function as laid out in this chapter.

[67] As concerns the teleology of reproductive organs the entire process of arousal through to ejaculation has as its natural end the deposit of semen

into the vagina. The destination of the semen in the woman's body is internal to the teleology of the process, not a mere extra: the natural end isn't just getting semen out of the man's body, but getting it into a specific place in the body of the woman.

[68] See below for clarification as to what counts as an 'attack'.

[69] I am imagining an extreme case where someone is liable to be raped and any resultant pregnancy will kill them – and where there is no possibility of defence or temporary sterilisation. I am not here concerned to examine the licitness or otherwise of permanent sterilisation for a contraceptive purpose where the one sterilised intends to engage in sexual activity of a reproductive type. For a convincing argument as to why the principle of totality fails, of itself, to justify the use of contraception within marriage see McInerny (1993).

[70] Whether we regard fertility in an aged woman a sign of health or not is moot. In the Bible the miraculous restoration of fertility in aged women seems to be regarded as a blessing brought about through a restoration of healthy functioning, rather than as a production of a dysfunction, albeit one with a valuable outcome.

[71] Braine (1994), 229.

[72] Crawford (2006), 257-258.

[73] Flannery (2004), 19.

[74] We do, however, need to remember that 'mega functions' (such as procreative acts) can't be exercised without the exercise of all sorts of mini-functions. A perverse act must involve some of those mini-functions, for a perverse act must have *something* in common with the natural overall function it is supposed to be perverting. Sterilisation, however, does not generally fall foul of this objection, because it is the complete disabling of a 'mega function' rather than the co-opting of 'mini functions'.

[75] Note that this formulation is about determining the perversity of certain activities. It does not of itself prove that such perverse actions are morally wrong. But it does show their undesirability *pro tanto* and that undesirability will be generally greater the more central the role the faculty

plays in human life. Moreover where the permanent disabling of a function is concerned, we may have an independent reason to regard such activity as morally wrong inasmuch it constitutes an attack on a basic good, at least if it is not intended to serve the same basic good for that person overall.

[76] Though we might think about the case where a deodorant is used with the intention to start but not end the sweating process. The example of chewing sugar-free gum is often used as an example against perversion-of-function-type arguments and I am grateful to Alexander Pruss for the thoughts below (unpublished).

"Firstly, it is not at all clear that chewing gum frustrates the functions of teeth. However, even if we don't accept this we might formulate the problem thus: Is it an empty-pleasure unconnected with any genuine good – and is it moreover perverse activity according to the above principle? One might say on this question that just as our eyes are there to provide us information about the shapes and colors of things in the world, our tongue is there to provide us information about the chemical compositions of things in the world. The pleasures of the palate (as opposed to the stomach) are not, strictly speaking, the pleasures of eating, but the pleasures of tasting. There is, thus, nothing immoral about the practice of wine-tasting. Tasting is good in and of itself because it is informative, like seeing. Nor is tasting necessarily connected with eating. For one of the points of our having the faculty of taste is so as to be able to recognize when food is wholesome and when it is not. In the latter case, obviously, the food that was tasted is not to be eaten. Moreover, it seems perfectly licit to taste food prior to feeding it to a child, even if one does not swallow the food oneself (e.g., because of scarcity). So the pleasures of the palate are pleasures of sense. Sense is good, since it is knowledge. So the pleasures of the palate are innately good. Tasting something is akin to looking out the window at the beautiful green tree, gently lit up with spring sun. It does not, however, seem to me that the pleasures of orgasm are like that. They are not discriminating in the same way (e.g., they are not a way of telling whether the other person would be good as a spouse)."

[77] Though sterilisation is not typically done 'through' a function but by an external operation (tubal ligation in the case of a woman). Strictly this is not 'perverting' a faculty in using it but it is certainly an attack on a function which is, arguably, an even more profound attack and one that is 'perverse' in a wide sense. See also McCarthy (2009) some material from which is reproduced here.

[78] We might compare this with the following. Imagine a boy with legs that are so fragile that if he walks on the ground he is likely to get gangrene very quickly and die. He belongs to a nomadic tribe with only intermittent access to medical care. As he is a lively young boy it is impossible to stop him from walking (or to stop him every time he tries). Can the parents have an operation performed on his healthy ligaments in order to stop him from walking permanently? Walking is a teleological activity (as is gestating) and this teleological activity, like the pregnancy of the woman with a dangerous heart condition, is causing a health harm. In this case it seems reasonable to say that, in order to save the boy's life, an intervention on his ligaments might be made. Such cases differ from a case whereby a terrorist threatens to kill his captive unless he severs his own healthy ligaments. Here the captive is being asked to mutilate himself (i.e. directly attack his health) in a way that has no intrinsic connection to his possible death. To deny the importance of intrinsic connections in this area would be to allow the aggressive actions of others to dictate what counts as medicine (surely the area that ought to be appealed to when considering direct attacks on health).

[79] Grisez (1997), 251-255, appears to contradict his own moral theory by endorsing tubal ligation for social reasons. The position he enunciates would also, if followed consistently, justify sterilization of males for reasons of social benefit to the male.

[80] In this context, 'attack', at least as far as Grisez-Finnis use the term, means an intentional act against a particular good. I use the term primarily to cover intended acts against a particular good which aim to do serious and lasting damage. It is not clear to me that the suppression of a particular faculty which is associated with a particular good (or goods), if it is temporary and aimed at the overall achievement of that same good or

even another good is in every case wrong (or accurately described as an attack). Nor, even on my understanding, need all 'attacks' be regarded as wrong. We can think of war and capital punishment: the way in which we arrive at non-negotiable demands of basic human goods is complex and requires deep reflection on the nature of individual goods and the guilt or innocence of bearers of the goods. None of this is to deny the general plausibility of viewing the basic goods (linked to virtues) as non-negotiable ingredients of a rational moral framework.

[81] An interesting case arises where someone is mentally ill and is greatly distressed by the existence of their own healthy leg. In other words, a symptom of their illness is a misperception of reality. Can one amputate the leg in order to alleviate a symptom of the illness? Such an operation is certainly not a 'cure' of the patient's illness – but might it be seen as analogous to sedation? The operation is a permanent mutilation that does not directly address the mental illness (any more than sedation addresses the illness causing pain). Unlike sedation which merely causes a temporary cessation of mental functioning, amputation actually plays along with and encourages mental dysfunction, albeit in an attempt to prevent other such dysfunction.

Chapter 3: pp. 101-126

[1] Douglas (1996), 72. For reflections on the relationship between radical social changes in the West and the 'reinvented body', see Juvin (2010) and the review by Anderson (2006). An earlier version of this chapter was published in Watt (2011), 45-70.

[2] This is presumably also true of transgressions which themselves presuppose a societal framework of understanding. Mauss did not give an argument for his claim that "nothing is more essentially transmitted by a social process of learning than sexual behaviour." Whatever the truth of this, it is uncontroversially the case that the learning of bodily techniques, including sex, takes place within a general context of learning symbolic systems. Douglas gives the following plausible analysis of Mauss's denial that there is no such thing as 'natural' behaviour: "It

falsely poses the relation between nature and culture. Here I seek to identify a natural tendency to express situations of a certain kind in appropriate bodily style. Insofar as it is obeyed universally in all cultures, the tendency is natural. It is generated in response to a perceived social situation, but the latter always comes clothed in its local history and culture. Therefore the natural expression is culturally determined." Douglas (1996), 76.

The novelist and composer Anthony Burgess (of *A Clockwork Orange* fame) once offered, on a late night UK television show, the following eloquent reflections on divorce:

"Liking involves no discipline; love does...A marriage, say that lasts twenty years or more, is a kind of civilization, a kind of microcosm - it develops its own language, its own semiotics, its own slang, its own shorthand...sex is part of it, part of the semiotics. To destroy, wantonly, such a relationship, is like destroying a whole civilization." (*After Dark – What is Sex For?*, Channel 4, 21st May 1988 available at https://www. youtube.com/watch?v=GFlF5rxOzec accessed on 20/08/2015.)

[3] While we might see certain 'instincts' as 'drives' towards the good, they are pre-rational – though their operation will in practice normally presuppose some learning.

[4] Scruton (2006), 348-49. Clearly Scruton in saying that desire is socially constructed is not just relying on the point that desire needs an object. For Scruton's reflections on desire (including what constitutes 'normal' desire) and intentional objects see pp.59-138. His fascinating account (building on work by Thomas Nagel and Jean-Paul Sartre, though taking it in a very different direction) focuses attention not on the procreative and non-procreative distinction, but rather on the nuptial and non-nuptial (or the personal/impersonal) distinction. For Scruton, emphasis on the reproductive nature of the sexual act is a further point, not so much about the act as about its social context (he is dismissive of Anscombe's arguments against contraception p.287). But then, why not say that the social context, in 'constructivist' style (see below), informs the act itself, together with its biological meaning?

[5] Moore (2003), 211.

[6] Moore (2003), 280. Moore also writes, in criticising the work of Germain Grisez and Livio Melina, "For them, the putative objective meaning of sexual activity is supposed to be inherent in it, independent of the existence of any community which understands sexual activity to have that meaning…Meanings do not inhere in things, independently of communities. Meanings are about human understanding and human communication, and that depends on there being a community." p.279. Here, Moore does not in any way anchor such community interpretations of meaning in anything other than the views of the community, thus making it impossible to assess the accuracy or veracity of any particular interpretation of meaning (e.g. a community which believed that the 'real' meaning of sexual activity was to express contempt for another could in no sense be said to be wrong about that meaning, and no reason concerning the nature and purpose of sexual activity could be given to rebut such a view). This kind of approach is also found in Stanley Fish's writings on 'interpretive communities' in the context of literary criticism, which fail to answer the question of where such communities derive their meanings from, not least because the 'text' has effectively disappeared. This leads to the absurd idea, expressed by Fish, that "When you think a view wrong, you don't see what is seen by those who think it right" so that "to say of an assertion that it is 'not true' is to say that you don't understand it."

As Garcia (1997) points out, "Of course, doxastically to accept proposition P (e.g. to "think it right") commits me to rejecting (as "not true") its contradictory proposition not-P, even as understanding an assertion of P is impossible unless I would understand an assertion of not-P. So, Fish's claim, if true, would render impossible all understanding and belief. I admit I do not see what Fish sees in his claim, but I think that is because what he sees is not there." pp.232-3 fn.37.

[7] In making the comparison Moore (2003) observes, "Our own primitive sexual values, the values that we have absorbed from our infancy like our native language, can also seem natural, obvious, a matter of course. And so they are, to us. But since sense of the natural is again a result of

socialization, nature is a social construct." p.211. This, however, does not follow: our sense of what is good or bad for our health is also a result of socialization, but responds nonetheless to a real, physically-grounded state of affairs which we ignore at our peril. Moreover, in choosing language as his example Moore would need to accommodate the findings of Noam Chomsky (2006) on Universal Grammar, suggestive of, at least, a highly 'natural' grounding for language itself, regardless of what particular form it takes.

[8] Moore's denial of 'natural meaning' entails, he assumes, that all meaning is socially constructed.

[9] Douglas (1996), 91.

[10] Moore (2003), 278. Instructive for thinking about this area is CS Peirce's semiology, especially his distinction between 'icons' (which actually resemble the things they signify) and 'symbols' (which are purely conventional). The terminology may sound slightly odd to modern ears because in general usage 'symbol' is often used to mean what Peirce calls 'icon', but the distinction is a potent one (the third in the trio is 'index' – smoke is an index of fire, the word 'round' is a symbol of circular things, without being circular, marriage is an *icon* of Christ and the Church in the belief of Christians). The semiology of sex is 'iconic' and thus different from the conventional semiology of language.

[11] For convincing arguments against anti-essentialism see Oderberg (2007). For an example of a denial of the idea of a fixed human nature see Sartre (1989).

[12] This remains true, I think, even if we follow Chomsky (1988) in holding that, "There is no longer any definite conception of body. Rather, the material world is whatever we discover it to be, with whatever properties it must be assumed to have for the purposes of explanatory theory. Any intelligible theory that offers genuine explanations and that can be assimilated to the core notions of physics becomes part of the theory of the material world, part of our account of body. If we have such a theory in some domain, we seek to assimilate it to the core notions of physics, perhaps modifying these notions as we carry out this enterprise." p.144.

An Aristotelian conception of formal and final causes and a focus on immanent teleology may provide a way out of the problem Pruss identifies (see for example Feser (2008)). Either way, Pruss's point holds.

13 Handshakes could, of course, become 'sexual' (if not 'sex' in any true unitive sense) if they were used as a source of sexual pleasure. However, this itself would involve fragments of sexual function such as orgasm.

14 Huxley (1937) reminisced, "The liberation we desired was simultaneously liberation from a certain political and economic system and liberation from a certain system of morality. We objected to the morality because it interfered with our sexual freedom; we objected to the political and economic system because it was unjust. The supporters of these systems claimed that in some way they embodied the meaning (a Christian meaning, they insisted) of the world. There was one admirably simple method of confuting these people and at the same time justifying ourselves in our political and erotic revolt: we could deny that the world had any meaning whatsoever." p. 273.

15 Anscombe (1972) makes the point, reflecting on marriage and its connection with the fact that human sex concerns the transmission of human life, that, "There is no such thing as a casual, non significant sexual act; everyone knows this. Contrast sex with eating – you're strolling along a lane, you see a mushroom on a bank as you pass by, you know about mushrooms, you pick it and eat it quite casually – sex is never like that. That's why virtue in connection with eating is basically a matter only of the *pattern* of one's eating habits. But virtue in sex – chastity – is not *only* a matter of such a pattern, that is of its role in a pair of lives. A single sexual action can be bad even without regard to its context, its further intentions and motives." p.24. In responding to Anscombe's article, Williams and Tanner (1972) object that Anscombe "seems to endorse [the idea] that if you treat some activity lightly on certain occasions, then you are very likely to adopt a frivolous attitude towards it in general." This, they add, is "simply absurd dogma" p.47. The matter is, I believe, best resolved by reflection on the meaning of marriage and its relation to the sexual act, something barely mentioned by Anscombe.

[16] The moral importance of certain chosen physical structures, and the 'sexual' nature of these structures in themselves, is seemingly denied by Grisez (1993) when he writes, "While self-stimulation to obtain a semen sample is physically the same as any other masturbation, it is morally different" (because the aim is not to experience orgasm). Grisez adds, however, that "obtaining a semen sample in this way is a grave matter, for it is a proximate occasion of grave sin (the more or less probable sexual fantasy and willing of the experienced sexual satisfaction)" p.648 fn.187. This passage makes clear that Grisez does not locate the wrongness of certain kinds of solitary sexual activity in physical structures intended by the agent – whatever the further intention – but rather in what he presumes to be the likely willed experience of certain sexual fantasies and pleasures. For more on this passage see Appendix.

[17] Brock (2008), 61-62. One way in which acts that are *contra naturam* (e.g. sodomy) can be distinguished from "normal fornication" is described by the Thomist scholar Lawrence Dewan, O.P. (2002): "Thomas argues, on the basis of teleology, that every emission of seed that takes place in such a way that generation cannot result or suitably result is against a good of the human being. Thus, if this is purposely done, it is a sin. He notes first the case of sins against nature (such as contraception). He goes on to take the case of an emission of seed that takes place in such a fashion that generation can indeed follow, but suitable education is impeded." *Summa Contra Gentiles* III, c.122 (Pera, ed., 2955) makes it clear that "the inordinate emission of seed opposes [*repugnat*] *the good of the nature*, which is the preservation of the species." Dewan comments on this, "the whole judgement is based on the justice involved in the common good of humanity and the particular good of individuals who may be born in unsuitable circumstances for wholesome human life."

The serious wrongness of sins against nature (as opposed to e.g. the sexual sin of normal fornication/adultery), is explained by Aquinas as follows: "It is to be said that in any domain the corruption of the principle on which all else depends is what is worst. Now, the principles of reason are those things which are in function of nature; for reason, those things being presupposed which are determined by nature, disposes the others in the way that agrees (with nature). And this is apparent both in speculative and in practical (matters). And thus, just as in speculative matters error concerning those things knowledge of which is naturally implanted in man is most serious and most unseemly, so also in matters of action to act against what is determined in function of nature is most serious and unseemly. Therefore, since in sins which are against nature a man transgresses that which is determined in function of nature regarding sexual activity, hence it is that in such matter this sin is most serious" (*Summa Theologiae* II-II, q.154, a.12 (2185b12-30)), 304-306).

One difficulty with the account of 'natural' and 'unnatural' acts in Aquinas is that it locates the perversion of the function of sexual activity primarily in the immediate physical/biological species of the act rather than in the *telos* of sexual activity insofar as it relates to the end of the proper nurturing and education of biological offspring and the kind of spousal relationship conducive to that. It is not immediately clear why the former should take priority over the latter. One way in which we might make sense of the distinction is to reflect on how a society which normalises sodomy is one which is far more likely (than, say, a merely heavily adulterous society) to lose sight of the fact that sexual organs and activity have any *telos* at all.

[18] See the list of references to Aquinas on this in Finnis (1998), 143-154. See also the exposition of Aquinas (and to some extent Aristotle) in Flannery (2004).

[19] It should be noted that the Catechism of the Council of Trent, in talking of the indissolubility of marriage, states, "Although it belongs to marriage as a natural contract to be indissoluble, yet its indissolubility arises principally from its nature as a Sacrament, as it is the sacramental character that, in all its natural relations, elevates marriage to the highest perfection. In any event, dissolubility is at once opposed to the proper education of children, and to the other advantages of marriage." (P. II. C. 8, qu. 11) *Catechism of the Council of Trent* (1982), 343.

[20] Boyle (1990), 7.

[21] We should note here that marriage, in the understanding of the Church, as expressed in the *Catechism of the Council of Trent* and the *Catechism*

of the Catholic Church and the 1983 *Code of Canon Law,* is broadly held as a covenant "by which a man and a woman establish between themselves a partnership of the whole of life." Flannery (2004), in discussing this passage in the context of marriage for mentally disabled people, tells us, "This mature joining of interests is what marriage *is*. This nature does not alter to conform to the condition of the potential spouses; rather, the potential spouses choose *it* as something that exists independently of whether they choose it – or are capable of choosing it – or not." p.23.

The literary critic Eagleton (1987), in discussing marriage in Shakespeare's comedies, describes sexual desire as finding its true (natural) form in that institution: "Marriage is not an arbitrary force which coercively hems in desire, but reveals its very inward structure – what desire, if only it had known, had wanted all the time. When you discover your appropriate marriage partner you can look back, rewrite your autobiography and recognize that all your previously coveted objects were in fact treacherous, displaced parodies of the real thing, shadows of the true substance...Marriage is natural, in the sense of being an outward sign or social role which expresses your authentic inward being, as opposed to those deceitful idioms which belie it. It is the true language of the erotic self, the point at which spontaneity of individual feeling and the stability of public institutions harmoniously interlock. It is at once a free personal choice and impersonal bond, 'subjective' and 'objective' together, an exchange of bodies which becomes the medium of the fullest mutuality of minds." pp.20-21. Such thinking complements well what I have tried to argue in this book.

[22] This usage is generally taken to require indissolubility. That said, it should be noted that writers such as Robert Bellarmine and Francisco Suarez held that the prohibition of divorce was a divine and not a natural precept. However, see also Pope Pius IX's *Syllabus of Errors*, which under the heading "Errors Concerning Christian Marriage," condemns as erroneous the following proposition: "67. By the law of nature, the marriage tie is not indissoluble, and in many cases divorce properly so called may be decreed by the civil authority." Ibid.; Allocution "Acerbissimum," Sept. 27, 1852.

[23] An institution, including a conventionally-established institution, can have a *telos*, just as a natural substance does. Sokolowski (2004) puts it well: "Artifacts and institutions, things brought about by human making and agreements, have essences and ends. It is not the case that only natural substances have a *telos*. Consider an institution such as an art museum. Its *telos* is to make works of art available for public viewing, and part of this activity will be the acquisition and preservation of such works...It is interesting and important to note that even though artifacts and institutions are brought about by human beings to serve our purposes and ends, we cannot change what they are...even as instrumental beings, they have their own nature or essence or ends...We may have brought them into being, but they do not become our purposes. They retain their own ends and we have to subordinate ourselves to them. To claim that institutions and artifacts have no definition, and they could be changed at will, would mean they could not be ruined or destroyed by us. Any change would just be a redefinition, carried out by us, who would have freely defined the thing in question in the first place," pp.510-511. Given that the essence is that which is the 'reason for the existence' of the institution, then if it is to remain the institution it is it must keep its essence. What is said here refers to humanly created rather than 'natural' institutions, but applies *a fortiori* to the latter which are in some sense 'basic' as regards human flourishing.

[24] St Clair (1989), 81.

[25] Donagan (1971), 102. Boyle (1990) draws attention to this statement.

[26] Kant (1996), 63.

[27] Scruton (2006) and others will further argue that such practices are ultimately not fulfilling of sexual desire. Lawrence (1979), a writer attuned to the mystery of sex, also sees sexual desire's fulfilment in faithful marriage: "All the literature of the world shows how profound is the instinct for fidelity in both man and woman, how men and women hanker restlessly after the satisfaction of this instinct, and fret at their own inability to find the real mode of fidelity. The instinct of fidelity is perhaps the deepest instinct in the great complex we call sex. Where there is real sex

there is the underlying passion for fidelity. And the prostitute knows this, because she is up against it. She can only keep men who have no real sex, the counterfeits: and these she despises. The men with real sex leave her inevitably, as unable to satisfy their real desire." p.343. Instructive on this topic are Mozart's operas *Cosi fan Tutte, Don Giovanni* and *The Marriage of Figaro*.

[28] Of course the increased practice of SS may not lead to a decrease, in all cases, of PS. But the point here is that dispositions are affected in important ways such that the possible commitment to PS is rendered more difficult. While various kinds of non-sexual activity can undermine commitment to PS, SS is especially relevant and serious in undermining it because it is, like PS, sexual activity (see below). Finnis (1994), (1997) has attempted to show how the practice of SS can undermine commitment to PS in terms of the effects of 'conditional willing'. This argument is challenged in the next chapter of this book.

[29] "Substitutionary" here encompasses activities which tend to engender in participants a lack of differentiation between that which needs to be distinguished (SS and PS) as well as activity which entirely 'displaces' PS both in terms of appreciation of its status and in the ability of practitioners to act upon that appreciation.

[30] James Alison, in his defence of the moral acceptability of homosexual activity, observes that "if it were the case that the homosexual inclination is simply a thing that just is "like that," and is not a disfiguration of anything, in that case the official characterisation [of the Catholic Church], and along with it the absolute prohibition, is false." He later adds, "if it were the case that not all human beings are intrinsically heterosexual, then extending the opportunity to marry to same-sex couples would present no threat to the existence of heterosexual marriage, and there would be no logical reason why same-sex couples should be deprived of that opportunity," Alison (2005). Note however that the movement for 'gay marriage' necessarily suggests that gay sex (and gay partnership built around sex) are *not* just "like that" i.e. they are related in important ways to heterosexual sex and marriage.

[31] It is relevant here that the sensation of orgasm is similar in SS and PS, which further supports the claim that couples are unlikely to treat SS and PS as completely separate kinds of activity. Indeed it is plausible to say that SS is an illusion of PS. But in order to say this one needs to support the claim that the sensation of pleasure is tied innately to PS. There is a plausible evolutionary story about this – namely that the pleasure is there to motivate PS (on the evolutionary story see Levin (2005) 171-190). And while evolutionary stories aren't conclusive teleologically (how could they be?), pleasure certainly does make sense teleologically if we think of it as something designed to motivate something as valuable as procreative activity. The orgasm, of course, distinguishes SS from handshakes (indeed, if a handshake were intended to produce the same pleasure as central cases of PS, the handshake would, on this account, be morally problematic).

[32] Primoratz (1999), 17.

[33] Primoratz (1999), 32. It should be noted that the concern here is with sex per se rather than marital/non-marital sex.

[34] Primoratz (1999), 32-33. Later in the same passage Primoratz announces that he is open to the possibility that "sex without love is actually better, as sex, than sex as part of a loving relationship." Quite how he would make this comparison, especially given his view that sex can have no inherent purpose or meaning (other than what its participants decide upon) is left unresolved. Primoratz shows no concern over questions of moral character, virtue or human flourishing, speaking instead of what might or might not be learned from "psychological research."

[35] Even these essentially conventional and therefore semantically highly mutable signs carry a symbolic charge in our culture, where a man holding hands with someone else's wife would not be morally neutral in many circumstances. However, holding hands is not, like intercourse (or not to the same extent) 'iconic' (in CS Peirce's terms) as the 'union' created is considerably less than that of a joint natural function; holding hands could thus have a different meaning in other cultures/subcultures. An extreme but not uncommon case of a highly mutable sign being

treated as not morally neutral (or at least treated in a highly 'special' and restrictive way) is kissing on the lips. Whereas Aquinas sees this as culturally variable in terms of symbolic charge, unlike sexual activity, the feminist and sexual liberationist Wypijewski (2009) notes that kissing on the mouth is so intensely intimate that, "there is a reason that kissing on the mouth is often the line that workers who are paid for sex will not cross." It is not clear though whether Wypijewski is referring to mouth kisses intended to sexually arouse and in a highly sexualised context as opposed to brief mouth kisses of affectionate greeting. Whatever one might make of the conventionality of such signs as this, they do not bear directly on the argument forwarded here concerning sexual acts per se.

On signs and meaning, recall Leontes' jealous words in Shakespeare's *The Winter's Tale* where he asks, "Is whispering nothing? Is leaning cheek to cheek?... Why, then the world and all that's in't is nothing; The covering sky is nothing; Bohemia nothing; My wife is nothing; nor nothing have these nothings, If this be nothing."

[36] As Flannery (2004) concisely put it when discussing marriage in relation to mental disability: "Marriage is something that exists apart from the question of whether these two persons are sterile or not – just as it exists apart from the question of whether a mentally *capable* couple are sterile or not. The *bonum prolis* which helps to define marriage refers not to the possible offspring of any particular couple but to what marriage is and to why it exists as a distinct, regulated human practice. This objective, institutional nature of marriage both makes it possible for mentally capable but sterile couples to marry *and* makes it impossible for those who are incapable of the appropriate consent to do the same. ...moral analysis begins...with *social* norms." p.24.

[37] Moore (2003), 280.

[38] Foucault (1990), (1980) does offer the thought that the basis of the relationship of power lies in the hostile engagement of forces and tries to apply this idea to sexual relationships. But "power" is not defined in any enlightening way, nor is it explained why "power" itself is something always to be "unmasked" and uprooted (if such a notion is even coherent),

as opposed to accommodated. Foucault, of course, famously talks of the "problematisation" of, among other things, sexual behaviour, as though this issues from the ascendant systems of society. He gives no plausible historical verification for his claims, which his own approach necessarily demands and without which the whole enterprise appears as little more than a way of distracting people from examining deep moral phenomena (the term "moral panic" is sometimes used in our day to do the same thing, often when no case has been made in a morally serious way to address the social reaction under consideration). Foucault's later attempts to explain sexual phenomena in terms of pleasure have a similar effect and suffer from the same problems as some of the approaches criticised later in this book.

Foucault's 'history of problematisation' is supposed to be a 'history of truth' but here truth is no longer anything absolute and transcendent but is reducible to mere unmoored 'discourse.' At a stretch we can say that Foucault tends to see sexual relations only in 'social' terms more appropriate to the analysis of political and economic relations. Yet the biological nature of the sexual sphere and the fundamental problems that are the subject matter of sexual ethics suggest that this approach is deeply misguided. The work in sexual phenomenology of Aurel Kolnai and Dietrich von Hildebrand (especially concerning notions of sexual purity and 'dirt') provides ample evidence for seeing such 'problematisation' as rooted in something far removed from social forces of the kind Foucault somewhat incoherently refers to. For a useful discussion of Foucault and his neo-Gnosticism and concern with power and knowledge together with that of his predecessors and successors see Preparata (2007). See also the overview in Scruton (1985), 31-45.

[39] With regard to physical structures it is useful to consider the following (deeply unpleasant) thought-experiment, which was suggested to me by Tim Wilkinson: Imagine a woman is injured so that her vagina is blocked and could not provide access to the uterus, but her rectum now does provide such access. Would anal sex be OK in this circumstance? I would answer - surely not, because the vagina still has a proper sexual/ reproductive *function* while the rectum has no such 'function'. One could

not say that the woman subsequently became 'infertile' if the rectum no longer provided passage to the uterus: her health would not be damaged by this but rather the reverse.

[40] Gormally (1997).

[41] For a searching philosophical examination of the ethical issues surrounding the bond of pregnancy see Watt (2016).

[42] See Pruss (2013).

[43] This point is ignored by Donagan (1977) who writes, summarising Aquinas, "since sexual gratification is obtained from procreative acts, the natural end of which is to produce children, and since it is impermissible to produce children except in a monogamous family, anybody who seeks sexual gratification except in nondeviant intercourse as husband or wife in such a family violates the fundamental human good of procreation." Yet this characterisation mentions nothing of the unitive aspect of procreative intercourse and goods. By not attending to these elements of Aquinas's thought Donagan too hastily concludes that "with regard to deviant sexual acts which do not lead to procreation, it does not seem to follow, merely because sexual gratification is obtained from them as well as from nondeviant intercourse, that to seek sexual gratification in them *eo ipso* violates the human good of procreation." pp.105-106.

[44] One way of envisaging this is set forth by Amerio (1996), 661: "Pius XI teaches [*Casti connubii* 24 and 25] that the mutual perfecting of the spouses 'can be called the primary reason and motive for marriage,' but it must be remembered that in his teaching, the mutual integration of lives that perfects the spouses includes the mutual gift of their bodies, which in the natural course of things is the source of offspring; and he regards offspring as the highest good marriage can produce. Without believing in the myths of the ancient world, we can still say that in their act of love, the spouses *are their offspring*: 'the marriage bed upon which' as Penelope says to Odysseus 'we were together in our son Telemachus.'" Such a view must not be confused with Schopenhauer's quite alien idea that an individual's sexual behaviour is essentially in the grip of a determinative impersonal force such that the 'will to life' of unconceived offspring

draws the sexual partners together, and couples are deluded if they think they act out of their own interests.

[45] On condomistic sex to prevent AIDS or other sexually transmitted infections see McCarthy and Pruss (2011).

[46] Read (2010), quoted in response to an imagined objection to Read's own pro-marriage position: "You may think that the link between people's sex lives and the suffering of children is tenuous."

[47] Crawford (2006), 256-257. Even Alison (2005) observes that he does not "question that as a matter of common sense, human *reproduction* is intrinsically dependent on the biological complementarity of the sexes." ftn4. He says this despite the fact that he holds it possible that human beings are not "intrinsically heterosexual." Alison might defend himself from the charge of contradiction by saying something like, pre or post-menopausal women – and therefore women generally – are not *intrinsically* fertile even if conception requires fertile women (though of course I would answer that as human beings we have a fundamental *fertile orientation* just as we are fundamentally masculine or feminine – see below).

[48] Vidal (1994) famously opined, before it was publicly fashionable, that, "Actually, there is no such thing as a homosexual person, any more than there is such a thing as a heterosexual person. The words are adjectives describing sexual acts, not people. Those sexual acts are entirely natural; if they were not, no one would perform them…Gay militants now assert that there is something called gay sensibility, the outward and visible sign of a new kind of human being. Thus madness begets madness." p.550. Vidal is I think correct to reject the idea that there is such a thing as a 'homosexual person', though note that an additional reason for thinking that sex might be 'special' is the extraordinary way in which many people are quite prepared to ground a deep identity around same-sex attraction and the predilection for homosexual acts. Where Vidal errs is in assuming that homosexual acts are perfectly 'natural' and not to be importantly distinguished from heterosexual acts. On this question see the arguments throughout this book; however, the distinction between SS and PS is the relevant moral distinction to be made here. Useful on the

identity question are the words of Check (2015), "So, I would offer this distinction to you: homosexuality is not first about sex or about relationships, *it is a misperception of identity*. In turn, that misperception can lead to a misdirected search to answer the desires of the heart. How we understand ourselves – our identity – influences, even determines, how we try to meet the needs and wants of the heart...*Agere sequitur esse*, action follows being or, if I may formulate it this way, actions follows identity, whether identity is properly understood or misperceived. I will act and make choices according to how I understand myself." p.224.

[49] Crawford (2006), 253-254. A liberal observer such as Nagel (1998) is aware of how changes in public recognition of certain fundamentally established social institutions – even if he thinks such institutions have no inherently rational basis – can have hugely significant consequences: "Although premarital sex is by now widely accepted, the institution of heterosexual marriage probably confers a derivative blessing on heterosexual partnerships of all kinds. That is why the idea of homosexual marriage produces so much alarm: It threatens to remove that contrastive protection, by turning marriage into a license for anyone to do anything with anybody. There is a genuine conflict here, but it seems to me that the right direction of development is not to expand marriage, but to extend the informal protection of intimacy without the need for secrecy to a broader range of sexual relations."

Chapter 4: pp. 127-140

[1] The argument for how conditional intentions can violate commitment to the good of marriage as expressed in the marital act is set out in most detail in a general paper by Finnis (1994) and also in Finnis (1997). In more condensed form, the argument is put forward in Finnis (1998) and in Finnis (2009). The latter paper is notable for the claim that "Humeian and *Kantian* models" (my emphasis) are those "in which sub-rational motivations set the ends, goals, purposes and reason comes in only to devise means and/or to eliminate the irrationality of contradiction" p.390. This tellingly erroneous claim, as any reading of Kant will confirm, fails

to take into account clear statements to be found in e.g. *Grounding for the Metaphysics of Morals* #413ftn3 where Kant asserts, as he does elsewhere, the existence of a "pure" moral interest in a course of action as intrinsically right. See also Allison (1990).

[2] For a brief summary of the 'basic goods' and what is meant by 'against,' see Chapters 1 and 2. As we saw in Chapter 1, according to New Natural Law Theory, sexual immorality can involve offences against the good of life, even if it necessarily also involves offences against the good of marriage.

[3] I am much indebted to Tim Wilkinson for valuable conversations, disagreements and observations about conditional intentions, especially in relation to the earlier Finnis paper, and for the useful term 'contingent intention.'

[4] Finnis (1994), 172-173.

[5] It would, however, be surprising if coldblooded book retention without current lustful feeling were not seriously unchaste as opposed to a momentarily roving eye which might be a lesser infringement of chastity.

[6] Finnis (1994), 173.

[7] Finnis (1994), 173-174 and refs therein.

[8] The question here is not whether such a mental stance is wrong, but rather whether it is the kind of thing Aquinas was referring to in the passage cited. Finnis (1994) 174 fn.42 writes, of de Scala, "he notes the explanation offered by Augustine and Jerome, that the phrase is equivalent to "so that he may look at her in order inwardly to lust after doing it [adultery] *if* the opportunity were to present itself (*ides ut eam eo fine videat ut faceret si facultas se offeret*)." With regard to what I here call "speculative preparation" it might be objected that all that is prepared for is a future decision, assuming that the husband has not yet decided to commit adultery (by analogy, we might think of a woman who has a prenatal test not knowing what she would decide concerning abortion if a disability were detected).

[9] Though I do not deny that if lusting after someone is adultery of the heart, even if there is no intention to actually commit adultery, then it

may not be at all unreasonable so to describe preparatory intentions for possible future choices to commit adultery.

[10] Finnis (1997).

[11] Finnis (1997), 119. Grisez (1993) discusses these and related issues at pp.553-737.

[12] This does not appear to differ from possessing a conditional intention.

[13] Finnis (1997), 119-120.

[14] We can distinguish between X's wanting to (perform-an-action-of-type) V-in-circumstance-C, on the one hand, and, on the other, X, when he's in circumstance C, wanting to V. The former will normally be immoral or at least morally problematic when V-ing-in-C would itself be immoral; not necessarily so the latter. As Francis shouldn't take and wear your coat when you've denied Francis permission, so Francis shouldn't want it to be the case that both (i) you deny him permission to take and wear your coat and (ii) he nevertheless does so. It is, however, less clear that in a situation where you've denied Francis your permission to take and wear your coat, it's wrong not just for Francis to do so anyway but even (avoidably) for Francis to (continue to) want to do so. Likewise, even if it's morally wrong for Howard (avoidably and with his own consent) to desire extramarital sexual contact, that may not exclude Howard's wanting (in the weak sense of finding appeal in the thought of) sexual contact with Cordelia, even though they are not in fact married to one another. That Howard isn't really married to Cordelia doesn't mean that Howard's wanting sex with Cordelia has to be Howard's wanting unmarried sex with her. Is it necessary for moral permissibility (better, to avoid vice) that Howard specifically imagine himself to be married to Cordelia whenever Howard thinks, perhaps in a vague and passing way, about touching Cordelia? What if Howard merely leaves that detail out of the imagined scenario? Does Francis have first to imagine buying or borrowing the coat licitly to take pleasure in thought of wearing it? Is sex different? I am grateful to JLA Garcia for this example and subsequent discussions and disagreements.

[15] Finnis (1997), 120. Consent here is understood, in Finnis's terms (fn.102) as "a disposition which (like all other acts) lasts in the will un-

less and until reversed by being repudiated (repented of, formally or in-formally)."

[16] Recall that Finnis is concerned not merely about 'damage to capacity' but about conditional intentions, as he sees them. It is not clear here how 'conditional intentions' are supposed to 'damage capacity' or whether they might be the result of a 'damaged capacity' in the first place and not vice versa.

[17] Ibid.

[18] As with Finnis's subsequent example, A is framed in the first person – i.e. as an *acknowledged* contingency. That means that Finnis's definition of conditional willing in terms of the truth of an objective counterfactual conditional is never tested in these examples. Perhaps this is a mistake, and Finnis only means to address counterfactuals that are acknowledged as true by the party at the time the spouse has sex (or some time before, and without repentance).

[19] Finnis (1997), 103.

[20] There is a distinction to be made between "I am not committed enough even to want to exclude alternative partners" and alternatively "I am so weak in these matters I don't know what I'd do."

[21] Finnis (1997), 121.

[22] Ibid.

[23] Finnis (1997), 122.

[24] Ibid.

[25] Ibid.

[26] Ibid.

[27] Ibid.

[28] Finnis (1997), 123.

[29] Finnis (1997), 122-123.

[30] Certainly the Catholic Church has not pronounced on this question, to the best of my knowledge, and many Catholic ethicists would accept

such tests. Nevertheless the man may, in fact, be mistaken in thinking of the structure of intercourse here as morally OK (or as 'having some value' in Finnis's terms).

[31] See for example Williams (1995), 35-45 and Smart and Williams (1973).

[32] That said, an error can occur when people assume that sex is necessarily unethical if one or both spouses do not feel fully reconciled after a quarrel, not seeing that where the preconditions are in place, such feelings, within reason, need not undermine the goodness (and indeed potentially reconciliatory powers) of the act itself. Certain modern religious writings on sex seem to encourage a focus on sexual and emotional perfectionism that is positively harmful to couples.

[33] A couple tired of NFP who decide on sterilization could still be having marital intercourse because they are accepting all the fertility that is here *now* (i.e. during the current infertile period). In contrast, a couple one or both of whom intend an act of infidelity in the near future cannot have genuine marital intercourse because fidelity is not, unlike acceptance of fertility (outside the context of getting married in the first place) a matter of individual acts but is a longer-term concept. My point about acts and moral agents in the main text should not be seen as similar to the kind of approach which Bennett (1995) has championed, namely the idea that an agent's 'intentions' are only of real relevance in assessing his/her moral character but not when assessing the 'first-order' moral question concerning the permissibility or impermissibility of an act. This view is addressed briefly in the next chapter. For now it is important to distinguish between a view about the significance for someone's character of the background positions that person holds, without this being assumed to affect radically the morality of an act (though it may of course affect the agent's appreciation of the goodness of the act) and the very different view of Bennett described above.

Chapter 5: pp. 141-168

[1] This depiction of a false chastity appears to lead to the despairing idea that where chastity is difficult it shouldn't be striven for. Thus does

Nietzsche reveal his opposition to Christianity, even while apparently (and it is only apparently) recognising the value of chastity. And to hold that the 'demandingness' of the virtue of chastity is something placing unreasonable burdens on someone is simply to postpone the question of why the ideal virtuous person is one to whom such a consideration is morally decisive in giving advice. While the traditional moralist might regard 'demandingness' as no objection to the duty to live a chaste life, many who reject such a view will, nevertheless, regard considerations of 'demandingness' as morally irrelevant in other areas of ethics such as justice.

[2] John Paul II (1997), 105 points out that, according to ancient translations, the text is "...has already made her an adulteress in his heart," a formula which seems to be more exact." I do not think this difference affects what I have to say on the passage, though I do think that it throws into sharp relief the difficulties with Gareth Moore's analysis below.

[3] For a slightly more theological take on these matters, see Appendix.

[4] Moore (1992), 17-18.

[5] Moore (1992), 20. Moore's words on 'imagination' do allow for a wide-range of 'morally permissible' fantasy. For example he writes, "If I imagine committing adultery with my neighbour's wife, it may be because I want to commit adultery with her – because I am committing adultery with her in my heart. But no such thing need be in question. It may just be a pleasant way to idle away a few spare moments...it is not a very laudable thing to do, and I should probably be discouraged from doing it, but it is not adultery of the heart. Or I may be confused about whether I want to commit adultery with her; in this case I may use fantasy as a way of thinking imaginatively about the situation, and that may show me that it is a bad thing to do. Or I may be an actor or a priest or some sympathetic person trying to understand what it is like to be in such a position." p.22. Here, however, we need to ask some precise questions which open the way for our later discussions of objectification and sexual virtue.

[6] Philosopher Blackburn (2004), 55 ignorantly conflates temptation with the intent of lusting by stating, "for Christians, the first jolt or movement

or agitation has become the hiss of the serpent, temptation. And even to hear the hiss of the serpent sullies you." What, then, of talk of Christian purity maintained through resistance to temptation? An example of what Blackburn, apparently an expert on lust (and proponent of lowering the age at which teenagers can purchase vibrators), regards as a serious philosophical argument can be found on p.71 of his book.

[7] Kolnai (2005), 107.

[8] John Paul II (1997) 150-151.On the subject of the 'heart' see Spaemann (2006) who states, for instance, that "the conversion of the heart is not an organic development; it is a prior moment of decision that fixes the direction in which any possible development shall go. It belongs to the level of 'secondary volitions,' i.e. how we orient ourselves to the concrete objects of our will." p. 206. Earlier Spaemann notes that, contra Socrates, the New Testament sees evil as the basis of ignorance and that the term 'heart' underlines this development "and so amounts, more or less, to the discovery of the person...the decision between good and evil, light and darkness, is not a decision about an idea, but about a person, who is the ultimate revelation of truth. The Johannine Christ sees sin as actually consisting in the fact that 'they do not believe in me.' In another place he can say: 'If I had not come...they would not have sin' [John 15:22]. Knowledge of the truth is thought of as a personal act of belief. Truth itself appears not as the universal that is greater than any individual, but as the unique countenance of another individual person." p.21. Regardless of our views about the existence or otherwise of a Divine Person, such speculations are useful in helping us to locate the place the 'heart' or internal choices ought to play in moral considerations.

[9] Watson (2004), 156.

[10] *De spiritu et littera,* 6.

[11] Watson (2004), 156-157. Watson also claims, and Augustine apparently agrees, that Romans 7.15 has a specifically sexual instance of concupiscence in mind.

[12] To this kind of objection Moore (1992) replies, "What I do not and cannot do in the matter of a fantasy partner is actually to set my desire

on somebody. I am at most imagining somebody on whom I imagine I set my desire. So this situation is far removed from what Jesus is actually talking about when he speaks of committing adultery in the heart." p.21. But if I am on a diet and think about an enticing chocolate cake, there is surely a sense in which I desire that (imaginary) cake. I may then proceed to look for a similar cake in a cafe – perhaps on my neighbour's plate if he is momentarily distracted. It should be noted that Moore later suggests of masturbation (very definitely a sexual act which typically will involve setting a desire on a fantasy partner in order to achieve orgasm), that "somebody might find in masturbation one of his few consolations in a life that is dreary and lonely, and quite sincerely thank God for that consolation. Thus, though he may have no human being to thank for his sexual pleasure (and he may regret this), he may be genuinely grateful to God for that pleasure, or for the organs which give him the power to give himself pleasure." p.89. Moore takes this to mean that masturbation per se need not be an 'ungrateful' use of the sexual faculties and is in no way an affront to God.

[13] John Paul II (1981), 161-162. A plausible reading of Robert Louis Stevenson's *The Strange Case of Dr Jekyll and Mr Hyde* understands it as a psychologically acute account of the effects of surrendered-to concupiscence.

[14] Nagel (1995), 100.

[15] Nagel (1995), 101.

[16] Nagel (1995), 105-106.

[17] Nagel (1995), 106-107.

[18] In Nagel (1979) the focus is different. More will be said about this paper later.

[19] This is not to deny the role of rights in sexual morality, merely to point out that an exclusivist limitation of the relevant subject matter is prejudicial and reductionist.

[20] Dancy (1993), 24.

[21] Quinn (1994). I am not here taking a position on the scholastic saying *omne appetitum sub specie boni*, but restrict myself to the less controver-

sial assertion that most of our desires *are* motivated by the good.

[22] Quinn (1994), 234-235.

[23] An example might be my pointless but otherwise innocent desire to turn left at a fork in the road when out for a stroll.

[24] Dancy (1994), 19. Such a point seems reasonable at least in the case of developed forms of lust. Dancy rightly adds that in many cases of lust what motivates is not the gap between before and after so much as what the action will be like while one is doing it. This is not incompatible with the view of desire he forwards but, as he says, "challenges the implication that all action motivated by lust is purposive." p.36 fn.1.

[25] John Paul II (1981), 161-162.

[26] Bennett (1995). Of course all sides agree with GEM Anscombe's point that as "a rule as you consider it in deciding to obey or disobey it does not run: do not *voluntarily* do such-and-such, for you cannot consider whether to do such-and-such voluntarily or not...The voluntariness is presupposed in [the agent's] *considering whether* to do so. Thus it does not come into his considerations of what to do, but it does come into a later judgement – his own or another's – of what was done." Anscombe (1963), 398-399.

[27] Scanlon (2010), 10-11. See also Anscombe (1958), 9. For Anscombe (1963) the "difference between voluntariness and intentionalness...is this: one cannot intentionally, but can voluntarily, do something without knowing one is doing it; e.g. some voluntary cases are like those of bigamy and adultery when the agent made no inquiry." p.398 fn2.

[28] Garcia (2007), 270. Garcia also notes that the centrality of 'thick' ethical concepts mentioned in the Introduction allows us to see that "many of the "thick" terms either themselves involve intentions (e.g., "malevolent") or imply further claims about intent (as does "lie"). That already indicates the difference between what an agent does and does not intend will carry moral weight." This distinction seems reasonable, although we should remember that terms such as 'callousness' can apply to lack of intent as well as intent.

[29] Whereas the *immediate* intention will always be morally relevant for the moral act to take place at all, to treat *further* intentions as morally irrelevant to assessing the permissibility of a prospective act makes little sense once we have conceded the role the immediate intention has in defining the act.

[30] On top of this some claim that hate crimes have distinctive bad effects on their victims.

[31] Hershfield (2009), 27.

[32] Hershfield (2009), 30.

[33] Hershfield (2009), 36.

[34] Hershfield (2009), 38.

[35] The classic paper exploring the issue is Tanner (1976). It is no coincidence that, as Tanner notes, an apt label for certain kinds of rancidly sentimental music is 'masturbatory'.

[36] Hershfield (2009), 37. I leave to one side the question of browsing one's emails while making love to one's wife!

[37] For example, in sexual ethics, people may be mistaken about the true nature of the beloved or of the desired union.

[38] Primoratz (1999), 45. Primoratz qualifies the statement in the following paragraph by telling us, "The notion of sexual pleasure, then, can be specified as follows: it is the sort of bodily pleasure experienced in the sexual parts of the body, or at least related to those parts in that if it associated with arousal, the arousal occurs in those parts." This qualification differentiates his position from Goldman's. He holds this belief alongside the extraordinary belief that unpleasurable sex isn't really sex at all, such that a couple engaging in consensual sex may either not be 'having sex' or one of them is and one of them isn't (or one or other or neither or both are 'having sex' during certain time slices of coitus and not others). It does no good to say in defence of such a thesis that someone being raped isn't 'having sex' because a) it is not impossible for someone to experience 'pleasure' while being raped and b) his/her experiencing it would

not make the difference, as would consent, between whether the person was 'having sex' or not.

[39] This does not, of course, mean that Primoratz and others who hold this view need think that extreme sado-masochism or rape are unproblematic – rather, they may simply think that if they are wrong they are wrong for extrinsic reasons and not on account of any wrong *sexual* desire. Moreover, who is to say that hunger itself can't admit of perversion, certainly in relation to eating: as Nagel says, "serious restrictions of the desire to eat could...be described as perversions, if they undermined that direct relation between man and food which is the natural expression." Nagel (1979), 42.

[40] Nagel (1979), 43.

[41] Scruton (2006), 90. Scruton appears to reserve the term "sexual desire" to something both interpersonal and specific to a person, whereas in common usage many would regard the sailor's generalised 'desire' as being something different from but importantly overlapping with the narrower sense of the term.

[42] As Scruton (2006) notes, drawing a parallel with anger, "The man who explodes in anger certainly relieves his feelings, and may afterwards feel pleasant sensations of relaxation, as the adrenalin ebbs from his system. But this temporary explosion is not part of the intentionality of his anger since it bears no relation to the thoughts which motivate him. If *this* is what he wants he would be as well fulfilled by an injection of adrenalin... the pleasure of release is here of no account in the project of anger, even if it may feature in a scientific explanation of what 'goes on'. Similarly with orgasm." pp. 90-91. Against this, one might argue that the angry person may be at least *subconsciously* motivated by the desire for feelings of enjoyment and release, such that this desire plays *some* part in his action, even if enjoyment is not a conscious aim (or at least, not the main conscious aim).

[43] Sartre (2003), 383.

[44] Nagel (1979), 47-48. Note though that Nagel's reciprocal model may, counterintuitively, reduce to the level of sexual perversion for example

marital behaviours where all the steps of reciprocity are not gone through due to low sexual interest on the side of one willing party. Nozick (1989) makes the related point that sex is not a mere matter of frictional force but is something from which, "The excitement comes largely in how we interpret the situation and how we perceive the connection to the other... What is exciting is interpersonal: how the other views you, what attitude the actions evidence." pp.61-62. He also notes that even in masturbatory fantasy people are not getting excited by thinking only about themselves!

[45] Soble (2014).

[46] It is worth noting, especially in relation to what was said in the Introduction, that this view appears reminiscent of the call of Greer (2006) for rape to be treated as common assault with a sexual element. Such a view sits uneasily with Greer's earlier complaint (1984) that widespread use of contraception has "demystified" women's bodies.

[47] In this they differ from Goldman, who coined the term "plain sex." Note, however, that the 'sex is about pleasure' model doesn't have to favour what Soble oddly calls the unitary approach: sexual pleasure is the pasta, not solitary sexual pleasure as such. Posner (1992), differs in his approach to paradigms, telling us that, "Economic analysis with its useful concepts of substitution and complementarity, search costs and signalling, inferior goods and externalities, and much else besides can explain a great deal of the variance in sexual behaviour and regulation over time and across cultures with a minimum of assumptions…" p.435. Despite what some economists claim, even as they smuggle in particular concepts of 'the good', economics is in fact normative, no less than medicine. It is interesting that Posner simply assumes that we can 'substitute' and compare, via a cost-benefit analysis, different sexual activities (e.g. masturbation, marital sex, homosexual activity, sado-masochism) perhaps in a way that even grounds moral analysis and does not simply provide us with assessments of the best means to achieve e.g. pleasure or wealth. Without analysis of the goods at stake in relation to sex itself it is unsurprising that someone like Posner cannot really distinguish, in any way that accords with reality, prostitution and marriage for which he sees prostitution as substitutable. p.131.

[48] A phenomenon which government-funded health and educational bodies, not to mention abortion- providers, are keen to eliminate – see O'Neill (2014); Jones (2005).

[49] *Summa Theologica* II-II, q.154, a.11.

[50] Kolnai (2005), 181.

[51] It is not, of course, wrong in itself to use the body 'instrumentally' for the sake of pleasure e.g. taking euphoria producing drugs as part of a scientific experiment (see Chapter 2). The point with masturbation is that the kind of bodily good we are concerned about here is of such importance to crucial expressions of human union and human life in general that instrumentalisation is undermining of a fundamental social function.

[52] Recall also the point made in Chapter 3 about degrees of social and physical departure from teleology, calling, *prima facie*, for taboos of different levels of intensity.

[53] Kolnai (2005), 184. Allers goes on to note the fact that the masturbator in doing what is forbidden does so without consequences and in avoiding every trace of responsibility for another human being need not step outside his own ego.

[54] Pruss (2013), 273-274.

Chapter 6: pp. 169-207

[1] See Luke 20:35-36. Some have, of course, argued that Christian marriage is not favoured by 'true' Christianity, the religion of Christ. Thus Kierkegaard (1996) can write "[True] Christianity says: Refrain from marrying; it is pleasing to God and a quite natural consequence of really being Christian. To this the human species replies: But if we all do that the species must die out. The species naturally regards the extinction of the species as the greatest misfortune." pp.628-629. This claim about 'true' Christianity is said to be in line with the teachings of Jesus and the desert Fathers. However, Jesus' presence at the wedding feast in Cana and his elevation of marriage (Matthew 19:3-8; cf. Mark 10:2-9; Luke 16:18 not to mention Ephesians 5:29-32) appear impossible to reconcile

with this interpretation. That the Catholic Church holds consecrated celibacy to be a higher calling than sacramental marriage is not in any doubt (indeed the Catholic Church regards the denial of this to be a heresy). But to hold this is not to treat marriage as something to be shunned as somehow incompatible with being a Christian. Indeed, according to an excellent paper by Mankowski (2011), "Once Jesus, by his teaching and by the emphatic example of his own celibate life, made it possible for marital love to be renounced "for the sake of the kingdom," he thereby declared it to be holy. Accordingly, St. Paul's conviction that the union of man and woman pertains to the mystery of Christ and the Church allows us not only to view the Church in a particular way, but it allows us to take an unblinkered and uncensorious look at the sexual embrace in marriage." p.15.

Passages sometimes cited in favour of an 'anti-marital' position include Luke 14:26 and Mark 3:31-35. However, continual admonitions to love one's parents (Matthew 15:4-6; Matthew 19:17-19; Mark 7:10-13; John 19:25-27) mean that passages talking of 'hate' must be understood quite differently (see Matthew 10:37). Just as putting oneself before the Kingdom is renounced (this is what it means for 'hate' of self to be encouraged), putting family members before the Kingdom is renounced. Some, though not all, Christians are invited to take this further and renounce the very possibility of marriage for the sake of the Kingdom.

[2] Nygren (1982). See also the discussion of Nygren in Pieper (1997), 207-232 and the criticisms in Seifert (2015).

[3] *Summa Theologica* II-II q.23-q.27.

[4] Pieper (1997), 164.

[5] Pieper (1997), 165.

[6] "Before" need not be understood in a temporal sense.

[7] The Nietzchean philosopher May (2011) argues that "By imputing to human love features properly reserved for divine love such as the unconditional and the eternal, we falsify the nature of this most conditional and time-bound and earthy emotion and force it to labour under intoler-

able expectations...the limits of the human can be ignored only at a terrible cost." pp.4-5. It should be noted that May feels it necessary to try to show, in Chapter 7 of his book, that the Christian God's love itself is not unconditional, an argument that ignores both the traditional Christian belief in God's unchanging and essential nature and passages from the Bible such as Romans 8:38-39 (God's love by its nature must be unconditional; it is we who are free to reject it).

[8] Whether that should apply to the 'goodness' of all Creation (i.e. existence as such) is an interesting question that cannot be explored here. Certainly nothing involving the three aspects of love listed below could possibly be involved in such appreciation.

[9] Pruss (2013) tells us "...unconditional love is a present love that the lover is obligated to persevere in no matter what (even if the beloved should no longer desire that perseverance—this is important in the case of children, who have the right to count on their parents loving them even at times when the children might say that they don't care about the parents' love)... Unconditional love... includes an obligation and an unreserved acceptance of the obligation. Sometimes the two seem to be disjointed. Thus, what generates the obligation to love my children is simply, and always, the fact that they are my children, and I have this obligation whether or not I accept it. At times, however, there is a closer relationship between the two aspects. Thus, while uttering one's marriage vows, one is both generating the unconditional obligation of future love and accepting that obligation. Of course, if Christianity is right that one always owes love to everyone, then even in marriage, the obligation precedes the acceptance. However, even so, the marriage vows generate an *additional* duty to love the spouse, and this additional duty is closely tied with its acceptance." p.42. Such an approach stands in stark contrast to that of (for example) the pious Polish Catholic couple who recently informed me that a spouse who no longer loves his/her wife has a duty to divorce them.

[10] Pieper (1997), 197-198. While this captures a truth about love it does not necessarily account for the kind of love a mother or father might instantly feel for their newborn baby.

[11] Pruss (2013), 46. Pruss explains: "The reason for loving someone... is the same for all people, while the reason for having a particular form of love differs from case to case. Indeed, sometimes this reason may include an element of Kierkegaardian choice —for instance, that the beloved is someone with whom I have chosen to start a family is surely relevant to the sort of love I should have for her — and the reason for love will also include Aristotelian ingredients. Likewise, someone's wit should not be *the* reason for loving her, since a sufficient reason is already present in the fact that she is a person (or a creature of God, and so forth). But it can be a reason for loving her *in the way I do*."

[12] Pruss (2013), 7 and 45. Similarly Pruss observes that "Our love is humble insofar as it is a response to reality. The central salient part of that reality is the beloved. But that is not all. We also need to humbly, i.e. realistically, examine ourselves and our relationship with the other, and there is an objectivity here. The nature of love calls on us to respond to reality, and this need to respond to reality is what makes the duties of love not to be subjective...The other-focus of love then goes hand-in-hand with a rejection of a relativistic approach to ethics." p.30.

[13] Pruss (2013) does not emphasise the phenomenon of falling in love without which, for many people, it will be harder to achieve the sense of the specialness and unique existential goodness of the person. Although this intense feeling is necessarily transitory, I would argue it is geared toward kinds of appreciation and commitment which are anything but transitory. Kolnai (2005) draws a parallel with religious conversion, and comments "The idea of a great experience does not imply that one should have as many of them as one can, but that, once the experience is given, it should also make itself fully felt. The glory of a conversion does not incline me to partake of this glorious experience, if possible, twice a year, but to become a stronger representative of the faith to which I have 'found my way home', and to satisfy its requirements..." p.133.

[14] This is perhaps an oversimplification in that people do not always will their own good either consciously or unconsciously.

[15] Pruss (2013), 31-32.

[16] John Paul II (1981), 37-39.

[17] Pleasure and pain in general can aid us perceptually in recognising what is generically good and bad for us, as with pleasure at a hot shower and pain at a too-hot shower.

[18] For Schopenhauer 'sexual love' is necessary but only as something which 'dupes' us egoistic individuals into an obsessive focus on one person appropriate for mating and reproduction for the perpetuation of what is in the end, it seems, a pointless existence!

[19] A procedure like IVF, while it is a project aimed at the production of new human beings, is not generally viewed as 'valuable in itself' as is spousal love-making. Indeed, in this case, it seems that the valuable activity of spousal love-making, precisely because it *does* have a value in its own right, is capable of realising and affirming the value of the child: a child who can be its outcome in a way which does not compromise the child's welfare by making him/her a product of a non-valuable-in-itself procedure too closely resembling other instrumental actions.

[20] If we say that someone is loved as irreplaceable, we are not merely saying that as a matter of fact they have *unique* qualities on the basis of which they must be respected but rather that their value as one who exists just for his or her own sake, their sheer selfhood, calls for respect in itself. Someone may be morally irreplaceable without being literally unique (for a related discussion see Brock (2005a)).

[21] Pruss (2013) makes the valuable point that, "There is something deeply problematic with having the pleasure of a deep interpersonal good, indeed a good consummation of love, in the absence of that good. For to do that is to distort oneself in respect of that which is central to human life – our loving relation to others. And the self-induction of orgasm in the absence of sexual union would be precisely such a distortion. For the same reason, one should not take pills that gave one the satisfying feeling of having acted generously when we in fact had not acted in this way, as that distorts one in respect of love. In respect of interpersonal relationships, truth is central." p.333. This is surely right, though it is not clear that someone could not take part in a genuinely useful scientific

experiment where their brain is stimulated in such a way as to produce, for a short-time, the pleasurable effects of a brotherly love that is in fact absent from their life. Of course, anything more than this begins to seem morally problematic for the kinds for reasons Pruss outlines. However, in the sexual realm such experiments do seem distinctly more problematic, perhaps particularly because of the intense interpersonal bodily nature of the goods at stake and the kinds of bonds connected with that unique 'one-flesh' union. An absolute taboo therefore seems more appropriate here than in the brotherly love case.

[22] In the same way parents through their personal interests not directly focused on their children can (incidentally) teach children how to 'lose themselves' in leisure or cultural pursuits and not see themselves as the 'centre of the universe'.

[23] See Scruton (2004), and Tanner (2008), 140-156. Examples of lovers such as Tristan and Isolde illustrate how sexual wrongdoing can take on an especially potent world-changing force, involving as it does fundamental distortions of moral reality as it relates to love and life. For a religious thinker like von Hildebrand (2010), sexual sin, given the nature of the inner core of the person, leads in unique ways to apostasy from God. Others point to how entire ideologies can be seen to have their roots in sexual wrongdoing – see Jones (2005).

[24] Garcia (1997), 231.

[25] Wood (2008), 226 and refs therein.

[26] Nussbaum (1999), 225.

[27] Schulz (2007).

[28] Interestingly there can be perfectly benign forms of fungibility e.g. the having of a tennis partner, but we do not say this of spouses where the core nature of sexuality of the person and her bodily meaning tell against this. It seems that, with regard to marriage, only death can make the person 'fungible' in that role, but I think this fact rather illustrates the radically non-fungible nature of the role in general.

[29] Schulz (2007).

[30] Kant (1996), 178-179 [6:425].

[31] Kant's suggestion that masturbation is more evil than suicide on account of its 'unnaturalness' seems, however, extraordinary. Could anything be more anti-teleological than a rational being deliberately destroying himself? Moreover, it is interesting to note that condemnations of masturbation in terms of what Kant calls 'self-violation' as well as what we hear from masturbators about feelings of 'self-degradation', are best explained by seeing masturbation as a perversion of the teleology of sex in terms of the emotions/sensations/sub-functions fitted to making oneself a gift to another, a gift realised through biological union expressive of love. Without such an ethical account, talk of 'self degradation" or 'self abuse' is hard to make philosophical sense of, even if intuitively these terms seem helpful.

[32] Here Kant's approach is an ancestor of much of the gender politics of today so well described in the citations of David S. Crawford in Chapters 2 and 3.

[33] Kant (2001) 156 [27:385]. It is worth noting here the point made by the highly unorthodox Hegelian philosopher Slavoj Zizek (2015) in relation to those who talk of the possibilities that Virtual Reality offers to the sexualised body. He tells us, "once the socio-symbolic order is fully established, the very dimension which introduced the "transcendent" attitude that defines a human being, namely *sexuality*, the uniquely human sexual passion, appears as its very opposite, as the main *obstacle* to the elevation of a human being to the pure spirituality, as that which ties him/her down to the inertia of bodily existence? For this reason, the end of sexuality in the much celebrated "posthuman" self-cloning entity expected to emerge soon, far from opening up the way to pure spirituality, will simultaneously signal the end of what is traditionally designated as the uniquely human spiritual transcendence. All the celebrating of the new "enhanced" possibilities of sexual life that Virtual Reality offers cannot conceal the fact that, once cloning supplements sexual difference, the game is over."

[34] Feser (2014).

[35] Those who think that only conditional love is possible or desirable tend to fall into two camps. On the one hand there are those who think unconditional love is not possible, that it is a notion that came about with Christian ideas about God and the afterlife (Nietzsche) and has had positively harmful effects. But it is surely only impossible if we view unconditional love in some intense romantic way, as opposed to an unwavering appreciation and well-wishing (more or less intensely experienced and acted upon). On the other hand there are those who will simply deny that mankind, or most of mankind (or reality as a whole) is in any fundamental sense good and therefore worthy of love, but for this they will need to show not just that human beings are flawed but that *human life itself* is somehow fundamentally not good. In the very act of arguing for this proposition they will be appealing to at least one good and very important (indeed defining) aspect of human beings: their capacity to engage in rational discourse with a view to achieving the good of truth. May (2011) argues for "conditional love."

[36] McMahan (2002), 359-361.

[37] John Paul II (1981), 190.

[38] John Paul II (1981), 191.

[39] Feser (2014) briefly raises this issue. I would say that reflecting on the appropriateness of sexual attributes for producing arousal, we might imagine someone who is instead aroused by and masturbates over broken glass. Aside from the moral problems surrounding masturbation itself, what seems particularly abhorrent about this is that the man is achieving orgasm by focussing on something entirely removed from the personal, the human and the bodily. He achieves the sub-function of orgasm – which should be part of the wider function of sexual intercourse – through a stimulus which has absolutely no teleological connection with that wider function, and as I have tried to show in this book, such a bypassing of normal teleology is especially problematic in the sexual realm. Here we have something that never issues in interpersonal sexual relations and so in one sense can't pervert them. And yet given the teleology of desire we can say that it *does* pervert the desire as such. It is worth

noting that sexual acts such as these, radically deprived of the personal, appear worse in some ways than those involving other persons which at least partially realise some teleological nature. That said, the latter may harm more people, and in profound ways. We might compare the wrongness of bestiality with the use of a prostitute (not 'unnatural' as such but anti-marital): surely one is worse than the other in certain aspects and the latter worse in other aspects.

[40] On double effect issues, see Appendix.

[41] The following section was inspired by some questions raised by JLA Garcia in an email exchange and previously summarised above. It is my attempt at an answer to these questions and I am very grateful to Professor Garcia for raising them and allowing me to defend certain positions which he may not share.

[42] Garcia (2010), 99.

[43] Garcia (1986), 242-245.

[44] Garcia (2010), 103.

[45] Garcia (1987), 411.

[46] Kolnai (2005), 242.

[47] For an argument as to why these and not other virtues are 'cardinal' see, as well as various writings of Aristotle (particularly the *Nicomachean Ethics*), Thomas Aquinas (especially *Summa Theologica* II-II, q.47-170) and also Oderberg (1999).

[48] For discussion and defence of the unity of the virtues see Thomas Aquinas, *Commentary on the Nicomachean Ethics*, Book VI, Lecture XI, 1279–1280; *Summa Theologica* I–II, q.57, a.4; cf. q.58, a.5, Aristotle, *Nicomachean Ethics*, Book VI; Annan (1993) pp.73–84

[49] John Paul II (1981), 161.

[50] John Paul II (1981), 168-172.

[51] Note too the names used, across many and varied cultures, to characterise women seen as unchaste (e.g. slag, slut, slapper, whore, filthy woman etc.). Such terms have no real male equivalents (terms such as

love-rat, cad or bounder have a very different resonance and refer more to how a man lets down women than to some 'dirt' within him) with the exception of the terms slime/sleazeball and the term 'dirty old man', usually reserved for elderly fantasists and masturbators. All of which suggests that, in matters sexual, it is women who have been regarded as the primary guardians of chaste living, in a way no doubt connected to the huge social importance of identifying paternity. Why women might have this particular responsibility could be explained by the fact that usually it will be they who are the primary carers for their young children and thus inevitably more responsible for safeguarding the child's psychological well-being. That well-being will, of course, crucially involve the child's sense of identity of which parentage is an important part. Note too that to make 'an honest woman' of someone traditionally meant to make their sexual relationship marital, whereas 'an honest man' would be a man of probity in other areas (e.g. financial). None of this is, of course, to deny the huge importance of the father's responsibility for his own (including future) children or to endorse what can often be an unjust double-standard in how men's and women's characters are judged in this area.

[52] Nagel (1995), 101.

[53] Insofar as one's desires literally only related to oneself – like someone who is not only masturbating but doing so thinking only of himself – this is an especially serious form of truncation.

[54] Riley (2000), 8, *Summa Theologica* II-II.q.141, a.8.

[55] Riley (2000), 9-10.

[56] Laing and Oderberg (2005), 328-356.

[57] *Summa Theologica* II-II. q58.a9, ad 3.

[58] Riley (2000), 15-16.

[59] Crawford (2007), 401.

[60] Crawford (2007), 382, citing *Compendium of the Social Doctrine of the Church* #125.

[61] Crawford (2007), 405.

[62] For an historical overview of these issues see Abbott (1981). For people like John Locke, interested, in his *Two Treatises on Government*, in promoting liberal toleration and social consensus among 'free and rational' men, the political order must be constructed upon premises respecting that 'truth' about individuals. As Abbott asks, "If we are free, rational, equal, and independent, how can we explain relationships of emotion and dependency separate from consent?" p.29. The family, as a natural unit and foundational to the other human associations that make up a polity, is on this view a 'problem' which needs to be reconfigured in line with a contract model of a rational individualistic order.

Moving towards the present we see that John Rawls in his *A Theory of Justice* and subsequent works argues for a 'social contract' theory which imagines people standing in an 'original position' behind a 'veil of ignorance', bereft of everything which makes them human except that which seeks for a social and political consensus acceptable to all (on the deep contradictions involved in the concept 'original position' (see Levin and Levin 1979). This approach to political philosophy based entirely on 'rights' and relying on no comprehensive theory of the good, makes the family something contingent and secondary, rather than the natural foundational unit of society from which our conception of moral reality and justice is necessarily born. For Rawls' theory seems to demand that the family cannot even enter into the 'basic structure' of society to which his principles of distributive justice apply. He thereby separates out the family from the political order.

Interestingly for Marx and Engels the family, as merely part of the 'superstructure', will be superseded in the communist utopia where 'natural bonds' (along with property, the state and religion) will wither away and purely affectional and dissoluble relationships unbound by 'nature' will be the norm. This vision of a society freed from marriage was echoed not so long ago by sociologist Anthony Giddens, a key advisor to former UK Prime Minister Tony Blair (see Morgan (2014), 99-123).

We are now seeing a logical outcome of this kind of political philosophy through the enactment of genderless marriage legislation, which treats the 'rational, free individual' as one without sexual capacities or roles related to them (what, now, do the terms husband, wife, father, mother amount to? Some have declared, following the logic of advocates of transgenderism and 'gender theory' that the last two role-bearers should be renamed Progenitor 1 and Progenitor 2). So what I have referred to as fundamental roles connected to a clear *telos* are now hollowed out at the level of law. Those things that are 'given', like our maleness and femaleness and all the fundamental relational aspects that go with them, have no place in what appears in some way a logical consequence of the liberalism just described.

For an account of the state of the conjugal family in a world of 'equal marriage' see Morgan (2014). For an argument about how liberal neutrality cannot sustain something like the prohibition of incest see Tralau (2013). For an argument as to why genderless marriage effectively abolishes marriage and why this is a 'good thing', see Nussbaum (2010). Quite how Nussbaum's argument could allow convincing justifications for laws against incest remains to be seen. For a robust argument highlighting the contradictions of the modern liberal tradition see Laing (2004). Note how the kinds of arguments set forth in this volume and by others in defence of the family are barely addressed by those who argue for the abolition of marriage and family.

[63] Which itself could be seen as a backhanded compliment to the specialness of sex. See also Appendix and reference to Max Scheler.

[64] James Dickey's great poem 'Adultery' captures both the futility of adultery and the intoxicating and apparently 'magical' power that can come from perverting in ourselves the instinct for fidelity and fruitfulness.

[65] A very public awareness of paedophilia as well as the increasing homosexualisation of the public square have clearly had an effect on personal relations of various kinds.

[66] *Catechism of the Catholic Church* (1994) #2521

[67] Nagel (1998), 3-30

[68] Something the writer Jonathan Franzen (2007), no defender of the kind of argument to be found in this book, notes with dismay pp.270-286.

The prevalence of pornography in our society and the normalisation of its use, which many social liberals are happy to defend, can hardly be said to have no effect on the chastity of its members. Nor can it be said, ultimately, to be respectful of the 'privacy' of those aiming to live virtuous lives in accord with the common good. For an historical account of how the deliberate undermining of modesty has since the Enlightenment served politico-financial ends see Jones (2005).

[69] Lawrence (1979), 345-346. Vidal (1994), while holding that "The sexual attitudes of any given society are the result of political decisions," further asserts with regard to traditional sexual morality, "A state of constant guilt in the citizenry is a good thing for rulers who tend not to take very seriously the religions that they impose on their subjects. Since marriage was the only admissible outlet for the sexual drive, that institution was used as a means of channeling the sexual drive in a way that would make docile the man, while the woman, humanly speaking, existed only as a repository of the sacred sperm...If one had set out deliberately to invent a religion that would effectively enslave a population, one could not have done much better than Judaeo-Christianity." p.546. That people with dependants might be easier for employers to push around in societies where jobs are scarce is hardly surprising. And that certain politicians may have ulterior motives in talking of 'family values' is similarly unsurprising. However, if the history of the sexual revolution teaches us anything it is that sexual liberation is a form of political control (see Jones (2005); Schooyans (2001); Lasch (1979) and in fiction Aldous Huxley's *Brave New World*): rootless individuals without strong families are far more likely to become playthings of powerful elites. Moreover, such elites can hardly be said in Western countries – certainly not in the UK – to favour the pre-political and formative institution of marriage which contributes to the strongly rooted sense of identity people need to resist the self-serving ideologies of those in power.

[70] Dabhoiwala (2012). A view of religious liberty which has been defended in recent times by leading figures in the Catholic Church (forcefully critiqued in Pink (2013)) has arguably contributed to a certain paralysis in responding to sexual liberalism at the political level.

[71] One way in which a society might treat sex seriously is through legislation against one or more forms of sexual wrongdoing. We have already seen how sexual wrongdoing of various kinds can radically affect the common good and how justice must concern itself with that good. However, as with any law, there are complex prudential questions concerning foreseeable negative side-effects which need to be raised when assessing how legislation might affect the common good. That said, there is no reason to presume *a priori* that the state has no business restricting or prohibiting any form of sexual wrongdoing whether private or public: there are, as we have seen, reasons for, at the very least, strong social pressure being brought to bear in this area to protect the common good. Strong social taboos and even laws against incest, for example, are not obviously inherently unjust. And where there are existing laws on the statute book criminalising sexual acts between consenting adults, it is undeniable that the lifting of such laws is seen in practice as sending out the message that the state now takes a neutral or positive stance on what was hitherto seen as seriously wrong activity. The history of legislation on homosexuality in the United Kingdom, for example, has followed this trajectory with homosexual sex now being elevated to the level of 'marital' activity in the eyes of the state and apparently a very large portion of the population.

[72] McCabe (2010), 107-108. A common situation in the case of marital betrayal, particularly where the male spouse is betrayed, is that the unfaithful wife and her lover rewrite the past, attempting perhaps unconsciously to demonise and/or dismiss the cuckolded husband and render their betrayal more 'marital' while denying the marital nature of the actual marriage. This appears to be less common when wives are betrayed by husbands involved with other women.

Appendix: pp. 208-218

[1] This article appears in *Studia Philosophiae Christianae* 51.2 (2015), 143-158.

[2] Karol Wojtyla (Pope John Paul II), *Love and Responsibility* tr H.T. Willets (London: Fount 1982), 143-144.

[3] I leave to one side extreme sexual revolutionaries like Wilhelm Reich and Gyorgy Lukacs who actively promoted unchastity through 'sex education' as the best way to undermine religious belief and marriage.

[4] By which I mean: exceptionless negative moral norms. I leave to one side the question of *positive* moral absolutes such as obeying a positive direct command from God. Of course, a certain kind of consequentialist will himself hold *one* positive moral absolute; namely to 'maximise good' where good can be measured by a single scale. And he must do that whatever the consequences!

[5] For a striking philosophical defence of the reasonableness of exceptionless moral norms and the incoherence of various consequentialist critiques of them see Nicholas Denyer, 'Is Anything Absolutely Wrong?,' in *Human Lives: Critical Essays on Consequentialist Bioethics* ed. David S. Oderberg and Jacqueline A. Laing (Basingstoke: MacMillan 1997), 39-58.

[6] It is worth recalling how developments in the history of metaphysics, not least philosophical theories which radically truncate the scope of metaphysical knowledge, have led to the kind of deep problems philosophers have had in relation to ethics generally and sexual ethics in particular: "According to St Thomas, the physical order was essentially made up of 'natures', that is to say, active principles, which were the cause of the motions and various operations of their respective matters. In other words, each nature, or form, was essentially an energy, an act. Now it is an obvious fact that such a world was no fit subject for a purely mechanical interpretation of physical change; dimensions, positions, distances are by themselves clear things; they can be measured and numbered; but those secret energies that had been ascribed to bodies by Aristotle and St Thomas, could not be submitted to any kind of calculation...Descartes could not possibly tolerate such a nuisance. Forms, natures and energies had to be eliminated then from the physical world, so that there should be nothing left but extension and always an equal amount of motion caused by God." Etienne Gilson, *The Unity of Philosophical Experience* (Dublin: Four Courts Press 1982), 203-204.

Displacing the role of metaphysics with regard to ethics has serious consequences with regard to thinking about sexual ethics and the ethics of homicide. Without an adequate metaphysics the body may end up being dissolved into parts. Neglecting deep consideration of the body's meaning and what that meaning practically implies, failing to pay due attention to natural kinds, formal causes, final ends, the teleological nature of our bodies and of the universe itself unsurprisingly leads to radically 'thin' accounts of sexual ethics.

'New Natural Lawyers' such as Germain Grisez, John Finnis, Joseph Boyle and Robert P. George, who have vigorously defended Catholic sexual ethics from critics both in and outside the Church, may argue that the theory they defend does not differ in its metaphysical worldview from other Catholic natural law approaches. For they contend (Finnis especially) that it is only by coming to know basic human goods that we can come to know adequately the metaphysics of human nature. Finnis holds that this is strictly entailed by Aquinas's repeated epistemological principle that one knows natures only by knowing capacities, and capacities only by understanding the actions for which they are the capacities, and only understands the actions by knowing their objects – and the objects of human actions are intelligible goods (at their various levels of specificity – see the table in John Finnis's *Aquinas: Moral, Political and Legal Theory* (Oxford: Oxford University Press), 71, or Finnis's critique of Fr. Kevin Flannery in *Reason, Morality and Law* ed. John Keown and Robert P. George (Oxford: Oxford University Press 2013), 491). Against this, it must however be asked why it is that when it comes to some questions, at least, concerning 'physical structures', such as the moral liceity of craniotomy discussed below, proponents of the New Natural Law approach reach such very different conclusions from their more traditional critics. I take this opportunity to thank John Finnis for his incisive and very helpful comments on an earlier draft of this paper.

A powerful critique of the New Natural Law interpretation of Aquinas, the good and human nature is Lawrence Dewan OP, 'St. Thomas, Our Natural Lights and the Moral Order,' in Lawrence Dewan OP, *Wisdom, Law, and Virtue: Essays in Thomistic Ethics* (New York: Fordham University Press 2008) 199-213). Dewan rightly points out, citing many texts from Aquinas, that even though a Thomist must grant that "ethics is prior to metaphysics in the order of learning, it is an ethics feeding on the sapiential seeds, conceived as Thomas conceives them; and the metaphysician does not merely *append* [Finnis talks of the 'natural' as a "speculative appendage" from the point of view of ethics] his observations but is able to tell the ethician what has been feeding his ethical reflections all along, and what the preethical human spirit already has somehow grasped." Dewan goes on to claim that "Reason puts nature first, not precisely because nature reveals its divine origin, but because reason sees ontological priority. Goodness is seen in ontological order, and reason's giving nature priority is the recognition of that order. The ontologically determinate (i.e., nature) has more of the aspect of being than has the ontological determinable (the operable or choosable)." 212.

[7] Robert P. George (*In Defense of Natural Law* (Oxford: Clarendon Press 1999), 181 note 2) claims that Pope John Paul II "specifically rejects" the 'perverted faculty' argument in sexual ethics at *VS*#48. However, this is not the case: what Pope John Paul II refers to here is any view which makes the body and its faculties *external to the person*: something 'biological' in a purely physicalist sense and thus without inherent moral significance. This is precisely the opposite of what the traditional moral theology manuals, in particular, say about human nature.

[8] For a discussion of 'transitive' and 'intransitive' significance see Karol Wojtyla, *The Acting Person: A Contribution to Phenomenological Anthropology* tr. A. Potocki (Dordrecht: D. Reidel Publishing Company, Inc. 1979).

[9] Stephen L. Brock, '*Veritatis Splendor* #78, St. Thomas, and (Not Merely) Physical Objects of Moral Acts,' *Nova et Vetera* (English Edition) 6.1 (2008), 1-62.

[10] GEM Anscombe observes that absolute prohibitions are inextricably bound up with the principle of double effect and that without the principle any act might be justified ('War and Murder,' in *Ethics, Religion and Politics: Collected Philosophical Papers Volume III* (Oxford: Basil

Blackwell 1981), 58). Perhaps, however, the making/allowing distinction might be sufficient for there to be moral absolutes, though Anscombe seems to think that more is required and that without the principle of double effect we can't have moral absolutes. For a sophisticated and unsympathetic critique of double effect reasoning see Jonathan Bennett, *The Act Itself* (Oxford: Oxford University Press 1995). For robust defences of double effect reasoning see Mark Murphy, 'Intention, Foresight and Success,' in *Human Values: New Essays on Ethics and Natural Law* ed. David S. Oderberg and Timothy Chappell (New York: Palgrave MacMillan 2007), 252-269; JLA Garcia, 'Intention in Medical Ethics', in *Human Lives: Critical Essays on Consequentialist Bioethics* ed. David S. Oderberg and Jacqueline A. Laing (Basingstoke: MacMillan 1997), 161-182; JLA Garcia, 'The Doubling Undone? Double Effect in Recent Medical Ethics,' *Philosophical Papers* 36.2 (2007), 245-270.

[11] See for example the paper by Josef Seifert, 'The Splendour of Truth and Intrinsically Immoral Acts: A Philosophical Defence of the Rejection of Proportionalism and Consequentialism in *Veritatis Splendor,' Studia Christianae Philosophae* 51.2 (2015).

[12] '"Direct" and "Indirect": A Reply to Critics of Our Action Theory,' *Thomist* 65 (2001), 1-44. The defence of craniotomy in this paper seems to contradict an earlier position taken by John Finnis with regard to the principle used in assessing the morality of a surgeon's treating the bodily substance of another human person as a mere subhuman object by subjecting that person to lethal organ harvesting - see John Finnis, 'Intentions and Side-Effects,' in *Liability and Responsibility: Essays in Law and* Morals, ed. R.G. Frey and Christopher W. Morris (Cambridge: Cambridge University Press 1991), 60-61. In the most recent version of this paper (in John Finnis, *Intention and Identity: Collected Essays volume 2* (Oxford: Oxford University Press), 173-198 (at pp196-97)), Finnis denies that there is any contradiction between the two positions and says with regard to the surgeon case "My discussion fails to consider sufficiently whether the surgeon's intent, which does not include death, does include mutilation – violation of bodily integrity as a means. In the postulated case the removal of the heart is a means to advance medical

knowledge; in routine cases of exceptionlessly wrongful mutilation the impairment of function and violation of integrity is a means, e.g. to facilitation of begging, not an end, e.g. when done out of a grudge...What is decisive for the intention-and act-analysis in such cases is whether the bodily position or activity of person V is itself a threat to the well-being of another or other persons and the cutting into or dismemberment of V is a means of mitigating that threat." Finnis makes clear in the following endnote that he restricts the term 'moral absolutes' (exceptionless moral norms) to "norms which exceptionlessly exclude a kind of act specified by its object, that is its intention." In which case, craniotomy cannot be condemned as violating an exceptionless moral norm.

Finnis believes that this clarification resolves any apparent inconsistency, but his clarified position can only convince if we assume that there is no such thing as an unintended yet morally determinative aspect to an act such as lethal organ harvesting. If lethal bodily invasion of an innocent person is such an aspect then this will mean that both the surgeon case and the craniotomy case violate an exceptionless moral norm, for the UMDA, though by definition unintended, is part of the moral object of the act (on one understanding of 'object' which is not confined to 'end' but concerns the state of affairs the end targets in effect).

For more on the issues raised here see Helen Watt, 'Beyond Double Effect: Side Effects and Bodily Harm,' in *Human Values: New Essays on Ethics and Natural Law* ed. David S. Oderberg and Timothy Chappell (New York: Palgrave MacMillan 2007), 236-252 and Stephen L. Brock, *Action and Conduct: Thomas Aquinas and the Theory of Action* (Edinburgh: T&T Clark 1998).

[13] Stephen L. Brock, '*Veritatis Splendor* #78, St. Thomas, and (Not Merely) Physical Objects of Moral Acts,' *Nova et Vetera* (English Edition) 6.1 (2008), 15.

[14] Germain Grisez, *The Way of the Lord Jesus Volume Two – Living a Christian Life,* (Quincy IL: Franciscan Press, Quincy University), 648 note 187.

[15] This passage makes use of material first published in Anthony McCarthy, 'Marriage and Meaning', in *Fertility and Gender: Issues in Repro-*

ductive and Sexual Ethics ed. Helen Watt (Oxford: Anscombe Bioethics Centre 2011), 45-70, especially 51.

[16] Pope Pius XII (address to delegates, 26th Congress of Urology, 8 Oct. 1953; address to 2nd World Congress on Fertility and Sterility, 19 May 1956).

[17] For a philosophical argument against the permissibility of using condoms for HIV prevention see Anthony McCarthy and Alexander Pruss, 'Condoms and HIV Transmission,' in *Fertility and Gender: Issues in Reproductive and Sexual Ethics* ed. Helen Watt (Oxford: Anscombe Bioethics Centre 2011), 157-169.

[18] Finnis, Grisez and Boyle argue in 'Direct and Indirect' that the Church has never authoritatively condemned the practice of craniotomy. I respectfully disagree and refer readers to Kevin Flannery SJ, 'Vital Conflicts and the Magisterial Tradition,' *National Catholic Bioethics Quarterly* 11.4 (Winter 2011), 691-704 and my own brief paper, 'Pre-viability inductions in vital conflict cases: are they really morally permissible?,' *Catholic Medical Quarterly* 64.1 (February 2014), 13-17 and subsequent correspondence in May, August, November 2014 issues. See also Chapter 15 of John Connery SJ, *Abortion: the Development of the Roman Catholic Perspective* (Chicago: Loyola Univ. Press 1977). I leave to one side the wisdom of publicly, as opposed to privately, advocating positions allowing craniotomy, a procedure still practised on babies during obstructed labour in some parts of the world.

[19] Violation of bodily integrity in the manner suggested would be wrong even if it didn't accelerate death, because of the way in which it treats another person: not all mutilation is death-hastening. In their discussion of craniotomy in 'Direct and Indirect,' Finnis, Grisez and Boyle raise the question "to what extent the life of the unborn child "depends on" not being subjected to craniotomy..." They claim that this is "far from clear in the obstetric emergency we are considering – a situation in which the child is expected to die no matter what is done." 26 ftn38). This very surprising statement appears to hold that the life of the unborn child is somehow less dependent upon his having an intact skull if he is soon to

die anyway. We would not say of someone who, minutes from death, were to have his skull smashed by another (possibly in order to save the life of a third party) that it is doubtful that the victim 'depended on' his skull to stay alive as he is expected to die whatever happens.

[20] David S. Crawford, 'Experience of Nature, Moral Experience: Interpreting *Veritatis Splendor's* "Perspective of The Acting Person,"' *Communio* 37 (Summer 2010), 277-278. I would, however, take issue with the aspect of Crawford's article which identifies the craniotomist's intention as necessarily being an intention to kill. Such a view makes a nonsense of standard distinctions between intentions and side-effects which Crawford would surely accept (e.g. giving morphine to a dying patient to alleviate suffering need not be done with an intention to shorten life). "In truth, this "change" or "reshaping" ("person-narrowing") entails the choice to change the baby into something other than a baby, for it is only a new substantial form—that of a corpse—that would be compatible with delivery. But this is just another way of saying that the doctor is in fact choosing to kill the baby." Contra Crawford, it needn't be the case that someone cutting into another in order to remove his heart (for example) is intending to create 'a heartless person', any more than a bicycle thief is necessarily intending, as he steals a bicycle, to create a bicycleless owner. In either case they can simply intend to remove.

[21] Stephen L. Brock, '*Veritatis Splendor* #78, St. Thomas, and (Not Merely) Physical Objects of Moral Acts,' *Nova et Vetera* (English Edition) 6.1 (2008), 62. See also 1 Corinthians 6.15-20.

Bibliography

This bibliography does not include the references to texts made in the Appendix, which are contained in the relevant footnotes.

Abbott, Philip. *The Family on Trial: Special Relationships in Modern Political Thought.* London: The Pennsylvania University Press, 1981.

Adler, Mortimer J. *The Time of Our Lives: The Ethics of Common Sense.* New York: Fordham University Press, 1970.

Alison, James. "Good-faith learning and the fear of God." In *Opening Up: Speaking Out in the Church*, ed. Julian Filichowski; Peter Stanford. London: Darton, Longman and Todd, 2005. Available at www.jamesalison.co.uk/pdf/eng17.pdf. Accessed 11/09/2014.

Allison, Henry E. *Kant's Theory of Freedom.* Cambridge: Cambridge University Press, 1990.

Amerio, Romano. *Iota Unum: A Study of the Changes in the Catholic Church in the XXth Century.* Translated by Fr John P. Parsons. Kansas, MA: Sarto House, 1996.

Anderson, Perry. "The World Made Flesh." *New Left Review* 39, no. 3 (2006): 132-137.

Annan, Julia. *The Morality of Happiness.* Oxford: Oxford University Press, 1993.

Anscombe, GEM. "Contraception and Chastity." *The Human World,* no. 7 (1972): 9-30.

——. *Intention.* Cambridge MA: Harvard University Press, 1958.

——. "Response." *The Human World.* no.9 (1972): 48-51.

——. "The Two Kinds of Error in Action." *Journal of Philosophy* 60, no. 14 (1963): 393-400.

Bibliography

Archard, David. "The Wrong of Rape." *The Philosophical Quarterly* 57, no. 228 (2007): 374-393.

Bayles, Michael D. "Harm to the Unconceived." *Philosophy and Public Affairs* 5, no.3 (1976): 292-304.

Benn, Piers. "Is Sex Morally Special?" *Journal of Applied Philosophy* 16, no.3 (1999): 235-245.

Bennett, Jonathan. *The Act Itself.* Oxford: Oxford University Press, 1995.

Bergoffen, Debra B. "From Genocide to Justice: Women's Bodies as Legal Writing Pad." *Feminist Studies* 32, no.1 (2006): 11-37.

Blackburn, Simon. *Lust: The Seven Deadly Sins.* Oxford: Oxford University Press, 2004.

Bourke, Vernon J. "Is Aquinas a Natural Law Ethicist." *Monist* 18, no.1 (1974): 52-66.

Boyle, Joseph. "Marriage Is an Institution Created by God." In *The Ethics of Having Children: Proceedings of the American Catholic Philosophical Association,* edited by Lawrence P. Schrenk, vol. 63, no.1 (1990): 2-16.

Braine, David, "Human animality: its relevance to the shape of ethics." In *Ethics, Technology and Medicine,* edited by David Braine and Harry Lesser, 6-31. Aldershot: Avebury, 1988.

———. "The Human and the Inhuman in Medicine: Review of Issues Concerning Reproductive Technology." In *Moral Truth and Moral Tradition:Essays in Honour of Peter Geach and Elizabeth Anscombe,* Edited by Luke Gormally, 226-241. Blackrock, Co. Dublin: Four Courts Press, 1994a.

———. *The Human Person: Animal and Spirit.* Indiana: University of Notre Dame Press, 1994.

Brock, Stephen L. *Action and Conduct: Thomas Aquinas and the Theory of Action* Edinburgh: T&T Clark, 1998.

———. "Is Uniqueness at the Root of Personal Dignity? John Crosby and Thomas Aquinas." *Thomist* 69, no.2 (2005a): 173-201.

——. "Natural Inclination and the Intelligibility of the Good in Thomistic Natural Law." *Vera Lex* 6, no.1-2 (2005): 57-78.

——. "*Veritatis Splendor* 78, St. Thomas and (Not Merely) Physical Objects of Moral Acts." *Nova et Vetera* (English Edition) 6, no.1 (2008): 1-62.

Burgess-Jackson, Keith. "A Theory of Rape." In *A Most Detestable Crime: New Philosophical Essays on Rape,* edited by Keith Burgess-Jackson, 92-117. Oxford: OUP, 1999.

Carter, Alan. "Can We Harm Future People?" *Environmental Values* 10, no.1 (2001): 429-454.

Catechism of the Catholic Church. London: Geoffrey Chapman, 1994.

Chappell, Timothy. "Natural Law Revived: Natural Law Theory and Contemporary Moral Philosophy." In *The Revival of Natural Law. Philosophical, Theological and Ethical Responses to the Finnis-Grisez School,* edited by Nigel Biggar and Rufus Black, 29-52. Aldershot: Ashgate Publishing, 2005.

Check, Paul N. "The Face of the Other: Ministering to Those with Same-Sex Attraction." *National Catholic Bioethics Quarterly* 15, no.2 (2015): 221-230.

Chomsky, Noam. *Language and Mind: 3rd edition.* Cambridge: Cambridge University Press, 2006.

——. *Language and Problems of Knowledge: The Managua Lectures.* Cambridge MA: The MIT Press, 1988.

Cohen, GA. *Karl Marx's Theory of History: A Defence.* Oxford: Oxford University Press, 1978.

Crawford, David S. "Liberal Androgyny: "Gay Marriage" and the Meaning of Sexuality in Our Time." *Communio* 33, no. 2 (2006): 239-265.

——. "Recognising the Roots of Society in the Family, Foundation of Justice." *Communio* vol.34, no.3 (2007): 379-412.

Dabhoiwala, Faramez. *The Origins of Sex: A History of the First Sexual Revolution.* London: Penguin Books, 2012.

Bibliography

Dancy, Jonathan. *Moral Reasons.* Oxford: Blackwell Publishers, 1993.

Denyer, Nicholas. "The Rape of Lucretia." Unpublished talk at Royal Institute of Philosophy Annual Lecture Series, 2002-2003.

Dewan, Lawrence. "Jean Porter on Natural Law: Thomistic Notes." *Thomist* 66, no.2 (2002): 275-309.

Donagan, Alan. *Theory of Morality.* London: University of Chicago Press, 1977.

Douglas, Mary. *Natural Symbols: Explorations in Cosmology.* London: Routledge Classics, 1996.

Eagleton, Terry. *William Shakespeare.* Oxford: Basil Blackwell, 1987.

Feser, Edward. "Sexual cant from asexual Kant." *Edward Feser* (blog), 30 May 2014. Accessed 12 September 2014. http://edwardfeser. blogspot.co.uk/2014/05/sexual-cant-from-asexual-kant.html.

——. *The Last Superstition: A Refutation of the New Atheism.* South Bend, Indiana: St Augustine's Press, 2008.

Finnis, John. "A philosophical case against euthanasia"; "The fragile case for euthanasia: a reply to John Harris." In *Euthanasia Examined: Ethical, Clinical, and Legal Perspectives,* edited by John Keown, 23-36. Cambridge: Cambridge University Press, 1995.

——. *Aquinas: Moral, Political, and Legal Theory.* Oxford: Oxford University Press, 1998.

——. *Fundamentals of Ethics.* Washington D.C.: Georgetown University Press, 1983.

——. "Misunderstanding the case against euthanasia: response to Harris's first reply." In *Euthanasia Examined: Ethical, Clinical, and Legal Perspectives,* edited by john Keown, 46-56. Cambridge: Cambridge University Press, 1995.

——. "Marriage: a Basic and Exigent Good." *Monist* 91, nos. 3&4 (2009): 388-406.

——. *Moral Absolutes: Tradition, Revision and Truth.* Washington D.C.: Catholic University of America, 1991.

————. *Natural Law and Natural Rights.* Oxford: Clarendon Press, 1980.

————. "On Conditional Intention and Preparatory Intentions." In *Moral Truth and Moral Tradition: Essays in Honour of Peter Geach and Elizabeth Anscombe,* edited by Luke Gormally. Dublin: Four Courts Press, 1994.

————. "Personal Integrity, Sexual Morality and Responsible Parenthood." In *Why Humanae Vitae was Right: A Reader,* edited by Janet Smith, 171-193. San Francisco: Ignatius Press 1993.

————. "The fragile case for euthanasia: a reply to John Harris." In *Euthanasia Examined: Ethical, Clinical, and Legal Perspectives,* edited by John Keown, 62-72. Cambridge: Cambridge University Press, 1995.

————. "The Good of Marriage and the Morality of Sexual Relations: Some Philosophical and Historical Observations.*" American Journal of Jurisprudence* 42, no. 1 (1997): 97-134.

Finnis, John; Grisez, Germain; Boyle, Joseph, ""Direct" and "Indirect": A Reply to Critics of our Action Theory," *Thomist* vol.65, no.1 (2001) pp.1-44.

Flannery, Kevin. "Marriage, Mental Handicap, and Sexuality." *Studies in Christian Ethics* 17, no. 2 (2004): 11-26.

Ford, John, Germain Grisez, Joseph Boyle, John Finnis, and William May. *The Teaching of Humanae Vitae: A Defense.* San Francisco, California: Ignatius Press, 1988.

Foucault, Michel. *Power/Knowledge: Selected Interviews and Other Writings, 1972-1977.* Edited by Colin Gordon. Translated by Colin Gordon, Leo Marshall, John Mepham, and Kate Soper. New York: Pantheon Books, 1980.

————. *The History of Sexuality.* Translated by Robert Hurley (3 vols). New York: Vintage Books, 1990.

Franzen, Jonathan. *How to be Alone.* London: Harper Perennial, 2007.

Bibliography

Freud, Sigmund. *Civilisation and its Discontents.* Translated by David McLintock. London: Penguin Books Ltd., 2004.

Garcia, JLA. "Evaluator Relativity and the Theory of Value." *Mind, New Series* 95, no.378 (1986): pp.242-245.

———. "Goods and Evils." *Philosophy and Phenomenological Research* 47, no.3 (1987): 385-412.

———. "Liberal Theory, Human Freedom, and the Politics of Sexual Morality."in *Religion and Contemporary Liberalism,* edited by Paul J. Weithman, 218-253. Notre Dame, IN: University of Notre Dame Press, 1997.

———. "The Doubling Undone? Double Effect in Recent Medical Ethics." *Philosophical Papers* 36, no.2 (2007): 245-270.

———. "The Virtues of the Natural Moral Law," in *Natural Law in Contemporary Society,* edited by Holger Zaborowski, 99-140. Washington: Catholic University of America Press, 2010.

———. "Topics in the New Natural Law Theory." *American Journal of Jurisprudence* 46, no. 1 (2001): 53-62.

George, Robert P. "Does the 'Incommensurability Thesis' Imperil Common Sense Moral Judgements?" In *In Defense of Natural Law,* Robert P. George, 92-102. Oxford: Clarendon Press, 1999.

———. *In Defense of Natural Law.* Oxford: Clarendon Press, 1999a.

———. *Natural Law & Moral Inquiry: Ethics, Metaphysics and Politics in the Work of Germain Grisez.* Washington D.C.: Georgetown University Press, 1998.

Goldman, Alan. "Plain Sex." In *Philosophy of Sex: Contemporary Readings,* edited by Alan Soble, 119-139. New Jersey: Littlefield, Adams and Co. 1980.

Gormally, Luke. "Contraception and Catholic Sexual Ethics." *The Linacre Centre.* Published in 1997, accessed 11/09/2014. http://www.linacre.org/contra.html.

Greer, Germaine. "Rape." *Independent on Sunday.* Published April 2, 2006, accessed 11/09/2014. www.independent.co.uk/voices/ commentators/germaine-greer-rape-472379.html.

———. *Sex and Destiny: The Politics of Human Fertility.* New York: Harper and Row, 1984.

Grisez, Germain. *Christian Moral Principles: The Way of the Lord Jesus, vol. 1.* Chicago: Franciscan Herald Press, 1983.

———. *Difficult Moral Questions: The Way of the Lord Jesus, vol. 3* Chicago: Franciscan Herald Press, 1997.

———. *Living a Christian Life: The Way of the Lord Jesus vol. 2.* Chicago: Franciscan Herald Press, 1993.

———. "Natural Law, God, Religion, and Human Fulfilment." *American Journal of Jurisprudence* 46, no. 1 (2001): 3-36.

Grisez, Germain and Joseph Boyle. *Life and Death with Liberty and Justice.* Indiana: University of Notre Dame Press, 1979.

———. "Response to Our Critics and Collaborators." In *Natural Law & Moral Inquiry: Ethics, Metaphysics and Politics in the Work of Germain Grisez,* edited by Robert P. George, 213-239. Washington, DC: Georgetown University Press, 1998.

Grisez, Germain, Joseph Boyle, and John Finnis. *Nuclear Deterrence, Morality and Realism.* Oxford: Clarendon Press, 1988.

———. "Practical Principles, Moral Truth, and Ultimate Ends." *American Journal of Jurisprudence* 32, no. 1 (1987): 99-151.

Grisez, Germain, Joseph Boyle, John Finnis, and William May. "'Every Marital Act Ought to Be Open to New Life': Toward a Clearer Understanding." *Thomist* 52, no.3 (1988): 365-427. In *The Teaching of Humanae Vitae: A Defense,* by John Ford, Germain Grisez, Joseph Boyle, John Finnis, and William May, 35-116. San Francisco, California: Ignatius Press, 1988.

Haldane, John. "Thomistic Ethics in America." *Logos: A Journal of Catholic Thought and Culture* 3, no.4 (2000): 150-168.

Bibliography

Halwani, Raja. *Virtuous Liaisons: Care, Love, Sex, and Virtue Ethics.* Chicago: Open Court Publishing, 2003.

Hare, RM. "Abortion and the Golden Rule." *Philosophy and Public Affairs* 4, no.3 (1975): 201-222.

Hershfield, Jeffrey. "The Ethics of Sexual Fantasy." *International Journal of Applied Philosophy* 23, no.1 (2009): 27-49.

Hewson, Barbara. "Is Rape Really a Fate Worse Than Death?" *Spiked Online.* Published 17 July 2013, accessed 8 September 2014. http://www.spiked-online.com/newsite/article/is_rape_really_a_fate_worse_than_death/

———. "Sex, Crime and Seduction." *Spiked Online.* Published 7 February 2003, accessed 8 September 2014. http://www.spiked-online.com/newsite/article/6776#.UeRfThbST8s.

Huxley, Aldous. *Ends and Means: An Inquiry into the Nature of Ideals and into the Methods Employed for their Realization.* London: Chatto and Windus, 1937.

Jones, E. Michael. *Libido Dominandi: Sexual Liberation as a Form of Political Control.* South Bend, IN: St Augustine's Press, 2005.

Juvin, Hervé. *The Coming of the Body.* Translated by John Howe. London: Verso, 2010.

Kamm, Frances M. *Intricate Ethics:Rights, Responsibilities, and Permissible Harm.* Oxford: Oxford University Press, 2007.

Kant, Immanuel. *Lectures on Ethics.* Edited by J.B Schneewind, translated by Peter Heath. Cambridge: Cambridge University Press, 2001.

———. *The Metaphysics of Morals.* Translated by Mary Gregor. Cambridge: Cambridge University Press, 1996.

Kierkegaard, Soren. *Papers and Journals: A Selection.* Translated by Alastair Hannay. London: Penguin Books, 1996.

Kolnai, Aurel. *Sexual Ethics: The Meaning and Foundations of Sexual Morality.* Translated and edited by Francis Dunlop. Aldershot: Ashgate Publishing, 2005.

Laing, Jacqueline A. "Law, Liberalism and the Common Good." In *Human Values: New Essays on Natural Law,* edited by David S. Oderberg and TDJ Chappell, 184-217. New York: Palgrave MacMillan, 2004.

Laing, Jacqueline A. and DS Oderberg. "Artificial Reproduction, the 'Welfare Principle', and the Common Good." *Medical Law Review* 13, no.3 (2005): 328-356.

Lamont, John. "Finnis and Aquinas on the Good of Life." *New Blackfriars* 83, no. 977/978 (2002): 365-380.

Lasch, Christopher. *The Culture of Narcissism: American Life in an Age of Diminishing Expectations.* New York: W.W. Norton & Company Ltd. 1979.

Lawrence, DH. In *A Selection from Phoenix*, edited by AAH Inglis. Middlesex: Penguin Books, 1979.

Lee, Patrick. "Is Thomas's Natural Law Theory Naturalist?" *American Catholic Philosophical Quarterly* 61, no. 4 (1997): 567-588.

Levin, Michael, "Why Homosexuality is Abnormal." in *What's Wrong?:Applied Ethicists and Their Critics,* edited by David Boonin and Graham Oddie, 171-190. (Oxford: Oxford University Press 2005.

Levin, Michael E. and Margarita Levin. "The Modal Confusion in Rawls' Original Position." *Analysis* 39, no. 2 (1979): 82-87.

Lisska, Anthony J. *Aquinas's Theory of Natural Law: An Analytic Reconstruction.* Oxford: Clarendon Press, 1996.

——. "Is Ethical Naturalism Possible in Thomas Aquinas?" Talk given at Ethics Without God? conference at University of Notre Dame, Jacques Maritain Center, South Bend, IN, 19 July 2003. Available at www.nd.edu/Departments/Maritian/ti03/eLisska.htm (accessed 10/09/2014).

Mankowski, Paul. "Fertility, Celibacy and the Biblical Vindication of Marriage." In *Fertility and Gender: Issues in Reproductive and*

Sexual Ethics, edited by Helen Watt, 10-16. Oxford: The Anscombe Bioethics Centre, 2011.

Marcuse, Herbert. *Eros and Civilisation: A Philosophical Inquiry into Freud.* London: Allen Lane, Penguin Press, 1969.

Martin, Christopher. "The Fact/Value Distinction." in *Human Values: New Essays on Natural Law*, edited by David S. Oderberg and TDJ Chappell, 52-70. New York: Palgrave MacMillan, 2004.

Masek, Lawrence. "The Contralife Argument and the Principle of Double Effect." *National Catholic Bioethics Quarterly* 11, no. 1 (2011): 83-97.

May, Simon. *Love: A History.* New Haven and London: Yale University Press, 2011.

May, William. *Catholic Bioethics and the Gift of Human Life.* Huntingdon, IN.: Our Sunday Visitor, 2000.

McCabe, Herbert. *The New Creation.* London: Continuum 2010.

McCarthy, Anthony. "Human dignity and the intellectually disabled person: Can prevention of harm justify sterilisation?" in *Incapacity and Care: Controversies in Healthcare and Research,* edited by Helen Watt, 37-58. Oxford: Linacre Centre, 2009.

McCarthy, Anthony and Alexander Pruss. "Condoms and HIV Transmission." in *Fertility and Gender: Issues in Reproductive and Sexual Ethics*, edited by Helen Watt, 157-169. Oxford: The Anscombe Bioethics Centre, 2011.

McInerny, Ralph. "*Humanae Vitae* and the Principle of Totality." in *Why Humanae Vitae was Right: A Reader,* edited by Janet Smith, 327-343. San Francisco: Ignatius Press, 1993.

McMahan, Jeff. *The Ethics of Killing: Problems at the Margin of Life.* Oxford: Oxford University Press, 2002.

Moore, Gareth. *A Question of Truth: Christianity and Homosexuality.* London: Continuum, 2003.

———. *The Body in Context: Sex and Catholicism.* Norwich: SCM Press, 1992.

Morgan, Patricia. *The Marriage Files: The Purpose, Limits and Fate of Marriage.* London: Wilberforce Publications Ltd., 2014.

Murphy, Mark C. *Natural Law and Practical Rationality.* Cambridge: Cambridge University Press, 2001.

Nagel, Thomas. "Concealment and Exposure." *Philosophy & Public Affairs* 27, no. 1 (1998): pp.3-30. Accessed 11 September 2014. http://www.nyu.edu/gsas/dept/philo/faculty/nagel/papers/exposure.html.

———. "Personal Rights and Public Space." *Philosophy and Public Affairs* 24, no.2 (1995): 83-107.

———. "Sexual Perversion." in *Mortal Questions,* by Thomas Nagel, 39-52. Cambridge: Cambridge University Press, 1979.

Noonan, John T. *Contraception: A History of its Treatment by the Catholic Theologians and Canonists.* Cambridge MA: Harvard University Press, 1986.

Nozick, Robert. *The Examined Life: Philosophical Meditations.* New York: Touchstone, 1989.

Nussbaum, Martha "A Right to Marry?" *California Law Review* 98, no.3 (2010): 667-696.

Nussbaum, Martha. "Objectification." in *Sex and Social Justice*, by Martha Nussbaum, 213-240. New York: Oxford University Press, 1999.

Nygren, Anders. *Agape and Eros: A Study of the Christian Idea of Love.* Chicago IL: University of Chicago Press, 1982.

Oaklander, L. Nathan. "Sartre on Sex." in *Philosophy of Sex: Contemporary Readings,* edited by Alan Soble, 190-206. New Jersey: Littlefield, Adams and Co., 1980.

Oderberg, David S. "Hylemorphic Dualism." *Social Philosophy and Policy* 22, no.2 (2005): 70-99.

——. "On the Cardinality of the Cardinal Virtues." *International Journal of Philosophical Studies* 7, no.3 (1999): 305-322.

——. *Real Essentialism.* Abingdon, Oxon: Routledge, 2007.

——. "Teleology: Organic and Inorganic." In *Contemporary Perspectives on Natural Law: Natural Law as a Limiting Concept,* edited by Ana Marta Gonzalez, 259-279. Aldershot: Ashgate, 2008.

——. "The Metaphysical Foundations of Natural Law." In *Natural Moral Law in Contemporary Society,* edited by H. Zaborowski, 44-75. Washington, DC: Catholic University of America Press, 2010.

——. "The Structure and the Content of the Good." In *Human Values: New Essays on Natural Law,* edited by David S. Oderberg and TDJ Chappell, 127-165. New York: Palgrave MacMillan, 2004.

O'Neill, Brendan. "The creepy campaign for masturbation." *Spectator.* 28 June 2014. Accessed 13 September 2014. www.spectator. co.uk/features/9247341/the-age-of-self-love/.

Paramahamsa, KR. *Buddhism in Scripture and Practice.* Friendswood, Texas: TotalRecall Publications, Inc. 2007. http://www.vedamu. org/Veda/KRP-Sir%5C4.%20Buddhism%20eBook.pdf.

Philosophy of Sex: Contemporary Readings. Edited by Alan Soble. New Jersey: Littlefield, Adams and Co., 1980.

Pieper, Josef. *Faith, Hope, Love.* San Francisco: Ignatius Press, 1997.

Pink, Thomas. "The Interpretation of *Dignitatis Humanae*: A Reply to Martin Rhonheimer" *Nova et Vetera* (English edition) 11, no.1 (2013): 77-121.

Pope John Paul II. *Love and Responsibility.* Translated by H.T. Willetts. London: William Collins Sons & Co. Ltd., 1981.

——. *The Theology of the Body: Human Love in the Divine Plan.* Slough: Pauline Books & Media, 1997.

Posner, Richard A. *Sex and Reason.* Cambridge, Massachusetts: Harvard University Press 1992.

Preparata, Guido Giacomo. *The Ideology of Tyranny: The Use of Neo-Gnostic Myth in American Politics.* New York: Palgrave Macmillan 2007.

Priest, Graham. "Sexual Perversion." *Australasian Journal of Philosophy* 75, no.3 (1997): 360-372.

Primoratz, Igor. *Ethics and Sex.* New York: Routledge, 1999.

Pruss, Alexander. *One Body: An Essay in Christian Sexual Ethics.* South Bend, IN: University of Notre Dame Press, 2013.

Quinn, Warren. "Putting Rationality in its Place." In *Morality and Action,* by Warren Quinn. Cambridge: Cambridge University Press, 1994.

Read, Piers Paul. "Can Catholicism save Christian England?" *Spectator.* 31 March 2010. Accessed 11 September 2014. http://www.spectator.co.uk/features/5879908/the-spectator-debate/.

Reich, Wilhelm. *The Sexual Revolution.* Translated by Theodore P. Wolfe. London: Vision Press Ltd., 1972.

Rhonheimer, Martin. "Contraception, Sexual Behaviour and Natural Law." *Linacre Quarterly* 56, no. 2 (1989): 20-57.

Riley, Patrick. *Civilising Sex: Chastity and the Common Good.* Edinburgh: T&T Clark Ltd., 2000.

St Clair, William. *The Godwins and the Shelleys: The Biography of a Family.* New York: W.W. Norton & Co.,1989.

Sartre, Jean-Paul. *Being and Nothingness: An Essay on Phenomenological Oncology.* Translated by Hazel E. Barnes. London: Routledge, 2003.

——. *Existentialism and Humanism.* Translated by Philip Mairet. London: Methuen, 1989.

Scanlon, TM. *Moral Dimensions: Permissibility, Meaning, Blame.* Cambridge, MA: Bellknap Press of Harvard University Press, 2010.

Bibliography

Schooyans, Michel. *The Hidden Face of the United Nations.* Translated by John H. Miller. St. Louis, Missouri: Central Bureau CCVA, 2001.

Schulz, Joshua. "Good Sex on Kantian Grounds, or A Reply to Alan Soble." *Essays in Philosophy* 8, no.2 (2007): Article 13. Accessed 11 September 2014. http://commons.pacificu.edu/cgi/viewcontent.cgi?article=1286&context=eip.

Scruton, Roger. *Death Devoted Heart: Sex and the Sacred in Wagner's Tristan and Isolde.* Oxford: Oxford University Press, 2004.

———. *Sexual Desire: A Philosophical Investigation.* London: Continuum, 2006.

———. "The Nature of Evil." In *A Political Philosophy: Arguments for Conservatism,* by Roger Scruton, 176-191. London: Continuum, 2006.

———. *Thinkers of the New Left.* Harlow: Longman, 1985.

Seifert, Josef. *True Love.* South Bend, Indiana: St Augustine's Press, 2015.

Singer, Peter. "Heavy Petting." *Nerve.* March, 2001. Accessed 8 September 2014. Reproduced at http://www.utilitarianism.net/singer/by/2001----.htm.

———. *Practical Ethics: Second Edition.* Cambridge: Cambridge University Press, 1993.

Smart, JJC, and Bernard Williams. *Utilitarianism: For and Against.* Cambridge: Cambridge University Press, 1973.

Smith, Janet. *Humanae Vitae: A Generation Later.* Washington, DC: The Catholic University of America Press, 1991.

Smith, Quentin. "The Metaphilosophy of Naturalism." *Philo* 4, no. 2 (2001): 195-215.

Soble, Alan. *Philosophies of Masturbation,* unpublished; available at http://faculty.plts.edu/gpence/PS2010/html/Philosophies%20of%20Masturbation.htm (accessed 11/09/2014).

Sokolowski, Robert. "What is Natural Law? Human Purposes and Natural Ends?" *Thomist* 68, no.4 (2004): 507-529.

Spaemann, Robert. *Persons: the difference between 'someone' and 'something.'* Oxford: Oxford University Press, 2006.

Tanner, Michael. "Sentimentality." *Proceedings of the Aristotelian Society* 77, no.1 (1976): 127-147.

———. *Wagner.* London: Flamingo, 2008.

Taylor, Charles. *The Explanation of Behaviour.* New York: Routledge & Kegan Paul, The Humanities Press, 1980.

Teichman, Jenny. "Review of *Sexual Ethics: The Meaning and Foundations of Sexual Morality.*" *Philosophy* 83, no. 3 (2008): 407-412. Accessed 8 September 2014. http://web.maths.unsw.edu.au/~jim/teichmanonkolnai.html.

Thomas, Alan. *Value and Context: The Nature of Moral and Political Knowledge.* Oxford: Oxford University Press, 2006.

Tralau, Johan. "Incest and Liberal Neutrality." *Journal of Political Philosophy* 1, no.1 (2013): 87-105.

Vacek, Edward C. "Contraception Again – A Conclusion in Search of Convincing Arguments." in *Natural Law & Moral Inquiry: Ethics, Metaphysics and Politics in the Work of Germain Grisez,* edited by Robert P. George, 50-82. Washington D.C.: Georgetown University Press, 1998.

Vidal, Gore. "Sex Is Politics." in *United States: Essays 1952-1992,* by Gore Vidal, 538-553. London: Abacus, 1994.

von Hildebrand, Dietrich. *In Defence of Purity: An Analysis of the Catholic Ideals of Purity and Virginity.* Perkin, Indiana: Refuge of Sinners Publishing Inc., 2010.

Watson, Francis. *Agape, Eros, Gender: Towards a Pauline Sexual Ethic.* Cambridge: Cambridge University Press, 2004.

Watt, Helen. "Beyond Double Effect: Side-Effects and Bodily Harm." in *Human Values: New Essays on Natural Law,* edited by David S.

Oderberg and TDJ Chappell, 236-251. New York: Palgrave Mac-Millan, 2004.

———. "Embryos and Pseudoembryos: Parthenotes, Reprogrammed Oo-cytes and Headless Clones." *Journal of Medical Ethics* 33, no. 9 (2007): 554-6.

———. *The Ethics of Pregnancy, Abortion and Childbirth: Exploring Moral Choices in Childbearing.* New York and Abingdon: Rout-ledge, 2016.

Webber, Jonathan. "Sex." *Philosophy* 84, no.328 (2009): pp.233-250. Ac-cessed 8 September 2014. http://cardiff.ac.uk/encap/resources/webber_jonathan_sex.pdf. pp.1-13.

Williams, Bernard. *Ethics and the Limits of Philosophy.* London: Fontana Paperbacks, 1985.

———. "Internal Reasons and the Obscurity of Blame." In Bernard Wil-liams, *Making Sense of Humanity,* by Bernard Williams, 35-45. Cambridge: Cambridge University Press, 1995.

———. *Shame and Necessity.* London: University of California Press, 2008.

Williams, Bernard and Michael Tanner. "Correspondence and Com-ments." *The Human World* no.9 (1972): 41-48.

Wood, Allen W. *Kantian Ethics.* Cambridge: Cambridge University Press 2008.

Wright, Larry. "Functions." *Philosophical Review* 82, no.2 (1973): 139-168.

Wypijewski, JoAnn. "The Kiss." *The Nation,* 12 Jan 2009. Accessed 11 September 2014. www.thenation.com/article/kiss#.

Zizek, Slavoj. "No Sex, Please, We're Post-Human!" Accessed 9 October 2015. http://www.lacan.com/nosex.htm.

Index of Names